Warren Goss

In the navy: Father against son

A story of naval adventures in the great civil war '61-'65

Warren Goss

In the navy: Father against son
A story of naval adventures in the great civil war '61-'65

ISBN/EAN: 9783337223564

Printed in Europe, USA, Canada, Australia, Japan

Cover: Foto ©ninafisch / pixelio.de

More available books at **www.hansebooks.com**

OR

FATHER AGAINST SON

A STORY OF NAVAL ADVENTURES IN
THE GREAT CIVIL WAR, '61–'65

BY

WARREN LEE GOSS

AUTHOR OF "JED," "RECOLLECTIONS OF A PRIVATE,"
"TOM CLIFTON," "JACK ALDEN," ETC.

NEW YORK: 46 EAST 14TH STREET
THOMAS Y. CROWELL & CO.
BOSTON: 100 PURCHASE STREET

ROCKWELL AND CHURCHILL PRESS
BOSTON

PREFACE.

The naval scenes of this story are laid principally on the inland waters of Virginia and North Carolina during our great Civil War.

The Dismal Swamp Canal connects Hampton Roads with Albemarle and Pamlico Sounds, and in these waters there is more internal navigation than is afforded by Long Island Sound and its rivers. The Neuse, the Cowan, and the Roanoke Rivers supply channels leading far into the interior of the country, where railroads branch to the main routes. There are numerous inlets or channels between these inland seas and the ocean, through which traders could carry supplies to the insurgents, and where blockading vessels could not follow because of shifting channels and shallow water.

The hardships endured and great services rendered by the sailors of our navy in capturing and holding for the Union these waters are but little understood or appreciated; for the drama of war, even during its progress, leaves upon the average mind only a few luminous points; a few great names and a few great victories. Yet such minor scenes as are here delineated, — individual sufferings and hardships,— which lie behind the smoke of war, unillumined by the glare of great battles, and which can only in part be described, show, as no statistics or official reports can, what was endured by those who fought on either side. Humanity might be less eager for conflict if the brilliant veil that hides the hardships and agony of war could be torn away, and its details more plainly seen. Not the least of these hardships in our war was the mental anguish caused by kindred fighting against kindred, brother against brother and father against son.

That portion of my tale that attempts to mirror some of these conditions has in it more of reality than of fiction, for such incidents were constantly paralleled during the progress of our Civil War.

The plot of this story is (in part) not imaginary but real, and, were it needful, the truth of most of its details might be substantiated.

The moral of this story is, that while there is but one right, it is none the less true that in a republic there must always be many standpoints from which the same questions may be viewed, by minds influenced by differing conditions of birth, education, and temperament. Happy are we when all differences can be settled by arbitration or an appeal to the ballot, and not to arms.

It therefore becomes Americans, while holding fast to cherished convictions, to avoid bitter discussions and misrepresentations, and, "with malice

PREFACE.

toward none, with charity for all," bind up the wounds and cement the friendships and loves between fellow-countrymen.

If I have succeeded in even a small degree in impressing these lessons of charity and love upon my youthful readers, the writing of this book has been justified.

W. L. G.

JULY 4, 1897.

CONTENTS.

CHAPTER		PAGE
I.	Fishing and Fished	1
II.	Phil at School	13
III.	A Failure and its Consequences	25
IV.	My Father leaves Wichnor	34
V.	A Mystery	45
VI.	On Board the Brig "Favorite"	56
VII.	At Newberne	68
VIII.	A Storm at Sea	82
IX.	The Wreck of the "Favorite"	93
X.	On a Barren Sand-bar	104
XI.	We make Discoveries	118
XII.	We Grope in Darkness	132
XIII.	We leave Chicamacomico	144
XIV.	Leaving Dixie	156
XV.	The Boot is on the Other Leg	170
XVI.	On Shore after the Battle	184
XVII.	Home, Sweet Home	197
XVIII.	In the Navy	211
XIX.	The Advent of the "Merrimack"	221
XX.	Iron meets Iron	236

CONTENTS.

CHAPTER		PAGE
XXI.	AFTER THE CONFLICT	246
XXII.	ON THE "SPITFIRE"	259
XXIII.	ATTACK ON SECESSIONVILLE	273
XXIV.	DOWN THE RIVER	288
XXV.	TRIED AND CONDEMNED	300
XXVI.	ENEMIES, YET FRIENDS	311
XXVII.	AT PLYMOUTH	325
XXVIII.	THE ADVENT OF THE "ALBEMARLE"	335
XXIX.	IN THE ENEMY'S COUNTRY	348
XXX.	UNDER TWO FLAGS	360
XXXI.	WITH OUR FLEET	369
XXXII.	UNDER THE SURGEON'S CARE	378
XXXIII.	IN THE HOSPITAL	390

LIST OF ILLUSTRATIONS.

Drawings by M. J. Burns.

	PAGE
The "Monitor" finally lay alongside the Huge "Merrimack" (p. 242)	*Frontispiece.*
I felt Phil holding me up	8
"Why don't you shoot me?"	40
"Let go that Rope, Hez!"	99
"Hold on," I said, "I can tow the Raft"	135
"Yes, they 're Uncle Sam's Barkers, an' no Mistake"	169
Landing of the U S. Troops at Hatteras	175
"Take those Handcuffs off that Young Man's Wrists!"	199
"Hullo," I said, "have you got a Contract to eat all that Stuff?"	250
I took her up again and strode resolutely to the House	285
The River was not Wide, and I was able to reach the Shore opposite to the Battery	296
The Order came, "All down!" and we struck the "Albemarle" like a Thunderbolt!	375

IN THE NAVY.

CHAPTER I.

FISHING AND FISHED.

I WAS named for my maternal grandfather. It was, however, a surprise to my mother when on my twelfth birthday my grandfather, Hezekiah Perkins, after turning a quarter of a dollar over in his fingers a great many times, gave it to me with repeated admonitions about saving. Heedful of these maxims, I hastened to invest it in a new fish-line and hooks, in order that I might make it pay a large dividend of fun, if not of fish.

I was, as my mother declared, a "chip of the old block," — like my father, — more fond of fishing than of work.

Even Jimmy Gager, the schoolmaster, with whom I was at times a favorite pupil, had accused me of bringing to school in my pocket more worms for bait than slate-pencils for ciphering.

I confess that the week I received the money mentioned, I was so intent on cutting a good fishing-pole, and on other preparations for fishing, that I lost sight of the birch sticks which Master Gager kept under his desk to quicken the memory of boys who, without a written excuse, forgot to go to school.

One of the traits of my character, if a boy has a character at such an age, was my disposition to form vagabond associations with boys of all kinds, and with dogs. A dog that had apparently lost its master had singled me out for that distinction, and became my constant companion and pet. My father gave him the name of Vagabond (which for convenience was abbreviated to "Vag"), and declared that he could always tell where I was by the dog's yelp, as well as if I had a bell tied to me. The Saturday after the purchase of my new fish-line, with Vag at my heels, I started on a fishing-trip.

The city of Wichnor, where I was born and then lived, was a Connecticut town of about sixteen thousand inhabitants. Its situation near the head of navigation on the Wild River, fifteen miles from the sea, is one of bewildering loveliness. Its streets climb and wind around Alpine-like heights, crowned in places by forest trees or gray boulders and ledges. Among these beautiful hills the homes and churches of its people cling and nestle like eagles' nests.

The house in which my parents lived was on an Acropolis-like hill which rose from the centre of the town, and from which could be seen two narrow tributary streams, one on either side, quietly mingling with the broader river, which flashed and gleamed like molten silver on its way to the sea. Its foliage-covered banks were as varied and beautiful as ever the light shone upon in any clime under the sun.

My father, who was by birth a North Carolinian, was accustomed to say, for the purpose of teasing my mother, who was a native of the town, that in selecting its site the original Puritan settlers had not thought of its romantic loveliness, but of the more practical fact that they could get house lots on both sides of the land.

On the Saturday mentioned I started out fishing, without thought of the beauty of the morning or of the surrounding scenery, and was soon on the wharf, absorbed in my favorite pastime, and waiting for nibbles and bites.

While fishing remained good, nothing distracted my attention. I had at first very good luck, but after a time the fish ceased to bite; even then, with Izaak Walton-like patience, I still persisted. But Vag, yelping with impatience at my inactivity, pranced around the wharf and then returned and looked solemnly into the water. Although I kept on fishing, my attention wandered to a steamer from New York, which was landing its passengers at an adjacent dock. With one eye on my bob, I watched a flood of people pouring over the gang-plank.

There was one passenger who did not land in the ordinary manner. While the tickets were being taken at the plank, a little ragamuffin climbed out on the bow of the steamer, and with an astonishing jump landed on his feet near me.

"Whew," I ejaculated admiringly, "but that was a jump!"

The boy made no reply, but gathering up his only baggage, a box containing boot-blacking equipments, turned to the outcoming passengers, and with "Black yer boots, sir?" spoken in an energetic manner, began that occupation, and served a number of customers before they left the wharf.

After a while he sauntered towards me and Vag, jingling a goodly number of silver pieces, which he had received for his work. Patting the dog, who seemed to recognize in him at once a congenial fellow-vagabond, he said:

"Did n't I catch 'em on the fly?"

Thinking he referred to his jump from the steamer, I said:

"It *was* a big jump. Why did n't you come down the gang-plank? You might have broken your neck by jumping in that way."

"Like ter jump; b'sides, had n't no money, an' them fellers at the plank would 'a' booted me if they 'd ketched me without the pasteboard."

"What 's pasteboard?" I inquired, not understanding his figure of speech.

"Ticket," he responded; and then asked, "Got any nibbles?"

"Yes," I replied, "and fish too: look in that basket," and I displayed a goodly number of perch and suckers.

"Better fishin' than in Ne' Yo'k," he said. "Say, can I take this fish-line 'n' fish?"

I assented with a nod, when he helped himself to bait and began fishing as if it were his only thought in life.

"Where did you come from?" I inquired.

"Ne' Yo'k," he responded, with the peculiar pronunciation of the Bowery.

"Your folks let you go 'round alone?" I inquired; "mine would n't."

"Ain't got none."

"No what?"

"No folks; old gran' died t' other day, had n't no place t' stay, an' the cops got after me t' send me away t' the Island; so I come on here."

"Where you going to stay?" I inquired; and then added: "Better go up to our house. Mother'll give you some supper an' you can sleep with me."

"See anything green?" said the little fellow, pulling down the corner of his eye. "You can't stick me. See this," he said, jingling the silver he had in his pocket; "made that in a jiffy; goin' t' sleep 'round here somewhere — don't see any cops."

"What's cops?"

"Why, p'lice, of course; them's cops."

During this conversation I took in the personality of the ragamuffin. His clothing consisted of trousers, much too large for him, held up by a single suspender; a ragged shirt that scarcely broke joints with his trousers; while a straw hat, the torn brim of which got constantly in his eyes, surmounted his head. The expression of his face was very pleasant, and in it I remember now there was a mingling of good-nature, shrewdness, and decision.

I give these seemingly trivial details because they made an impression on me, young as I was, and also because without this new acquaintance I should not, in all probability, be here to tell this story. The afternoon approached and we continued to talk and fish, although the fish had ceased even to nibble.

After a long silence my comrade said, "Le's go in swimmin'."

"No," I responded, "mother says I can't go into the water until I learn to swim."

Phil Gurley, for that he informed me was "all the name he had," gave a half laugh and sniff of disdain; then, after a moment's attention to his nibbleless bob, said, "Can y' box?"

"Yes," I responded, "father has taught me to box some, and gives me fencing lessons too sometimes."

"Ever seen a real fight?" asked Phil.

"No," I replied. "Did you?" and then added, "Father says 't isn't manly to fight, 'less some one hits you; then to promote peace you must hit 'em back so hard that they'll never want to strike any one again."

"I see the fight between the Ne' Yo'k Chicken an' the Bully Plug," said Phil. "The Ne' Yo'k Chicken got knocked out; made me sick. I never begins a fight, but I don't 'low no duffers to punch me. No, siree!"—then added, "Le's get into that boat," pointing to a little craft with her sail up. "I see a fish break water out there."

Suiting the action to his words, he began to slip down the rope that held the boat to the wharf, and I, forgetting the often-repeated admonitions of my father to keep out of boats, followed.

I had just got aboard when I noticed two important facts: first, that the rope had in some way slipped over the low rounded post of the wharf and we were drifting with the tide; and, second, that my father was just coming down the wharf, probably in search of a boy who had gone fishing that morning and had forgotten to return for dinner.

My father, although kind and forbearing, would tolerate no disobedience of his orders, and I feared his displeasure should he find me in the act. So I hastily tried to pass Phil with the intention of getting behind the sail, just as a flaw of wind struck it. The narrow boat tipped, and overboard I went, clutching at air and water.

As I went under water the second time I seemed to hear my mother's voice saying, "Hez, how could you?" and I knew nothing more until I felt Phil holding me up and shouting for me to catch hold of the gunwale of the boat instead of himself; and was conscious that Vag, my poor dog, was trying to help by swimming frantically around me, and yelping. I afterwards learned that when Phil saw me go overboard he seized an oar, and jumping with it to my rescue caught me, and with the aid of the oar got me to the boat, which fortunately had been brought near us by the wind.

There was a bustle of excitement, and a circle of people around me, when I regained consciousness. They were, as I thought, punishing me by rolling me over a barrel. I was at last able to make them understand that I was alive, by yelling, "Le' me go, an' I won't do so again."

The incident had one important result besides saving me from the water, and that was that my father took Phil, as he termed it, "home to dry," clothed him in a dry suit of my clothes, and in some way persuaded him to remain at our house.

The part Phil had taken in my rescue drew favorable attention to him, and the city "Daily News" had a scare head-line in its next morning's issue, with the caption, "A RAGGED HERO," giving with some detail an account of my rescue.

Neighbors fond of excitement and gossip dropped in to talk the matter over with my mother, and

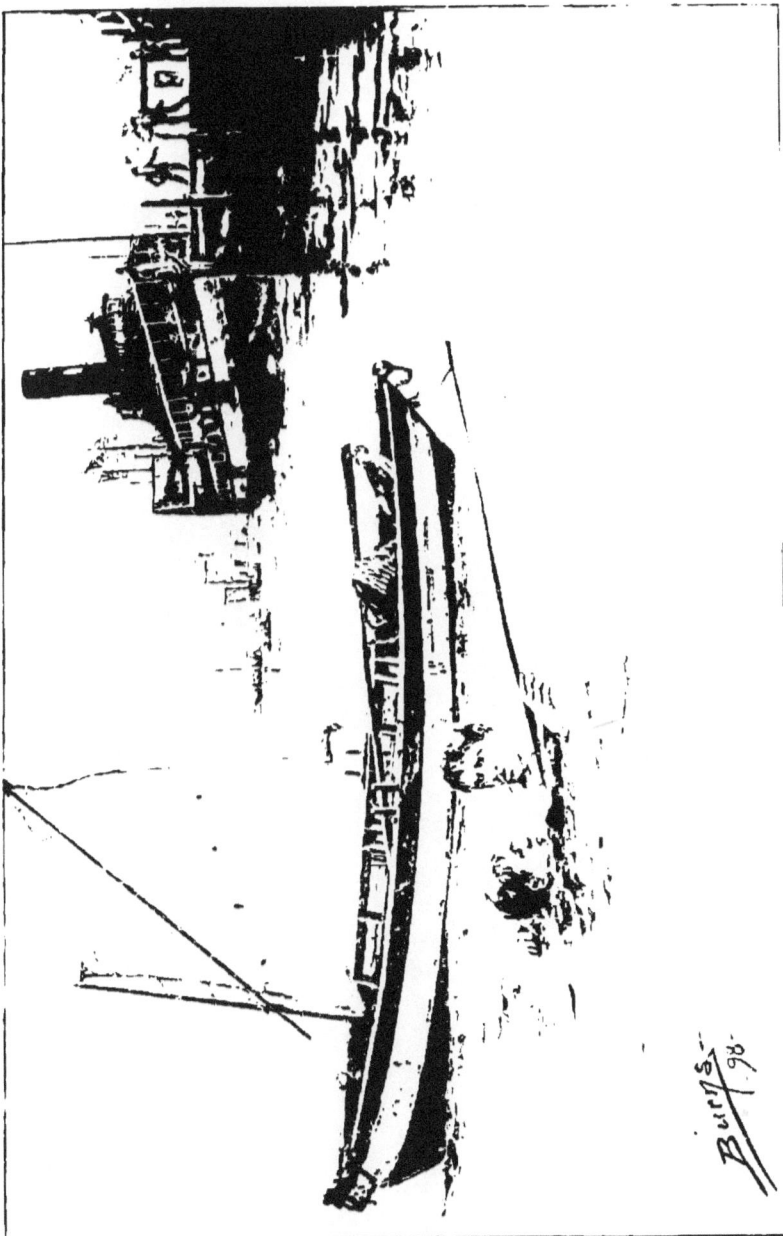

I FELT PHIL HOLDING ME UP.

to bring goodies to the supposed invalid, until my father facetiously proposed to hire a man to help Andy (a mulatto servant-boy that he had brought with him from the South) do the eating.

Among these callers was a childless lady, Mrs. Josephus Nonfit, a widow of independent fortune, distinguished among her neighbors as a prominent member of the State Peace Society.

After one or two visits, in which she talked much to Phil, Mrs. Nonfit brought her brother, who talked with him as if to test his intelligence. Finally she proposed that he live with her and do errands and light chores. In payment for this service she would clothe him and send him to school, "so long," she added, "as we can agree."

Phil had been somewhat nervous at first at the attention shown him, and confidentially told me he was afraid the cops would get after him; but, gaining confidence in the people who showed him so much kindness and sympathy, after asking my father's advice he assented to the proposal.

Thus it was that Phil became my neighbor, and before long my most intimate friend; and although my mother demurred at my constant association with him, my father replied, "I played with our servants when I was young, and I'd share my last dollar with that boy Andy."

"You always call him a boy," said my mother, "but he is a man grown."

"That is what we at the South call all of our

male servants," explained my father, and then resuming said, "It doesn't hurt a lad to play with any kind of boys so long as he has a proper spirit. Phil seems to me to be a good kind of fellow, and I somehow think that he comes of good stock. Did you notice the other day he wouldn't take the money the people wanted to give to him, because, as he said, he had done nothing for it? It seems to me that is the kind of spirit that any gentleman's son might be proud of."

A word of explanation here seems in order regarding our family. My father, Rufus Johnstone, Jr., while at a Connecticut college, had made the acquaintance of Miss Rose Perkins — afterwards my mother — while she was visiting her aunt at the town in which the college was located. The acquaintance thus formed resulted in a marriage without the consent of the parents of either.

When Rufus Johnstone, Jr., informed Rufus Johnstone, Sr., of his marriage, no answer was made to the letter except through a lawyer, who wrote: "Mr. Rufus Johnstone desires me to communicate for your information that he will hereafter furnish you with no money and will pay no debts of your contracting. He also desires me to say that there is an unexpended balance belonging to you as an inheritance from your mother, an account of which will be given and the money turned over to you whenever applied for in proper form."

From the tenor of this letter Rufus Johnstone,

Jr., inferred that his father was not pleased with his marriage. It proved, however, a love marriage as well as a love match, and neither of the contracting parties had occasion to repent at leisure of that which had been consummated in haste.

My father and mother had come to Wichnor, and at the time when this story opens were living on a small estate which was my mother's by inheritance.

My maternal grandfather, of whom I have already made mention, was a man who, by shrewd management and penuriousness, had got together what was in those days thought to be a large property. He grudgingly paid money, and had never been known until the incident recorded in a foregoing page to give away anything.

When his daughter Rose came to Wichnor with her husband, he offered to the young couple neither help nor interference.

The year after their marriage I was born, and my father found himself without trade or profession, and with but a few hundred dollars in money and the estate mentioned as my mother's.

Fortunately the care and control of money were largely intrusted to my mother, who had the Yankee gift of management and economy in an unusual degree, and, as my father used to say, "could buy with both sides of a dollar."

I never heard a tart or unpleasant word pass between them but once, and that was when my father had referred to the stock joke that Connecticut people made wooden hams and nutmegs. Then my mother sharply responded by saying, "Yes, but we have to go South to sell them, as there are no New England people stupid enough to buy such wares."

My father, at this answer, at first flushed with vexation, but finally laughingly said, "There's one little nutmeg that is not wooden, but all spice right through, and that is my wife!"

CHAPTER II.

PHIL AT SCHOOL.

PHIL at once began going to the same district school that I did. He had previously learned to read and write, and when questioned as to how he learned said his father had begun to teach him and he had picked up the rest. All he could remember about his father more than this was of there being a crowd at the house where he lived, of his mother's crying as if her heart would break, and that he never saw his father after that.

Of his mother his memory was more distinct: he remembered that she was continually crying, and that one day when she lay on her bed, as he thought asleep, he tried to awaken her because he was hungry, and was told she was dead.

From this account it was concluded by father that both of Phil's parents were dead.

The only thing Phil had that had belonged to his mother was a small picture of her, in a gold locket. My father suggested keeping this in a safe place, as it might sometime be important as a means of Phil's indentification.

A neighbor was captain of a coaster running to New York and other places, and on hearing Phil's history offered to take him to New York sometime to see if anything more could be learned of his parentage, but this was not thought at the time to be advisable.

Neither Phil nor I, as these pages will disclose, was a model boy, so far as conduct was concerned. Phil was quick tempered, while I, though slow to wrath and in the main good tempered, was, if provoked too far, subject to fits of ungovernable rage, which Grandfather Perkins denominated "a slave-holder's temper."

A boy has, I suppose, the savage instincts of the original man, and teachers and parents are the ordained instruments for training or subduing these instincts. Neither Phil nor I was an exception to this rule.

On our way to school he often made inquiries which showed that his mind was agitated over problems suggested by his new surroundings.

"Does some of your togs hurt you, Hez?" he asked, with a wiggle and twist and grimace, and with his hand to his shirt-band to illustrate. "Mine does, an' the shirt scratches me all over sometimes."

"They starch 'em all over, I guess," I explained. "They do mine sometimes; but they don't mean to, though."

"Do you have to eat with a fork, an' sit up to the table as stiff as a lamp-post?" again inquired Phil. "I have to — won't let me eat fast when I'm hungry. Marm [so he called Mrs. Nonfit] combs my hair an' scrubs my face, an' thinks it's awful if I get my finger-nails dirty. Is your marm so partic'lar?"

"Yes," I said hesitatingly, for my mother had intermittent seasons of being very particular. "When she's busy she ain't so fussy about me. She's quilting now," I said, showing Phil my very dirty hands, "and lets me off light."

That a boy revolts against discipline and soap and water, and gravitates toward mud-puddles, dirt, and danger, to my mind shows that nature is not a safe guide for him.

Civilization consists of an attempt to take crude nature out of boys and other savages and refine it.

That boys can be disciplined to keep the peace, wear whole clothes, give attention to cleanliness, study and work, is one of the wonders, and I almost said miracles, of the achievements of civilization and of Christianity. For Christianity, when brought down to practice, is in great part the putting of one's better self in dominion over his natural savage self, which, as Grandfather Perkins often said at prayer meeting, "is as prone to evil as the sparks fly upward."

For illustration: the natural boy, before being broken to the home harness, loves to go with his feet untrammeled in summer, and to wriggle his toes in the mud and sand, and is never so proud as when he has a rag on a stubbed toe. He loves to climb a tree better than he likes good clothes, for is not nature one vast gymnasium, impelling boys to muscular exertion? Should he be unstintedly blamed, as he often is, because his instincts are at war with maternal anxiety to keep him clean, and his clothes and cuticle whole?

"Boys," Andy often said, "is powerful fon' ob raisin' ructions an' dirt."

Again, the best of boys and men and nations feel, when driven to the wall by brutal bullying, that they must fight in the interest of peace. Instinct in either case leads us to hit the other fellow so hard that he will not want to hit us again. Christ teaches us to forbear, and return good for evil; but who will restrain evil if it is encouraged by non-resistance?

Boys should not be taught to become men too soon, and thus outgrow much that is unmixed loveableness inherent in them, for they can never be boys again.

In school neither Phil nor I was anything more than moderately good. "Our youthful hearts for learning burned" less than for a holiday. It was a serious though undebated question, as it ever will be with boys, what parents and guardians are for except to feed and house boys and trouble them by being fussy about them.

Phil, especially, had led the free, untrammeled life of a vagabond in a great city so long that sometimes his guardian seemed to him a kind of domestic "cop," to check fun and administer reminders that he was under surveillance.

I have been thus particular in my estimate of Phil and myself because I want my boy readers to understand that Phil was a real boy, and not a Sunday-school-book boy — an author's creation and not nature's. This is not an apology for his wrongdoing, but a simple statement of facts.

One day, not long after Phil began his attendance at our school, we both had to stay in at recess for being late, on account of stopping to climb a tree to inspect a squirrel's nest.

One of the scholars was a neighbor's boy, named Dudley Burton. He was two years older than Phil, and a head taller and correspondingly larger than either of us. When we went to the playground that noon, Dudley, evidently presuming that after punishment neither of us would complain to the teacher, began to pull Phil roughly by the jacket collar, and to say with sneering, tantalizing emphasis, "Wharf rat! Wharf rat! Wharf rat!"

Phil, with flushed, piteous face, said to me, "Marm wouldn't like to have me fight or I'd give him one on the nose. She said this morning I must always be a little peacemaker.

"Yes," I said, "fighting is disgraceful;" while I must confess that all the time I was itching to get hold of the bully. "Mother says so, but father thinks it is our duty to resent bad treatment sometimes, otherwise bullies would rule the world and good people be at a discount."

In the afternoon Dudley Burton, or, as the boys called him behind his back, "Bully Burton," was very provoking; he not only called Phil bad names, but pulled his hat from his head and trampled it under foot. I was sure from Phil's flushed face that nothing but his good resolution kept him from fighting.

That night as he walked thoughtfully by my side he said, "I suppose Dud thought I was afraid, but I ain't goin' to get into a mess an' have marm feel bad, would you, Hez?"

"No," I said hesitatingly, "it wouldn't be proper." And yet all the time I felt as if I would like to pound Dud.

"I'm goin' to tell marm about him," said Phil, "an' see what she thinks; if 't wa'n't for makin' marm feel bad, I'd punch him! Do you think she'd really care?"

"Oh, my!" I said; "she belongs to the Peace Society, and they don't believe in fighting!"

"Well," said Phil, after a moment's silence, and kicking at a stone in his way, "nobody was ever so good to me as marm is, except your marm when I was wet that time, an' I'm goin' to be good."

At recess on the Saturday forenoon following, Burton threatened to strike Phil with a cat-stick, as we boys then called a bat.

"Stop that, Burton!" I exclaimed, picking up another bat.

"Two of yer, hey? Perhaps you want to pick a quarrel," said Burton in a sneering tone.

"No," I said, "but we want you to stop bullying."

Just then the bell rang and put a stop to further angry talk.

On Saturday afternoon there was no school, and the boys gathered on the village green to play "Four Old Cat," a game similar to base ball, but not so intricate.

In selecting players I was appointed to choose on one side and Dudley Burton on the other. The cat-stick or bat was thrown up, caught, and first my hand and then Dudley's, alternately, was closed around it one above the other, to determine first choice of players. It resulted in my being able to get four fingers on the cat-stick last. This should have given me the first choice, but Dudley jerked the bat from my hand and declared that I'd cheated. I was indignant, but yielded for the sake of peace, and that the game might not be spoiled. So we tossed up once more, and Dudley won the first choice. He had already chosen his first player when one of the best players in the school came on to the ground and I at once chose him for my side. This Dudley declared was unfair, and as I was in doubt I yielded again.

During the progress of the game we were beating the other side, when Burton called a foul on one of Phil's runs, and not being sustained in his assertion struck Phil with his cat-stick as he reached the home goal. I was now not only getting angry, but was of the opinion that we had yielded enough for the sake of peace, and said, "Look here, Burton, you've bullied us from the beginning, and we've let it go so as not to have a fuss. Now cheese it!"

"I don't associate with wharf rats and gutter snipes," snarlingly said Burton; and to emphasize his remarks he struck Phil once more a cruel blow.

At this I pulled off my jacket, and advancing angrily towards Burton exclaimed, "I'll show you how to treat a coward and bully!" The boys formed a ring and cried, "A fight, a fight!"

Just then Phil pushed his way into the ring and said, "Fellers, this chap begun it by callin' me names an' strikin' me, an' it's my fight!"

"Dud 'll lick spots out of yer," growled the boys. "He's bigger'n you; 'tain't fair."

Phil persisted; there was a murmur of assent, and I was obliged to give way to him.

"Fellers," he said, "I ain't goin' to have Hez blamed f'r fightin' f'r me."

Phil stripped off both jackets and even his undershirt, and resolutely stood on the defence. Dudley threw off his jacket and made an angry rush to finish Phil, who quickly stepped one side and put out his foot, and Dudley plunged forward, falling on his face. He now was furious, and again rushed upon his small opponent, but Phil, while facing his antagonist, kept stepping back nimbly as he struck Dudley, so that every blow aimed at him was warded off or avoided. Dudley was now out of breath as well as out of temper. He had lost his head. This was Phil's opportunity, and soon he had given the bully a black eye and a bloody nose. The boys cheered Phil; when Dudley, thoroughly infuriated, and in defiance of fair play, kicked Phil in the stomach and then rushed upon him, while the boys cried, "Foul! Shame! Shame!" and other exclamations of disapproval of Dudley's conduct. But when we thought Phil was down and conquered, by a skilful trick he turned the bully and was on top of him. Upon this a tremendous cheer went up from the boys, and they exclaimed, "Give it to him, Phil!"

"No," said Phil pathetically, "I fights fair, if I is a wharf rat," and with this he let Dudley get upon his feet.

Once more Dudley attempted to kick, when Phil caught his foot and sent him heels over head to the ground. He did not get to his feet so readily as usual, and when he again approached Phil it was with such total lack of self-command that Phil caught the bully's head under his arm and punished him "until he bellowed," as the boys said, "like a big calf."

When Burton had gone from the field of his defeat, crying "enough," Phil turned to the boys and said, "If any of Dud's friends wants to call me or Hez names, or take up Dud's fight, now's y'r chance."

But no one wanted to fight. They all agreed, even Dudley's supposed friends, that Phil had been more than fair. One of them set up a cheer for Phil, and called him "Philibuster," and seemed glad that the bully had been vanquished.

I helped Phil put on his clothes, and then he said soberly, "Won't you go up to marm's with me? I s'pose she won't want me f'r a boy any more, now I've been fightin', f'r she said this mornin' that I must be a peacemaker."

"I don't think she'll turn you out of the house for that," I said.

"I don't care so much 'bout that," said Phil, "as I do that she'll think I've been bad a-purpose. I've tried all along to be good an' to be a peacemaker, as marm told me I must, 'cause she's good to a feller."

And Phil began to snuffle with his arm up to his face, saying between snuffles, "an' now — I've been an' — an' - knocked Dud Burton into pieces, an' tore my best briches!"

And with this Phil began to cry like a good fellow. So I went home with Phil to help him make his confession to marm, as he called Mrs. Nonfit. "Marm," said Phil, very humbly and tremblingly, and catching his breath with agitation, and snuffling, — "marm — I've been an' torn them new briches a-fightin' Dud Burton." And then Phil began to howl, as if he had got the whipping instead of Dud.

"Dudley kicked him dreadfully, too," I put in sympathetically. "He's hurt him bad, marm."

"Why, why! What *did* you fight for?" she exclaimed in reproachful tones.

"He called me names, an' Hez a liar, an' struck me with a cat-stick. I had n't touched him then, neither. And I did n't want t' fight. I don't s'pose you 'll want me for a boy, now I've been fightin'. But you 've been good to me," said Phil, with the tears running down his face, "an' — an' — I love y', if I is bad."

The good woman could restrain her motherly instincts and expressions of sympathy no longer, and throwing her arms around Phil's neck said between her sobs, as I told her about the fight, "My poor, dear boy, your marm loves you. Don't cry, don't cry, Phil," and then, woman-like, she set the example by another burst of tears.

The president of the Peace Society, who happened to be visiting her that day, came in while this was going on, and Mrs. Nonfit explained the situation to him and said, "He's a manly little fellow, if he did fight, Mr. Stanley."

When the white-headed advocate of peace heard the full particulars he said to Phil, "It's very bad, very bad."

"You would n't have stood it to be abused yourself!" indignantly said Mrs. Nonfit. "You know you would n't, Mr. Stanley!"

"No!" emphatically responded the good old man, as he lifted up Phil's tearful face. "It's a bad practice to fight, but you seem simply to have defended yourself, and plague me if I would n't have liked to have seen you wallop the brute!— H'm:" and the good peace president, remembering his peaceful nature, ejaculated, "Bad, bad!— Humph;" and then breaking out again said, "But he deserved all you gave him, though, the brute!"

When I told my father and grandfather about this interview they laughed immensely for a time, and then father said to mother, "I guess if Phil conquered Burton by force, Mrs. Nonfit has conquered Phil by love." So it proved.

Phil had one of those noble natures in which good seed planted by kind and loving hands quickly germinated. If at times after this he felt an inclination to fight, the impulse was quickly curbed by the thought of the pain it would cause to those who were kind to him. And after this the boys knew he could defend himself, and were but little inclined to provoke him.

CHAPTER III.

A FAILURE AND ITS CONSEQUENCES.

The events narrated in the foregoing chapter, although in themselves trivial, were not without influence on our family. They show how the smallest incidents may turn the current of one's life. My mother, although reared in democratic New England, was ambitious of social distinction. My father, born and reared in the aristocratic surroundings of the South, and his father an aristocrat among aristocrats, cared but little for such distinctions except so far as they pleased my mother. For her he had at times made efforts to break through the cold crust of Wichnor society reserve. Mrs. Burton, the mother of " Bully Burton," had taken my mother up at one time and patronizingly declared that my father had a very distinguished manner; but after the episode recounted in the last chapter she had socially dropped her, as grandfather sneeringly declared, " like a hot potato."

In Wichnor two conditions were essential to those who desired social recognition (and no doubt in this it is different from other towns and cities in New England): first, they must belong to the leading church of the town; second, they, or rather the male members of the family, must be in some kind of prosperous business, or have undoubted claims to wealth. With these qualifications a person might take a high place in the church or in society, though having but little claim to either high birth or good breeding, and though his life as well as the means by which his wealth was acquired might be a trifle shady.

My father jestingly said that in practical Wichnor, piety was kept from contamination by keeping it from unduly interfering with avarice and money-getting. He continued, "What though the Master said, long years ago in Judea, 'Ye cannot serve God and Mammon,' and 'Where your treasure is, there will your heart be also'? It does not apply to the practical affairs of our churches, where large sums of money are needed for sustaining a fashionable society and a high-salaried minister, and for converting the heathen. Christianity, under modern conditions, must make concessions to the pursuit of wealth, or suffer defeat."

Grandfather Perkins poked the fire fiercely and his face turned red — or was it a reflection of the blaze? — as he said, "Rufus, I don't believe in a man's being such a heathen as not to belong to a church, or so dumned poor that he can't help support it; that is — moderately. It is written, 'The meek shall inherit the earth,' isn't it?"

"I reckon, then," said father, with a smile,

"that a good church member must n't be too particular how he comes into possession of his inheritance — is that it?"

"How can a man be respectable without money?" querulously inquired grandfather, with another impatient poke at the fire. "Besides, did n't St. Paul say, 'If any provide not for his own . . . he is worse than an infidel'?"

"Wal," drawled Jim Bisbee, an ex-tin-peddler, who had dropped in for a neighborly talk, "a little money ain't a bad thing to hev, Mr. Johnstone, but if a feller pinches a dollar harder 'n — he pinches on to other good things, it is t' my mind a sign that his heart is in the dollar ruther than in the good he can du with it. If a feller's bound t' make money by hook or crook, an' takes more pleasure in gittin' it than in usin' of it for some good purpose, then it 's agin Scriptur."

"Well, then," said my father, "it 's a good idea to offer the high places in our churches not to those who are most Christ-like, but to those who can put up the money; to the highest bidder, as you might say?"

"Wal, naow, Mr. Johnstone, that 's one way o' puttin' of it, but I don't say it ain't a good scheme t' make the rich ones contribute money if they can't contribute a good example; but, goodness! you know I think the way t' keep men lib'ral an' good is t' keep 'em givin' t' some good purpose: then they feel they 've got an int'rest in it. So the church is all right when you look at that side of it. Don't you see, Mr. Johnstone?"

My father smiled at Jim's presentation of the moral use of money in church affairs, while grandfather dropped the poker, looked at his huge silver watch, got up, and with a sour look at Jim Bisbee went out for the night.

I have recorded my recollections of this conversation because it reveals my father's contempt for mere money-getters. I have often heard him express the opinion that the lowest use to which the human intellect could be put was to convert it into a machine for turning out dollars and cents. In this will be seen how alien were his methods of thought from the ordinary New England mind.

Notwithstanding these views and his contempt for sordid gains, my father surprised all his neighbors, not long after this conversation, by entering into partnership with a sharp-faced, sharp-dealing man, a Mr. Cyrus Katchem.

Father's explanation of his reasons was, that although a gentleman and in the main a good Christian, yet being in no paying business he had no proper recognition in either the church or in society, and in consequence would receive no consideration, should he die, in a New England or a Wichnor heaven.

"It's because you've got no proper gauge of your own capacity for business, Rufus. I'll agree with you in one thing, you are too much of an honest man and a gentleman to take a partnership with Cyrus Katchem," said grandfather; and having had his say he did not again mention the partnership until his attention was called thereto by the following circumstances:

At first father had put into the business only a little ready money that he had in bank, but after a time Katchem declared that father's abilities had "made things hum," so that the business was extending beyond their capital.

Grandfather Perkins, on being consulted about putting in more money, very wisely said: "If the business is extending, your credit ought to extend with it. Don't risk money when you don't see where it's going to."

What arguments were used to counteract this very common-sense view I know not; but a short time afterwards my mother's estate was heavily mortgaged for money to put into the firm of "Katchem & Johnstone."

A few days later Cyrus Katchem declared that the business had got into a terrible snarl, and some one would have to put in more money to untangle things.

As my father had no funds on which to draw, and as Katchem said that he had begged and borrowed for the firm to the extent of his abilities, the snarl became a knot, which, it was soon found, could not be untied without an assignment.

Burton, shortly after this, took the opportunity

to seize my mother's estate by foreclosing his mortgage, but was checkmated by Grandfather Perkins, who furnished the money to pay up the mortgage on the estate, taking one himself at six per cent. interest.

Among some of our fair-minded neighbors there was a strong opinion that Cyrus Katchem had defrauded his partner.

On an examination of the books of the Katchem concern, there was such unmistakable evidence of recent unfair and fraudulent transfer of property to Katchem's wife, that father began a suit at law against him. Grandfather Perkins was opposed to this on the ground that it would be, as he said, "throwing good money after bad."

My father engaged as his lawyer the able Whitcome Cute, an influential man, and before Katchem had a chance to convey all his property by safe transfer it was promptly seized on account of the suit brought by my father.

After the usual "law's delay," judgment was rendered for the plaintiff Johnstone. The defendant appealed, and after a vexatious re-hearing the judgment of the lower court was sustained. Exceptions to the rulings of the court were then carried before a full bench, which again sustained the judgment of the lower court, and my father triumphed. There was rejoicing in the house of Rufus Johnstone, but Grandfather Perkins was a wet blanket. "Wait," he said, "until you hear from your lawyer. You've beaten Katchem, and now your lawyer will beat you."

"The Hon. Whitcome Cute is the soul of honor," exclaimed my father: "I'll vouch for his integrity anywhere."

The day of settlement with the lawyer came. Father, the Hon. Whitcome Cute and his young partner, and Grandfather Perkins were seated at a table where various papers were displayed and examined and explained. Everything so far was satisfactory. The Hon. Whitcome Cute then presented an itemized account for his services.

As the Hon. Whitcome Cute handed over to my father the account he said:

"Mr. Johnstone, I've known your father-in-law a great many years. I knew his good wife — God bless her! — before he married her; I attended her funeral and was one of the bearers. I knew your wife, Mr. Johnstone, when she was a little girl. Our family has always thought a great deal of her; and in consideration of our long, unbroken friendship I've made my bill just as reasonable as is consistent."

A tear glistened on the cheek of the Hon. Whitcome Cute as he made these feeling remarks. All present were affected except Grandfather Perkins. He had unsentimentally put on his spectacles and was running his eye over the long, itemized account.

As the Hon. Whitcome Cute concluded and was

wiping his eyes with his spotless pocket-handkerchief, Grandfather Perkins, passing the paper to father, said with an angry grunt, "It's durned lucky, Rufus, that the squire did n't know your father and mother and all your connections, or he'd 'a' skinned you alive!"

Father, as he mastered the import of the items, exclaimed, "But what do I get, Mr. Cute? Your bill seems to cover the whole sum recovered from the thief."

"Get? Get, my dear sir?" exclaimed lawyer Cute. "Why, my good friend, *you get your case!*"

I have often since that time had occasion to observe that, in going to law, a client may get his case without obtaining much else of justice or satisfaction for himself, except the doubtful pleasure of punishing an opponent, and of paying the well-earned fees of his lawyers. Finally, the Hon. Whitcome Cute, at grandfather's suggestion, threw out several items from the account and reduced others until the bill had shrunken somewhat in its proportions, grandfather sarcastically saying that as lawyer Cute had n't known any of his son-in-law's folks, he thought it no more than right that these abatements be made. Thus it was that the original bill was so reduced that some four hundred dollars remained after paying the bill rendered for lawyers' services.

The Hon. Whitcome Cute seemed pleased when the settlement was concluded, and father courteously said, while bowing him to the door, "I do not consider the bill as it stands, Mr. Cute, in the least unjust."

Father's means had now become so meagre that at last, after several months' waiting, he humiliated himself so far as to write to his father, the Hon. Rufus Johnstone, Sr., offering, like the prodigal son, to become as one of his hired servants.

There came no answer direct to father from Rufus Johnstone, Sr., but one from an uncle, William Johnstone, saying that, as he had heard that my father was willing to accept employment, and as he needed a manager for his business, one who was trustworthy rather than of great business ability, he took the liberty of offering that position for his acceptance.

After family consultation, father decided to accept the position.

In a few weeks an answer was received inclosing a draft on New York for his expenses, one-half of which my father deemed sufficient, leaving the balance to defray family expenses until he could remove my mother and myself to the South.

But while men make their little plans, and make them seemingly well, a higher power than man's often overrules them.

CHAPTER IV.

MY FATHER LEAVES WICHNOR.

It was in December, 1859, that the incidents of which the foregoing chapter is a record occurred. At that time the agitation of the slavery question was at its height. During the previous October John Brown, with a few devoted followers, had made a raid into Virginia at Harper's Ferry, with the avowed purpose of raising the standard of insurrection, and of arming and liberating the slaves.

The personal bravery of this fanatical old man had excited the admiration even of his enemies, and aroused more sympathy throughout the North than the anti-slavery men had ever been able to gain for the slaves of the South. He was tried, convicted, and sentenced, and was hanged on the second of December.

The main effect of this incident was to exasperate the temper and to increase the bitterness of political discussion everywhere. Some men execrated Brown as a dangerous fellow; others exalted him as a saint.

Several of our neighbors had dropped into our sitting-room to express their regrets that father was to leave Wichnor, and perhaps, incidentally, to learn his opinion of the hanging of John Brown. Father had always encouraged these gatherings, and his neighbors, in their self-contained manner, appreciated his unfeigned hospitality.

"We understand," said Jim Bisbee, "that you're goin' hum South. We're mighty sorry t' hev y' go, tu; you've been a good neighbor an' we hope we hain't seen the last of y'. I know somethin' 'bout you Southern fellers — pooty good breed; ruther pep'ry. tu, sometimes, I snum! when y' happen ter git on the off side of 'em. I've peddled tin down South, an' some o' them chaps would buy things they did n't want, an' never ask the price ef they happened t' like a feller, but ef they took a contr'y notion y' could n't tech 'em with a ten-foot pole. But say, Mister Johnstone, what du y' think o' hangin' that ole feller Brown? Kind o' tough on him, wa'n't it? That ole feller hed more grit 'n all the rest o' the abolitionists goin'."

Father made no reply, for Grandfather Perkins was fumbling a newspaper and clearing his throat, and he knew that more was coming.

"I see they have had a meeting in Boston," said grandfather, "regarding the hanging of this Captain Brown."

"Should n't wonder," said father laughingly; "they get up meetings there on very slight provocations."

"Theodore Parker said at that meeting," continued grandfather in his most stately manner (for he did n't like to be interrupted when he had anything that he considered of great importance to deliver). "'The road to Heaven is as short from the gallows as from a throne, perhaps as easy.' Thoreau said, 'Some eighteen hundred years ago Christ was crucified; this morning, perchance, Captain Brown was hanged; these are two ends of a chain which is not without its links.' Emerson said, 'John Brown is a new saint, waiting yet for his martyrdom, who, if he shall suffer, will make the gallows glorious like the cross.'"

Grandfather folded his paper and took off his spectacles with unusual stateliness, and said impressively, "That's what I call eloquence. What do you think of it, Rufus?"

"With all deference to you," said father, with his usual politeness, "I think it is grandiloquent nonsense. Old Brown was a brave man; he believed he was in the right, and was willing to die unflinchingly for it. Such traits always ennoble men. I believe there is more of that kind of grit in your people than they get credit for. But all this about John Brown being a saint and martyr is far-fetched. He was simply, so far as I can see, a brave old man."

It will be seen by this that my father was a moderate and reasonable man in discussions which concerned the South.

"The truth is," said my father, "the angry feelings between the North and the South could not live a day if the two sections understood each other's point of view as I do. There are but few gentlemen in the South who will not agree when not angry that slavery is wrong. They claim, however, that it is made more tolerable at the South than it has ever been elsewhere; that they have inherited slavery and its attendant problems, and if let alone could deal with its questions better than Northern men. Now, instead of endeavoring to solve the problems, they are busy in inventing replies to Northern criticisms."

Grandfather Perkins poked at the fire, hitched uneasily in his seat (for he was an extreme abolitionist in sentiment), and finally said:

"What can we expect of men, Rufus, who deny a man's right to possess himself? Such unreasonableness leads to all kinds of violence, until a man gets adrift, as it were, and can't tell right from wrong;" and grandfather, while holding the newspaper before his face to shield it from the heat, gave the fire another great thrust, sending a tongue of flame, accompanied by a shower of angry sparks, up the chimney. A murmur of something like assent was heard in the room.

"Andrew! Andrew!" called my father; and Andy, father's colored man, or, as some one had called him sarcastically, Rufus Johnstone's shadow, at this call came from the kitchen, and stood respectfully waiting for father's orders. Andy was a mulatto, compactly built, and though nearly six feet in height did not look it, because of his symmetrical proportions. His face, though ordinarily pleasant, had at times an expression of almost savage determination rarely seen in one of his race. Father gave a few directions, and as Andy turned to go called him back again, saying, "Andrew, get the guns out and clean them, and we'll try a little shooting to-morrow."

"Yes, sah," responded Andy, as he bowed himself out.

"He's a mighty handy feller," said Jim Bisbee, "an' he knows as much as anybody, tu."

"Yes; and for my part, Rufus, I can't see what in the world he wants to work for you for," said grandfather; "you pay him only small wages. I offered him double to work for me, and the fellow hardly treated me decent; acted— dummed if he didn't!— as if I'd insulted him."

Father smiled, and said in his soft Southern undertones, and as if to himself, "No, Andy wouldn't leave me;" and then added as he mused: "You wouldn't think that Andy was once considered intractable, and a very bad servant, would you?"

"The idea of such a man being held as a slave!" exclaimed grandfather, interrupting father. "Why, Andy can cipher and read about as well as you or I can! I don't see how he learned it, though."

"Andy," said my father thoughtfully, "was always interested in everything I was fond of except Latin and Greek, and I dare say he knows more about them than I do; he always labored on anything that was hard for me, because that boy," said father dropping his voice again, "loves me as well as I love Hez, or better; you would scarcely believe if I should tell you how much. Here, Andy is free as you or I, and yet the relations between us are the same that they were when we were at the South, only he works a great deal harder here because we are poorer. Slavery has its disagreeable points, I'll admit, and there are hard masters in the South, as there are here. I shouldn't like to have Andy fall into the hands of such men, but," and father laughed as he said it, " they wouldn't get much service out of Andy if he didn't approve of them."

"Well," said Mr. Stanley, who was present, "a man like that stands a chance to get a bad master, doesn't he?"

"I think he does," said father. "There are some men South, as there are everywhere, who would coin blood into gold, who care neither for God nor Caesar, only the superscription on the coin. It isn't safe to give such men too much power. But they overreach themselves, for bad masters make bad servants everywhere. I could tell you a story to illustrate that, one which came under my own observation, if I wanted to."

"Oh, do tell us a story!" I exclaimed.

"Well," said father, "it is a true story, and it may interest you older men, but it isn't much of a story to tell, though the affair was a great deal talked of around where I lived at the time it happened.

"A man who owned a plantation adjoining my father's had a boy that no one could manage. He had, so his master said, a very bad temper, and he was finally whipped, and being as high-strung as any one of you he became worse instead of better.

"One day, while my brother Bob and I were on this plantation, we came upon him when the overseer was about to whip him again. I gave the overseer my new rifle to let the boy off from further whipping at that time, for he had been given two or three cuts with the whip already.

"A day or two after this the boy ran away to the swamps. Here he lived, and couldn't be caught. He was so fierce and savage that after a time his owner offered a reward for his body, dead or alive. He killed pack after pack of bloodhounds sent out to track him, and I haven't any doubt he would have killed the men sent after him if they had come within his reach. After a while no one cared to meddle with him. He was nicknamed 'Yellow Jack.'

"One day, while brother Bob and I were hunting near the swamp, there stood Yellow Jack on a hummock close to us. He was ragged and bareheaded.

"'Hello! what are you doing here?' said Bob, not a bit frightened.

"'Why don't you shoot me? I ain't nothin' but

"WHY DON'T YOU SHOOT ME?"

a poor runaway servant,' said he. He looked so miserable that it made me sorry for him, and I said, 'My poor fellow, we wouldn't hurt you if we could. We would much rather help you.'

"'Don't you want some dinner?' asked Bob, at the same time passing the lunch basket. The fellow sat down and ate like a starving man. We gave him some fish-lines we had with us, a knife, and some matches, and after that saw nothing of him for a long time.

"I was very ill that winter. It was a cold winter, one of the coldest I ever knew in our country; at one time the swamp was frozen over.

"I lay in my room burning up with a fever; sick, it was feared, unto death. Somehow, I don't know exactly how, perhaps from my brother, or more likely from the servants, Yellow Jack learned of my sickness, left the swamps, and came to the house; some one let him in, and the first I knew of it he was bathing my hands and face as tenderly as a woman. My father came to the room, and seeing this — as he thought — dangerous fellow, reached for his pistol to shoot him.

"I don't know how I did it, but I got from the bed and stood between my father and the boy, while my brother, who had come in, pushed in between us, exclaiming: 'This boy is here on my parole of honor, father. If you touch him I shall be dishonored, and shall resent it.' Yellow Jack, meanwhile, had taken me in his arms and put me into bed again.

"My father stood a moment as if uncertain, then, as if comprehending in part the situation, turned on his heel and left the room.

"In an hour he came back and handed me a paper. 'What is this for?' I said. 'Read it, my son,' said father, with unusual tenderness. It was a bill of sale of Yellow Jack, from his master to me.

"'There,' said father, 'the boy is yours; I have bought him for you! You can set him free or do anything else you have a mind to with him.'

"From that time the boy nursed me faithfully. I don't think he slept for a week, and the doctor said his nursing saved my life. You would hardly believe that the fellow who had been so disobedient and savage became the most devoted servant a man ever had. He never took to the swamps after that."

"What became of him finally?" we all asked.

"He is out there in the kitchen — it was Andy."

There was silence in the group for an instant, when Jim Bisbee ejaculated, "I snum!"

The incident was a revelation to our neighbors of the relations sometimes existing between master and slave.

"I'd like to see Uncle Robert," I said. "Where does he live, father?"

"Bless you, Hez, so would I like to see him! Where does he live, did you say? Well, when I came to this State to enter college, he came to New York. He lived a rather fast life, so it was said, though it was supposed he was studying law there. I saw him once or twice after we came North. After that he was married, to an actress, it was said, and then father was angry, broke with him as he did with me later, and I've not seen him since. He wrote me once about going to sea, and I've never heard from him since."

"Perhaps he has made up with your dad and is at home now," I said.

"No," said father, "he would starve before he would acknowledge himself wrong when he believed himself right. No, he's not gone home."

The next day — and I remember it as if it were yesterday, though nearly forty years have passed since then — I accompanied father and Andy to the woods.

The reserve and pride which at times seemed to shut me out from father's heart was broken down that day, and he was sunny and at his best. I was allowed to shoot, under his direction, to my heart's content, for he was a famous shot; and both Andy and father declared that I would make an excellent marksman.

Before leaving for home, while Andy was cleaning the rifles, father said to me:

"As you know, I am about to leave Wichnor for

the South; that unfortunate failure has made it needful for me to make an effort to do something for those I love. My uncle has offered me a position with a good salary, a place, he says, that doesn't require much business talent, — which is fortunate for me, — but fidelity." Then he hesitated as he said: "Hez, I've had, in some indefinable way, a feeling of trouble — I might call it a presentiment. I suppose it is simply low spirits. Still, I feel in some way that possibly I may not see you again for a long time. I want you always to remember that you are a gentleman's son. If you are ever tempted to do or consent to a low-down act, remember this. I do not wish you to despise useful employment, such as a trade; if I had a good knowledge of some useful trade I would not leave you now. But whatever you do, do it in a manly, self-respecting way. If you must work for a living, work like a gentleman and don't be ashamed of it. Never take advantage of the weak nor cringe to the strong; never abuse a trust nor betray a confidence; defend your honor as you would a weak woman or a child — if need be with your life."

This talk made a deep impression on me at a time when such impressions are indelible; and if I have ever proved myself manly and strong where I might have found excuse to be otherwise it was because of such impressions, received from my father.

The next day he took his departure by steamer to New York *en route* for North Carolina.

CHAPTER V.

A MYSTERY.

Shortly after the arrival of my father in the South we received a letter written in a very hopeful and happy tone. His uncle treated him as a son rather than as a dependent, he said; his surroundings were pleasant, and he anticipated a speedy reunion with his family; at least, as soon as he had the means, and could arrange properly for our removal South.

After this letters came at regular intervals for a while, some of them containing drafts for money, and all expressing the love he felt for mother and me.

In one of these letters he alluded to the threats of dissolving the Union, so commonly heard at that time among Southern men, if the Republican party should elect a president; and said it was mere bluster and talk, which would disappear after the elections were over.

About four months after his arrival we were somewhat surprised by the intelligence that his uncle was attempting to effect a reconciliation between him and his father. Soon afterwards another letter from father announced that a complete reconciliation had been effected. "So you will see, my dear Rose," he wrote, "that the days of our poverty are about over, and also, which is of more consequence to me, the days of our separation from each other."

A short time after this there came still another letter, saying that his father had consented to an arrangement by which he was to come North to remove mother and me to his home in North Carolina, and that he should not write again before starting for Connecticut.

We were glad and somewhat excited over the prospect. Each day thereafter I visited the steamboat landing to welcome him home, but he did not come. Days and weeks passed, and yet he did not come; neither did we receive any message from him. Mother wrote to Grandfather Johnstone, but received no reply.

Andy, who was consulted, said very positively, "Mas'r Rufus is sick, an' de res' ob dem fokes dar doan' car' f' nobody but demselves. Mas'r Rufus would write if he could. If an't'ing is de matter, de ol' mas'r would be too sorry for hisself to car' for you uns."

After this the atmosphere at home became very gloomy, and I often found my mother crying by herself. "Something dreadful has happened to your father," she said, "and I would go South to see what, if I only had the money." Grandfather Perkins said, "Yes, something has certainly happened to prevent his coming, but not necessarily sickness or accident. When Rufus Johnstone says he will do anything, and fails to do it, there is some good reason for the failure; it is not his fault, I am sure."

The fact that he was starting for Wichnor when last heard from, and had not been seen or heard from since, though months had elapsed, became the talk of our town. Some of our neighbors — and among them the Burtons — put a sinister construction upon his non-appearance, saying he had deserted his Northern wife. Jim Bisbee, when the subject came up for discussion, said:

"Like 's not Mr. Johnstone has had some dis-'greement with some o' them political hot-heads there. Y' know he ain't the man t' keep his mouth shet when there 's anythin' that orter be said; an' like 's not he 's ben sayin' their secession tin ain't silver. It 's a word an' a blow down there, an' the blow is likely t' come fust. I snum, they shoot at each other instid o' sassin' each other as they would here! For my part, I think sass is more moral an' civil, an' y' can git over it easier."

"Nonsense! what kind of talk is that?" said grandfather, sniffing as if he smelled something unsavory.

"Wal," persisted Jim, assuming an argumentative attitude, and poking his index finger at grandfather's vest, "Naow, I tell y' how 't is: I 've peddled tinware 'mong 'em, an' y' know y' kind 'o see inside of a man when y' ar' tradin' with 'im. If y' say anythin' 'bout politics they don't like, they say, kind o' pleasant-like, that they hev the highest respect f'r y'r opinions, but y'd better not express 'em round there. Then y'd better be a-gettin' away if y' hev any respect f'r y'r carcus. I snum, them that never owned a nigger or a shingle on the roof of a shanty is the wust! I guess that's the way 't is daown there 'baout talkin' 'g'inst secession; I'll bet my hat 'g'inst a tin pan it's got somethin' t' du with Rufus Johnstone's not comin' hum when y' expected him; jest like 's not he told 'em that it was consarned nonsense!"

Others of our neighbors suggested that he might have been foully dealt with in coming through New York City.

But speculations and conjectures regarding him and his whereabouts proved as unavailing as had letters written to him and to Rufus Johnstone, Sr.

The gloom caused by father's absence, and the suspense caused by uncertainty as to his fate, was intensified by poverty, which stealthily crept upon us.

This gloom was lightened for me by Phil's coming to our house to board. Mrs. Nonfit, who had been complaining for some months of not being well, was at last prostrated by a hemorrhage of the lungs, which was so serious as to call forth from her physician, doubts if whether or not she could ever recover from its effects. On his recommendation she went to Minnesota for a change of climate.

Before leaving, with many kind admonitions to Phil, she committed him to my mother's charge to care for during her absence. As she paid quite a large sum of money in advance for his board and clothing, this was a great assistance to mother.

Poor woman, she never came back alive. Two months or more afterward a telegram was received saying that she had died suddenly from a hemorrhage of the lungs.

After her death it was ascertained that the only will she had left was one in the hands of her legal adviser, which was made long before she knew Phil, and that the papers for Phil's adoption had never been executed. The lawyer said he had no doubt, from what he had heard her say, that she had intended to make a provision for Phil, yet, he said, it is very common for people to put off such matters until too late to carry out their good intentions.

Thus it was that Phil was once more thrown on his own resources. But the kindly influence of Mrs. Nonfit remained. Her love had left such an impression on Phil that in proportion as he regretted her death he heeded the good advice and teachings she had given him. Such is the transforming influence of kindness and love.

We were in much the same situation so far as our immediate prospects were concerned.

Andy, after moping around the place for several weeks after this, left for parts unknown, to find, as he explained in a note which he left in his room, "Mas'r Rufus."

As there was now no one in our family competent to care for the place or cultivate the land, mother removed to Grandfather Perkins's, where she took charge of his house. Grandfather said that the boys, alluding to Phil and me, were big enough to pay for their keep by working on the farm.

Farm work was distasteful to me, and grandfather was very exacting, and, as I thought, needlessly fussy. Phil looked upon farming much as I did, though he did not openly complain.

After we were in bed at night it was a favorite pastime with us to talk of going to sea. From the standpoint of two boys in a comfortable home a sailor's life appeared alluring. I declared to Phil that I had always wanted to be a sailor. While his former hard lessons in life taught him that there would, as he said, "be some hard knocks in it," yet in the main he agreed with me that going to sea was preferable to "digging."

I finally began to urge mother to consent to my going to Rivermouth with Captain Zenas Williams to ship with him for a sea-voyage. My mother's reply to these importunities had always been unfavorable. Grandfather had "poohed" at it, and said it was "hare-brained nonsense." "Did n't you ever read Peter Parley's Geography?" said he. "Isn't there a verse in it that reads:

> ' Water and land upon the face
> Of this round world we see.
> The land is man's safe dwelling-place,
> But ships sail on the sea'?

"I'd 'a' made an amendment to that verse if I'd had the making of that geography; I'd had it read:

> 'The land is man's safe dwelling-place,
> But fools will go to sea.'"

One evening Jim Bisbee visited us, and on account of his quaint talk (which was sprinkled with more than accidental wisdom) he was a welcome and entertaining visitor.

"Heard from y'r father yit, Hez?" he inquired; then added, as if in answer to his own question, "It's awful queer he or some 'n' else don't write."

I said, "Yes, Jim; and I'm trying to get mother to consent to my going to sea, on some vessel bound for Southern ports, in hopes to learn something about where father is."

"Sho!" said Jim slowly, looking fixedly at me. "Goin' t' sea ain't what it's cracked up to be, by a long chuck. I've ben t' sea myself, an' I ruther guess ef y' knew what kind o' duin's an' the topsy-turvy kind o' life 't is y'd never say 'nother word."

Just then mother came in, and Jim, to my surprise, turned like a weather-vane, and began to intercede with her in line with my wishes.

"Naow, Mis' Johnstone," said Jim, crossing his legs in a deliberate manner, and running his fingers through his hair as if to clear his thoughts, "y'r son he's ben a-tellin' he wants t' go t' sea; he says he thinks in that way he may fall in with his father. Hez is oneasy as he c'n be, an' the way he's goin' on he'll soon be a trouble t' y' an' like 's not no advantage t' himself. He don't like farmin', an' the squire here, he thinks a good deal o' Hez, an' Hez sets a store by his gran'ther; but he's like lighted touchwood an' the boy is like powder, an' I guess 't is a good idee t' keep sech things in differunt parcels if y' do n't want t' blow up, I snum! Hez wants t' go t' sea; or at least he thinks he doos, an' ef y' don't look aout he may feel es ef he'd a call t' go, anyway. He's jest said t' me that in touchin' at Southern ports he may find aout somethin' 'bout his father. Naow, Mis' Johnstone, why don't y' let him hev a lick at sea-farin' life? There's Nathan Gallup, he did n't maount t' shucks on a farm; jest see what a mighty smart feller he makes as cap'n of a ship; at least that 's what they say. He'd 'a' made a poor stick of a farmer. T' git ahead in the world, a feller's got t' work at somethin' he likes. Naow, I kind o' whopped 'raound from one thing to t' other till I got t' tin-peddlin'. It fitted me jes' like a glove. I knew the minnit I got on t' a tin cart that

I was made for the biz; an' I've made a pooty fair fort'n at it, tu. Say, Mis' Johnstone, why don't y' let Hez go? Ten chances t' one 't'll knock the conceit out on 'im ef y' let him try it. Naow, I wanted desp'ritly t' go t' sea once myself. Father up an' says, 'Go ahead, Jim; an' when ye've got tired o' sleepin' on a shelf, come hum an' try an' behave y'rself an' sleep in a reg'lar bed.'

"Wal, I went daown t' Rivermouth, an' after lookin' up at them tall masts an' understan'in' I'd got t' shin 'em ef I went b'fore the mast, I ast the cap'n ef thar wuz any place behind the mast whar I would n't hev t' shin them tall poles. He said, guess I meant a cook's berth. Fin'lly, after peekin' 'raound kinder anxious-like most o' the day, I did ship as cook on a thunderin' gre't coal skuner.

"Wal, we sot sail an' for 'baout an hour everything was slick as greased sunshine, I snum! An' then the wind cum up, the waves sloshed, an' jest jumped that ol' skuner raound like popcorn in the hot ashes. I wuz washin' up the dishes, when them tin pans 'n' plates b'gun t' roll 'raound an' slide 'bout like all p'sessed. An' then I was consumedly sick, an' thar I wuz, tryin' t' hold on t' sumthin' an' tryin' t' ketch the pans an' things that wuz a-sloshin' fust this side an' then that side like mad. An' thar I wuz gittin' sicker an' sicker, an' sech a mess raound that air skuner's kitchen y' never see, but y'll stan' a chance ef y' go t' sea, I snum!

"Fin'lly, I hed t' lay daown; the pots an' dishes rollin' raound with me on the floor, an' I gittin' sicker every dummed minnit t'll I thought I sh'd die. I went on in that poor sick an' dyin' style, the cap'n jawin' an' all the rest on 'em mad 'cuz I could n't git grub f'r 'em, an' usin' bad language I would n't use tu a sick pig.

"Fin'lly," continued Jim, very solemnly, "the cap'n put inter Bridgeport, ''cuz,' he said, 'it looked as it were a-goin' t' blow.' Jewhitaker! Jest 's ef it had n't begun!

"When that craft got inter Bridgeport, I jest left everythin' I had — clothes an' sea-notions — an' I did n't turn t' look at that skunner agin; ef I hed I b'lieve I 'd 'a' puked.

"'Whar be y'r goin'?' yelled the cap'n.

"'Goin' hum,' says I, withaout turnin' my head, the land heavin' an' onstiddy-like, like the swashin' deep. An' I put f'r the steam-cars an' got hum that night jest 'baout milkin'-time.

"Mother said when I walked inter the haouse, 'Mercy sakes alive, James, y' look like a ghost! Whar did y' come frum?' An' I said, 'Mother, I've come f'm the ravin' deep an' f'm death's door.'

"When father come in, he said very kindly an' smilin'-like, 'James, eat your supper an' go an' milk the caows an' du the chores.' Y'd ought t' see me spring tu it. Why, farm work wa'n't nothin' arter that v'y'ge!"

And Jim chuckled and rubbed down his trousers legs, which were some distance from his shoes.

"Haven't you ever been to sea since, Mister Bisbee?" inquired Phil.

"Wal — no, not 'zactly; I've been t' the medders t' mow salt hay, but I've alla's kep' withi n wadin' distance o' the shore, by gum! I say, Mis' Johnstone, give the boy a trial at seafarin' lif , an' let him hev money enough so he c'n git hu n f'm any reasonable distance 'thout walkin'."

My mother, perhaps because she thought, like Bisbee, that I should get sick of the sea and be thereafter contented to stay at home, finally consented to my going on a voyage with Captain Zenas Williams, if he would take me.

CHAPTER VI.

ON BOARD THE BRIG "FAVORITE."

Now that it was at last settled that I was going to sea, at least one voyage, neither Phil nor I could talk of anything else, for Phil had made up his mind that if Captain Zenas Williams would take him he would go with me.

We were talking at the breakfast-table about it, when grandfather said: "I suppose it is all settled now, Hez, except what position you'll take, whether before the mast or, like Jim Bisbee, *behind* the mast; or perhaps you'll take Cap'n Williams's place as master?"

"I expect," I replied, "to begin at the bottom and learn the business, grandfather."

"Well," said he more seriously, "whatever you do, Hez, do it well, and remember that honesty is the foundation of success. Be respectful to every one — your father has taught you that; and remember that a dollar in your pocket is a good friend."

When night came Phil and I lay awake as long as we could, talking of adventures on the sea. We seldom got to sleep before being cast away on what Phil called a "desperate" island apiece, for we did not agree as to the material to be cast away with us. I wanted to be left on a desolate island with nothing but a suit of clothes, while Phil would not consent to be cast away without a shipful of good things with him to make life cheerful. We usually compromised by Phil's being wrecked on an island near to mine. "Then," he would say, "it would be handy for you to come over and borrow the things you needed."

Captain Zenas at last came home from a voyage, and mother waited on him, accompanied by Phil and me.

The captain was a rosy-cheeked, sedate-looking man, with very little of the appearance of a sailor; but at times there was an expression in his face that showed to me that he was a man not to be trifled with.

Mother made her application, to which the captain at first replied adversely, saying, "I don't like to take my neighbors' boys to sea, because at sea no favors can be shown to any one; even boys have got to be men at sea, ma'm!"

At last he yielded to many flattering persuasions urged by mother, and agreed to take us with him on what he called a trial trip. "Then we can see," he said, "how the brig and the boys will jibe together."

Then came the excitement of getting us ready, for clothes had to be made especially for service at sea.

While these preparations were going on, Jim

Bisbee came in to talk things over, and make suggestions drawn from his experience on the deep in a coal schooner.

"Cap'n Zenas, did y' say?" said Jim crossing his long legs and assuming a look of fox-like sagacity. "Wal, naow, Mis' Johnstone, he 's a good man ashore, he 's one o' the pillars o' the church, ef not half o' the hull o' the Bethel daown there t' Rivermaouth where they du say he runs the hull thing an' preaches, tu, sometimes. But y' know a man is kind 'o diff'runt when he 's on the rollin' deep; the best on 'em 'll act kind 'o tearin' like, when things is a-cuttin' up an' howlin' an' tossin'," and Jim heaved a profound sigh of sympathy at what was before us. I had hard work to keep from laughing outright, for I had not forgotten Jim's description of his sea voyage.

"Captain Williams," interrupted mother, "is different from ordinary rough and profane sailors, and that is the reason I want Hez to go to sea with him; he 's a Christian man."

"Hum!" ejaculated Jim, stroking his chin thoughtfully; "yes, he *is* a pooty good man, an' well spoken, but then — Say, did y' hear 'baout their church maulin' him at Rivermaouth f'r cussin', once?"

"No," said mother, "and I don't believe anything said against such a man, either; envy loves a shining mark."

"Bill Hardin', one o' them Rivermaouth men,"

continued Jim, not noticing my mother's remark, "went t' sea 'fore the mast with Cap'n Zenas; an' when he come hum — y' see he b'longed t' the Bethel tu — he put in a complaint t' the church, an' they hauled him over the coals f'r cussin' his men at sea.

"Wal, Cap'n Zenas he stood up t' the rack an' took it like a man. He owned up that he swore sometimes, but not in any irreligious manner, but as a cap'n of a brig, perfessionally. Then he turned on Bill Hardin' an' said, 'Brethering, I had a duty t' perform f'r the owners an' underwriters, an' there ain't a man here,' he said, 'that can skipper a craft an' not swear, with such men 'fore the mast as that air Bill Hardin'!'

"The officers an' brethering was mostly seafarin' folks, an' they brought in 'ginst the cap'n thet it wuz in evidence that he hed used strong language at sea, but it wuz also shown thet it wa' n't used in a profane or irreligious manner, but as the cap'n of a ship, I snum ef they did n't," and Jim chuckled and added, "but Cap'n Zenas is a respectable man, Mis' Johnstone, an' I don't think the sea hes hardened his heart like it had the ole chap I sailed with, — sailors ain't like other people; the terrors o' the deep are awful provokin', Mis' Johnstone. Ef y' could hev jest seed me on thet ole coal skuner y' would n't wonder sailors lose the'r presence of mind, an' — mos' everything else, I snum, sometimes."

It was a moment of great excitement when Phil and I, in our sea rigs, went on board the brig "Favorite," at Rivermouth. The creaking of the blocks and the smell of tar all had a charm for us which cannot be expressed in words, but which many will understand.

We first got our chests into the forecastle, which was a small, black, ill-smelling hole, in which six men besides us boys were to have a home. An old sailor named Tarbox showed us our berths and where to stow away our "duds," as he called them, after which we went on deck.

The brig was a trim-looking craft; her white decks, and well-set up rigging, and fresh paint showing advantageously in contrast with the dingy colliers and lumbermen and other coasters which lay at the wharves.

We soon began to explore her, after which we amused ourselves by going aloft and seeing which could first reach the masthead. While thus engaged the captain came on board, and for a while looked on at what Bill Tarbox called our "skylarking."

I heard the captain say, "They'll do; they git round 'mong the riggin' as quick as cats."

"Ay, ay," growled Bill Tarbox, "but it'll be diff'rent for the youngsters in a gale o' wind!"

That night we slept in the forecastle, but got our supper up town. The next day, the last of the brig's cargo — several hundred quintals of dried fish, also a large quantity of salt, and several large boxes or cases — was stowed below decks. In the afternoon we pulled out into the stream ready to sail on the morrow, "wind and tide," as Bill Tarbox said, "permitting."

I had my first meal on board that evening, and then learned that in the forecastle of a ship there are no such things as a table, knives, forks, spoons, or crockery. The "kid," around which we sat on the deck, contained a piece of "salt junk" and a few boiled potatoes, to which we helped ourselves by cutting from the meat with our sheath knives. (The kid, let me explain, is a tub bound with iron hoops.) As we crawled out of the dismal forecastle after this unpalatable meal, Phil nudged me and said, "Say, Hez, we're livin' like pigs, ain't we?"

That night I stood my first "watch" on board ship. I walked "fore and aft," looking over the taffrail and bows at every round, feeling that the safety of the ship depended on my vigilance and fidelity. When I was at last relieved, one can imagine how horrified I was to see the old sailor who relieved me stow himself away in a snug spot, and light his pipe for a smoke!

"Is that allowable on shipboard?" I asked.

"Avast there and belay!" ejaculated the old salt; "the barnacles can't come up through the bottom o' the brig, nor th' sky tumble on to th' mainmast when she's in harbor an' safe at anchor."

I went below and turned in "all stan'in'," as Bill Tarbox called it (that is, with my clothes on). It seemed to me I had no sooner got to sleep than I heard thumping on the hatch and the long-drawn out call from the deck,—"All-star-bow-lines ahoy! Eight bells there below! Do you hear the news?"

If I thought it a hardship to be awakened and called on deck at that time, how much harder was it afterwards, when at sea, with the attendant discomforts, I answered similar calls to duty.

I scrambled on deck with my eyes but half open, wishing I could only just sleep a few moments longer. On assuming my duties, I was instructed to call the captain if the wind changed. My watch was nearly out when the wind came around to the northward and eastward, and I called the captain. It was broad daylight when he came on deck. He told me to call all hands at once. I did this as instructed, though I was aware that neither my manner nor voice had a very nautical style. Bill Tarbox afterwards said "it sounded more like 'cock-a-doodle doo' than "all hands on deck ahoy!"

The men came on deck at the call, however, like magic. They loosened the sails and braced the yards amidst what seemed to me a babel of unintelligible sea-cries and sounds. The orders were rapidly given and executed, we manned the windlass, and in a few minutes the anchor was up and we were laying our course down the Sound.

The first mate, through whom came all orders to the men on the deck, was a weather-beaten old sea-dog, with a face the color of Russia leather, and a voice that sounded as if a squall of wind had struck the rigging. He was a good seaman, so Bill Tarbox said, but, to quote the same authority, "too much given to splicin' the main brace."

I did not understand the term until Bill had accompanied it in pantomime, as if taking a drink from an invisible glass. As the mate walked the deck, his hands hanging by his sides, like hooks spliced to handspikes, he seemed to me arbitrary, tyrannical, and in all respects the reverse of what a gentleman should be.

The wind was blowing quite fresh, and before we had been out in the Sound an hour both Phil and I were dreadfully sick. We took Bill Tarbox's advice, and made just as little of our sickness as was possible, though the smell of bilge-water in the forecastle, when I went below while off duty, did n't help me to any appreciable degree. So, following the advice, we both did our best to keep on our feet and at our duties, though, I must confess, it was tough. But on a ship there is no coddling, and sickness of any kind gets but little sympathy, for, as Bill said, "A man don't come to sea for his health."

By the time we had reached New York we got over being sick, for that time at least. I was sick several times after this, however, during rough weather, and sometimes when it was not rough, in going aloft. During our trip down the Sound, I waited on the captain, and learned the names of the sails and ropes, and the meaning of "port" and "starboard."

We arrived in New York on Sunday; and as that day was a day of rest, after a fashion, even on shipboard, we were allowed to go on shore.

Here Phil showed me the places with which he was familiar, and, as I had not been in New York before, I was very much interested. We rambled around near the Bowery, when, stopping before a dingy, dilapitated building, in a dirty alleyway, Phil ran up a pair of creaky, narrow stairs and knocked at a door that seemed dropping from its hinges.

A blear-eyed woman, slatternly and sour-faced, answered the call. "There," said Phil, "is where I lived with Marm Gurley, but they don't know anything about her, and I s'pose it's like looking for a chip thrown overboard on Long Island Sound to try to find her in this big place."

As we were making our way back to the "Favorite," we encountered the mate coming out of one of the many drinking-places that defile that quarter of the city. His eyes were bleared, his steps loose and uncertain.

"Whew!" said Phil, in a low tone, as the mate passed without noticing us; "he hasn't been to church or Sunday-school; his breath sticks out like the flying jib-boom of the brig; you can hang your hat on it, it's so strong!"

That afternoon, after we had got back to the brig, the mate came on board, as Bill said, "with three sheets in the wind, an' t'other shiverin'!"

The captain, who had been to church, also put in an appearance on the quarter-deck. An hour later we pulled out into the stream, the wind being favorable, and were off Sandy Hook by sundown.

The next day the weather was fine, and I began to think that I should like a sailor's life. I said something like that to an old salt, when he made me the unexpected reply, "So would any old woman in the country," and then crossly added, "There ain't wind 'nough to fill y'r hat."

That night, however, we had a disagreeable change. I was fast asleep, when I was awakened by three thunderous blows on the booby-hatch, and the call, "All hands on deck!" On reaching the deck we found a heavy cloud darkening the sky. We had barely time to haul down and clew up, before a squall struck us, and the water was pouring in the port bows and the hawser hole, while at the lee scuppers it was over boots in water. The decks were as steep as a roof, and the brig was tearing through the water like mad with a lather of foam at her bows. Both Phil and I sprung aloft with the rest, and though we were of but little assistance, much is forgiven to green hands that show good will, and we did our best. In a very short time the sails were furled or reefed, but we remained on deck, sea-sick, chilled, and benumbed with wet and cold.

I thought we had escaped great peril, and said as much afterward to Bill, but he took the wind out of my sail, as sailors say, by laughing and saying, "It wan't nothin' but a puff o' wind, you lubber! Wait till a gale comes so y'll have to hold y'r hair on."

We arrived at Norfolk in the course of a week, and by that time both Phil and I had become in part accustomed to the life, and could at least do a little good service. But it was a dog's life, as the growling old sailors justly called it. There is nothing regular about life on shipboard; there are no stated hours of sleep that may not at any time be broken in upon by an emergency, or by the caprice of the captain or some other officer of the ship. "A good sailor," said Bill Tarbox, "sleeps when he can, for when at sea he don't know when he'll git another chance."

On our arrival at Norfolk we began discharging a portion of our cargo.

While in this port I went up town, and while waiting for a reply to a note from the captain, which I had delivered, heard much talk about "Yankee abolitionists."

"What have the Yankees done?" I innocently asked of the clerk at the office where I had delivered the note.

"Why, the rascals have elected a president of

their own," he replied, "and that will oblige us to go out of the Union."

We sailed from Norfolk to Newberne, N.C., where, after a rough voyage, even when measured by Bill Tarbox's standard, we arrived in due season. Long before this we had occasion to remember Jim Bisbee's saying, " Goin' to sea ain't what it's cracked up to be!" All its romance had faded, and we had got down to its grim, prosaic, and uncomfortable reality.

CHAPTER VII.

AT NEWBERNE.

During the trip to Newberne the first mate, who at best was what Bill Tarbox called a "cross-grained stick," was made more than usually ugly by being partially under the influence of liquor which he had brought on board at Norfolk.

The second mate, Mr. Robert Bell, was a good sailor and, as the sailors all agreed, a gentleman. He had shipped on the "Favorite" at Rivermouth, where, it was reported, he had just before arrived as first mate of a ship, from a voyage around the world. Mr. Bell was as fine a specimen of an American sailor (and I now speak with a much wider knowledge than I then had) as I have ever seen. Not only was he a fine sailor, educated in seamanship, as one of our old salts declared, "way to the tips of his toes," but his strong and handsome face was set off by unusually good taste in dress, graceful carriage, and scrupulous personal neatness.

The second officer of a ship, as most sailors will agree, has an exceedingly difficult position to fill, for he has no associates among the common sailors for he is not one of them, and yet he is expected to lead them, and be foremost in their duties aloft, and in reefing he takes the weather earing. He has the captain's watch at sea, and while he takes his meals and sleeps in the cabin, he rarely associates on terms of equality with the captain and his first officer. In port he is the ship's stevedore, and at sea he is the ship's servant, as sailors say.

Mr. Bell's manner was pleasant though decided; never familiar to his superiors in rank, nor to the sailors in the forecastle; he never assumed nor condescended; he listened respectfully, and obeyed orders quickly, as a sailor should. Owing to his apparent superiority in seamanship as well as in manners, there were many surmises among the men in the forecastle why he had accepted a position as second mate on board of the "Favorite," and that too at a time when good officers were in great demand on first-class ships and sailing crafts of all kinds.

From Mr. Bell's coming on board the brig at Rivermouth, the first mate, either through jealousy or natural ugliness and an unreasonable temper, had in every way possible for a man in his position tried to make the second officer's place unpleasant. But the latter adroitly avoided the nautical traps set by his superior, and passed unnoticed his crossness, anger, and want of good manners, as he would an angry gust of wind or a dash of salt water.

"It's because Mr. Bell's a first-class sailor an'

a first-class man," said Bill, "that he takes the mate's hazin' so coolly an' as a matter o' course; he's a better sailor an' a better man than that old duffer of a first mate."

Those, however, who were students of human nature might at times have seen on the face of Mr. Bell an expression which boded no good for the first officer.

Mr. Bell not only treated Phil and me considerately, but was seemingly much interested in us and in our progress in learning the duties of sailors. He not only spoke to us in a pleasant manner, but "put himself out" to instruct us in our duties. This was in marked contrast with the manner of the first mate toward us. He, from our first coming on board, treated us as intruders and interlopers; especially was this true of his treatment of me, for whom he seemed to have taken a special dislike.

On the trip from Norfolk to Newberne Mr. Harding had called me to stand by the wheel. It was rough weather, and I, being not accustomed to the duties of helmsman, of course did not suit him at a time which would have tried the skill of one much more experienced. I did my best, however, and I doubt if he would have been better suited had I been able to steer much better. As it was, when the brig varied a point at times, owing to my lack of both skill and strength, he began to curse me in a very foul and abusive manner, and finally, though I had made no reply (though some of my contempt and disgust for the man may have been seen in my face), he exclaimed, "I'll teach you, you surly dog, to sulk and look black at me." And with this he seized a rope and struck me, and was about to repeat the blow when the captain, coming out of the cabin, arrested his hand, saying in his coldest tones,

"None of that, Mr. Harding; I will have no punishments on board this brig without my orders, and in no case while a man is at the wheel."

Some hot words followed.

"You take a land-lubber on board," said the mate angrily, "to boost through the cabin window, but you must n't expect me to help you do it."

"Let me hear no more of this. You have hazed the men ever since we began this voyage, so I am afraid we shall be left short-handed before we get back to New York," said the captain. "I won't have any more of it. Let me hear any more such talk and I will send you to the forecastle to do duty."

"You darsn't do it," growled the mate under his breath, but at the same time cowering and obeying the captain.

There was a good deal of talk and many conjectures among the men in the forecastle, why, after such a breach of discipline as well as unusual provocation, the captain did not "break" the mate as he had threatened and send him to the forecastle to do duty as a common sailor, as was the captain's right, and perhaps his duty.

"I'll tell you," said Jim Conklin, a red-headed sailor and a sort of a "ship's lawyer," as sailors call the species, "he's got some kind of a hold on the old man or he wouldn't take so much slack from him."

"Wal," said Bill Tarbox, slowly turning his quid in his cheek, "I've sailed with Cap'n Zenas off 'n' on quite a spell, an' he's a very considerate an' just man, but I never knew o' his takin' back talk or slack o' the jaw from any one b'fore, an' 'tween you 'n' me 'n' the mainm'st it looks 's though the mate *had* got a round turn 'nd a bight on th' ol' man."

Such was the general opinion in the forecastle, where it was agreed by all that the captain, though an easy-going man when things went to suit, was as hard as iron when any one didn't "mind his eye," or was lacking in respect to officers.

It must not be inferred from the foregoing incident that I was dull in learning the duties of a seaman. On the contrary I had (as no less an authority in seamanship than Bill Tarbox declared) improved wonderfully. I had learned to knot and reef, could box the compass, knew the meaning of most of the orders for working the ship, and could steer a trick at the wheel in fair or ordinary weather.

Phil had made progress equal to if not greater than mine. Of the two he was the nimbler in laying aloft, and from the first, if not a better sailor, was a more ready one than I.

From our coming on board he was in greater favor with all on the brig than I. In temperament we were opposites: I was by nature grave, cold, and unsmiling in my manner, and did not relish familiarity, such as being slapped on the shoulder by a casual acquaintance, while Phil, though not lacking in proper dignity, had a laughing, smiling manner that thawed, like sunshine, the coldest natures into a liking for him. In learning there was also a difference. Phil learned as if by intuition, or, as Bill said, "as if he 'd learnt it all 't once an' was simply pickin' up ag'in what he 'd partly forgot."

On the other hand I learned by patient application and careful attention to the minutest details; but what I learned I did not forget, and could always make use of it, or, as Mr. Bell once flatteringly said, "could apply in practice what I had learned in theory, and make a little knowledge go a great way."

Phil had a wonderful liking for Mr. Bell, and could not sound his praises too highly; he often said, "He puts me in mind of your father." This offended me, for I felt in my heart that there was no one to be compared with him.

"You compare Mr. Bell with my father," I said, "but there is no resemblance."

"Now, don't get in a freeze, Hez," said Phil, "for I agree with you that your father is hard to beat. I 'll tell you where the resemblance is — it 's because they are both of them gentlemen."

I had to acknowledge that in this Phil was right.

On our arrival at Newberne, we found that weather-beaten and sleepy-looking place, for a Southern town very much excited.

At least a dozen men, headed by a fifer and drummer, were parading the streets, and all on board the brig who had been at Newberne before said that a wonderful liveliness prevailed. On inquiry we learned that a recruiting office for the Confederate army had just been opened.

"What is that for?" inquired one of the men on the brig; "what is the matter?"

"Matter? Why, haven't you heard the glorious news?"

"No," said the captain, who was listening; "what is it?"

"Why, Fort Sumter has been bombarded by our folks, and the fort and the whole Yankee army has surrendered. There was about a thousand Yankees killed, I reckon, and not one of our folks was hurt. We are going to declare our independence, and raise a company to fight the Yankees if they come down this way."

"Has North Carolina seceded yet?" asked Captain Zenas, in a tone of alarm, glancing from stem to stern of his brig.

"No," responded the man, "but we won't stand a Yankee president; we'll go out of the Union first; we won't stand it to be governed by Yankees and niggers, sar."

"These folks *are* awful excited," said Bill; "I never heerd one o' these kind o' loafers make so long a speech or put so much shout in one sence I 've sailed to a Southern port."

As we were not posted in news of the events that led up to the attack and subsequent capture of Sumter, we were greatly astonished, and for a time could talk of little else. The sentiment of the crew, so far as heard, was that of Union men; the general trend of which was that the South Carolinians must be crazy to attack a national fort and tear down its flag. Though Jack Tar is not thought to be very sentimental, he regards the old flag with reverence, as representing a government that is respected in every port of the world.

We began at once discharging the remainder of our cargo, which among other things consisted of some large cases or boxes which I have elsewhere mentioned. While being taken from the hold, one of these was accidentally broken open, and disclosed some of its contents, which consisted of muskets.

A significant look was exchanged among the men, but no remark was made except by the first mate, who said with a leer, "What a purty cargo! Wonder what the folks at home would say ef they knew it."

Mr. Bell hastily repaired the box, and for the first time since we knew him spoke angrily to the men for their carelessness.

Afterwards, while eating our supper in the forecastle, one of the men said, "Our craft is carrying arms for these secessionists, an' I'm goin' to leave her when I git home."

"I don't care what the cargo is," said a sailor we called Old Bluff, while critically examining a piece of meat he had taken from the mess kid, "but the grub is stinkin', an' here we are in port without fresh provisions. I c'n stan' that slush pot of a mate, but I won't stan' such stuff as this," and Bluff gave a solemn sniff of disdain.

The old salt was a chronic growler, but it must be confessed that the food was very bad. Whoever feeds Jack Tar seems to have a genius for the selection of poor "grub."

Others of our men growled about the brutality of the mate, and with all complaints combined there was much dissatisfaction. I think, however, that a knowledge of what our cargo in part comprised was that over which the men growled the worst. Bill Tarbox said, "What 'r' ye growlin' 'bout? Most o' y' w'd growl anyway; y'd growl ef y' was goin' to be hanged, an' ef y'd nothin' to grumble 'bout y'd grumble 'bout that."

After discharging the cargo we began putting below deck a cargo of Southern products, consisting, among other things, of barrels of tar and sweet potatoes.

The first mate took it upon himself to have the small space of the forecastle encroached upon by putting some of these barrels into the narrow quarters belonging to the men, and these were held in place only by ropes fastened to the sides of the bunks.

On Saturday afternoon, when the loading of the brig was almost completed. I was sent up-town with a note from the captain to the office of the firm to which that portion of the cargo landed at Newberne had been consigned. The captain said to me, "You can receipt for anything they may send to the ship by you."

While waiting in the dingy outer office, to my surprise Mr. Bell came out of an inner room with Mr. Orton. The second officer, as he saw me, spoke in an undertone to the principal of the firm, he then nodded to me pleasantly, and after a ceremonious leave-taking with Mr. Orton, as I thought very unlike that of a sailor, he went out. This ceremonious manner on the part of the second mate was not less observable than was the air of respect and deference in the manner of Mr. Orton to the second officer of the " Favorite."

I delivered the note from the captain.

" Your captain should have come to the office for a matter like this," said Mr. Orton, as I thought in a needlessly sharp and irritable tone. " There are important papers to send on board, which must be receipted for."

I replied respectfully that the captain had said I could receipt for anything that was sent to him.

Mr. Orton glanced at the captain's note again,

and said, "I see," and then, in an abstracted manner, drummed on the table with his fingers, then said, "My clerk is out; can you - will you - write a line at my dictation?" and then very courteously added, "I usually dictate to him."

I began to write at his dictation, he constantly referring to a bundle of papers which he had taken from his safe, and for which, in detail, I had been writing a receipt. Taking the paper in his hands he glanced it over, and said in a tone of surprise, "You write a very fine hand, spell correctly, and punctuate properly, — quite extraordinary for a young - man."

I prided myself on the neatness, correctness, and rapidity with which I could write, and was pleased with a compliment which I knew was not undeserved.

"Please sign it," he said, after looking it over the second time.

After going over the papers carefully and checking each one so as to make sure that all mentioned were there, I signed it, tied the papers together, and just then the clerk (whose absence had annoyed Mr. Orton) came in.

"Your name is Johnstone," he said pleasantly, "and I see you spell it as — as — our Johnstones do."

"Yes," I responded. "My father is a North Carolinian."

"Ah, indeed?" he said inquiringly, and in a tone of surprise.

"My father," I said, "is Mr. Rufus Johnstone, Jr. Do you know the family?" Instead of answering, Mr. Orton looked at me with an air of astonishment.

"Do you mean to say," said the clerk to me, "that your father is the Rufus Johnstone, Jr., of Pine Grove Hall?"

"Yes, sir," I replied; "do you know where he is? We have not heard from him for quite a while; he has been absent from home for several months, and we don't know what has happened to him."

I noticed a look of intelligence pass between the clerk and his employer — a look such as people exchange when they have some common thought not conveyed to a third party. Mr. Orton's face did not change, however, and he presently said: "I heard some time ago that Rufus Johnstone, Jr., had returned from the North, but I had not heard before that he had a family, so naturally I am a little surprised, — but I know very little of the Johnstones, except what I've told you, and that only from hearsay."

I attempted to inquire further, but as the questions I desired to ask might imply distrust of my father they stuck in my throat unasked, and I took my papers and with a bow left the office. I had not, however, got far when I discovered that I had left my penknife on the table where I had been writing, and returned to get it.

I was at the door, and before I had put my hand

to the old-fashioned fastening I heard a voice from within say, as if in continuation of a conversation, "Is it the one that is reported as going to be married to the —— (I did not understand the name) girl?"

"Yes; and wasn't that one of the Johnstone boys" — and I did not hear the rest of the question. Then the same voice, which I took to be Mr. Orton's, said, "The boy looks like the family."

All this time I had been standing as if in a dream, but now, realizing that I was doing a dishonorable act in listening to conversation not intended for my ears, I knocked at the door, and then at the call, "Come in," went in, made my excuses, and reclaimed my knife.

After I got out of the office I found my thoughts busy with the purport of the conversation I had overheard. It puzzled me. Did it have any reference to me? I will say, in justice to myself, that I did not for one moment give to it an interpretation which might imply dishonorable conduct on the part of my father; yet I was not unaware that it would bear such interpretation. I dismissed from my mind this standpoint, and at last concluded that the conversation I had heard could not refer to me.

When I had delivered the papers I said to the captain: "Can you pay me my wages and let me leave the brig here?" For answer the captain stared at me a moment as if he thought I had lost my mind, and turned away without other answer.

That night I "turned in," as sailors term going to bed, debating if I would not better run away in the morning and go in pursuit of my father.

In the midst of this mental debate I fell asleep, to be awakened by the call, "All-star-bow-lines ahoy!" and then I knew it was my watch on deck.

When I got there I was not a little astonished to find that we had hauled out into the stream, and were under full sail.

CHAPTER VIII.

A STORM AT SEA.

It was six o'clock when I came on deck in the morning watch. The wind, though light, was fair, and we were already in the broad waters of Pamlico Sound headed for the ocean beyond.

The captain stood on the weather gangway, the mate on the lee side, while the second mate stood in place on the weather side.

The morning's work of washing down, coiling ropes, and scrubbing decks began.

I now learned that the brig was short-handed; three of the men had run away at Newberne, and though another had been shipped there as an ordinary seaman he proved to be but little better than a green hand. He had been hurt while at work the afternoon before we sailed, and was in his bunk.

It was said that the captain had sailed in a hurry for fear of losing more men.

It was observable that the manner of the chief mate was more subdued than usual, from which it was inferred that the captain had been reading him a lesson in private.

Discontent was seen in the faces of the men, and they obeyed orders in a very surly manner.

Not only were they dissatisfied at being short-handed, but also at the encroachments on their quarters; and that this was a real and not an imaginary grievance any one familiar with the narrow forecastle (which is the sailor's only home on shipboard) will understand.

Phil, who had been observant of the mood the men were in, said to me, "The men don't like the way things are going on; they say we are being used like dogs. They don't blame the cap'n so much, but they're ugly 'bout the hazing they've got from the mate. If he's got whiskey on board they say it'll make trouble."

Though, as it proved, the mate did have liquor on board, and indulged in it freely, trouble, as will be seen, did not come wholly from this, but from another and an unexpected source.

The weather continued fair, the sun shining in unclouded splendor during the entire day; but the temper of the men did not accord with the weather. They grumbled in dangerous undertones unlike the ordinary sailor growl, which is one of habit rather than of deep-seated dissatisfaction. The grumbling was general and indefinite in its character; there was no special grievance. The men, as it were, egged one another on in expressions of discontent.

"This is purty grub an' a purty craft, an', blast my eyes, a purty lot o' stuff to come to sea with!" said Jim Conklin, glancing at the barrels that encumbered the forecastle, as we sat around the kid eating our dinner.

"What did y' come to sea f'r?" said "Spouter" (so nicknamed because he had been a whaleman). "What did y' ship f'r a ship's dog f'r? y' ain't a man 'board here."

"Belay there, y' lubbers!" said Bill, who seemed to be endeavoring to turn their minds from their grievances, and to get them started on some other tack. "See here, mates, I've seen wus men 'an ol' Hardin'."

"He's a purty officer f'r a 'zample," growled Conklin.

"I'll tell ye, mates," continued Bill, rounding his shoulders and assuming a "yarning" position, "Hardin' lost his only son — fell from the masthead in a gale; as likely a boy as y' ever see."

"Took after his dad, I s'pose," interrupted Conklin sarcastically.

"As I said," continued Bill, scowling at the interruption, "he was lost off the Cape three year ago. Hardin' has n't ben himself sence. Then, t' make matters wus, he took t' drink. Y' see," said Bill, turning to me, "when rum gits the least holt 'f a man, an' then anythin' runs athwart his hawser 't don't agree with him it don't seem t' make him better, as 't would a sober Christian, but he takes t' drink 'til he 's like a craft with a thunderin' big deck-load an' nothin' in the hold. An' when a man takes rum aboard t' drownd sorrer

I've noticed it gen'lly drownds out everything else that's good. I've sailed with Hardin' 'fore the mast sev'ral v'yages, an' a better shipmate an' all 'round sailor I've seldom sailed with. When he got to be fust mate, y' see, he didn't climb through th' cabin winder but got t' th' quarter-deck through th' fo'cas'le, an' by hard knocks, an' he was a purty fair officer to sail with till he took t' rum — for if I be a common Jack Tar that says it, if y' want fust-class treatment y' must sail with officers who was somebody 'fore they got to be sailors; men like our second mate an' the cap'n."

There was a moment's silence as the men ate their dinner, and it was evident that this attempt of Billy to get the men's thoughts on another tack was partially successful, but not wholly so, as will be seen by the sequel.

The weather continued fine all the next day until nearly sundown, when it began to blow from the north-east a very lively breeze, kicking up a rough sea. That night the order came, " All hands on deck ! " and at eleven o'clock it was, as sailors say, " blowing great guns " from north-east to east-north-east.

It was four o'clock before we got the brig under easy sail, for in addition to being short-handed the deck-load of cotton hindered us, and besides, the men did not work at their tasks with their usual heartiness.

At six o'clock the wind was screaming, and the

sea increasing, and the brig was laboring in an ugly and heavy cross sea, under reefed topsails and foresail. In addition to other discomforts it began to rain; later it turned to sleet and hail, the wind steadily increasing all the time. At ten o'clock orders came to double reef the topsail and reef the foresail. They were frozen, and of course as reefing can only be done with bare hands it was trying work. The frozen canvas was like sheet-iron, and to hold on to the yard was very difficult; but at last, with over an hour's work, we got the reefs in and came down on deck once more.

That night we got but four hours below, and when my watch on deck came I found the brig laboring heavily and going at a tremendous pace, her course partially in the trough of the sea and partially over the waves. Such was the situation the next morning, the wind still increasing, when to our astonishment the mate ordered the reefs thrown out of the foresail.

"We've got too much sail on already," growled Spouter as he sprang up the rigging following the second mate, I following closely after.

It was still cold, and the sleet cut like needles as it struck my face, and at times almost blinded me.

At last we had the sail loosened, and it was caught by the wind and bellied out before the terrible gale.

When we got on deck we found the mate giving other orders, which to us seemed still more wild and unusual. His face was inflamed, his eyes distended, and in manner he was very unlike his usual self (for with all his shortcomings none could deny that ordinarily he understood the duties of his office).

The brig, in spite of her heavy cargo, was leaning over to the gale so that her lee gunwale was partly under water. The mate had called Bill to the wheel, and that was sensible at least. Although the weather was cold the effort of steering the brig was so great that Bill was wet and dripping with sweat, when hours after this he came down from his duties on the quarter-deck.

"Keep her off four points," ordered the mate.

"Hi yor, sir," responded Bill.

As she swung off, with her big foresail bellying out before the gale, it seemed as if the masts would be taken out of her. She stuck her nose into a tremendous sea, which swept the deck, washing two of our men off the forecastle hatch, stove in the weather door of the cook's galley, and washed "King Sambo," as we called the cook (his name was Sam King), and some of his cooking utensils into the lee scuppers.

Distressing as was the situation — one which ordinarily it would be difficult to find a subject of mirth — I laughed to see Sambo spouting water from his thick lips, and crawling to a dry place on a cotton bale, and with an angry but comical expression on his face shake his fist towards Bill, as much as to say, "I'll pay you for this." And to a man before the mast it is no laughing matter to be out with the cook, for in such case he will be deprived of many small favors (which do not look small, however, to a foremast hand), such as the privilege of drying his wet clothes before the galley fire, or getting a sly sip of coffee or tea, when in the cold on deck.

To add to our general trouble, word came that the barrels in the forecastle had broken loose, and in so doing they had fetched away the sides of the bunks to which they had been fastened, and having nothing to keep them in place, the contents of the bunks were spilled on the deck.

I, with others, was sent to secure the barrels, when we found some of them were smashed, and had spread their contents of sweet potatoes, bacon sides, and tar on every side; while the unbroken barrels were dancing, chasséeing up and down, back and forth, with hams, sweet potatoes, and tarpaulin hats for partners.

After conquering the barrels and securing them, we went once more on deck to find that, in obedience to an order from the chief mate, we were about to go on the shore tack.

The brig was meanwhile going at a tremendous pace; her masts bending, her gunwales half under water, and her bow churning the sea. As we went slowly around, the brig, with seeming malice, stuck her nose under another sea, which deluged the decks; then as she swung off on the other tack the upper yards to which sails had just been set seemed to bend like bows. The cords cracked, and then with a report like that of a gun (heard above other clamorous sounds of the air and sea) the yards snapped, and with the sail whipped and banged the foremast with angry blows.

The captain, half-dressed (for he had been on deck nearly all the previous night, and had been sleeping at the time mentioned), rushed on deck, gave a sharp look aloft and over the decks, brushed the mate aside with a sharp word and manner, then thundered out his orders in a hoarse but commanding voice.

The mate went below; the men sprung into the rigging to obey the orders, and the wreckage of spars and sail was soon cleared away.

The sail was shortened, and though the sleet and cold made the work very difficult it was quickly accomplished.

I was very cold when I got to the deck once more, and was thrashing my hands to get up a little circulation, when there came an order to go about on the other tack. The weather made the atmosphere thick, notwithstanding the gale, so that we could see nothing plainly a quarter of a mile distant.

Before the order could be executed there came a shock, and then another. Our craft had struck bottom! At first I thought that it was the sea beating against her, so strong was the force of the waves.

The stanch brig, however, went about with seemingly no other mishap than shipping a sea that deluged the decks, but in view of a greater danger we did not mind that.

I had been clinging to the rigging on the weather side, almost holding my breath, but seeing that the brig was seemingly uninjured I breathed more easily.

The relief from suspense was but for a moment; other dangers menaced us. The cry went up, "We've sprung a leak!"

One can imagine, but not realize, these awful moments as the brig drove forward amid the fury of the storm, while we waited for — I knew not what.

Mr. Bell and Billy went below to search for the leak, while the men were sent to the pumps.

Mr. Bell soon came on deck again, and it was noised around that the leak had not been found on account of the cargo's being in the way.

There was then two feet of water in the hold. This was, however, thought to be in part due to the water from the deck. It was for a moment thought that the pumps were gaining on the water. The spirit of discontent, if not of mutiny, had disappeared before a common danger, and the men worked with a will. The first officer, however, was still sullen.

Meanwhile the brig drove forward in the howling gale, while the men, occasionally assisted by the steward and the cook, labored at the throbbing pumps.

All the sail on the "Favorite" at that time was the reefed main topsail, and this was enough. The second mate, the cook, the steward, and even Blarney, the injured man, were laboring at the pumps with desperate energy. But it was useless to deceive ourselves longer; the brig was steadily sinking. Phil, Sambo, Blarney, and I relieved the men at the pumps, while they threw over the deck load. While this somewhat lightened the brig the water still gained on the pumps.

A cloud rested on the captain's usually placid face, for he saw that unless something unusual happened the "Favorite" was doomed.

The brig was hove to, the long-boat carefully launched, and men stationed with boat-hooks to keep her from being stove to pieces against the side of the brig. But the men treacherously abandoned their posts of duty and piled into the boat. In an instant retribution followed; the boat was broken and crushed like an egg-shell by being dashed against the brig.

I saw for an instant the despairing faces of the wretches as they drowned alongside.

There were now on board only the captain, the two mates, Tarbox, Blarney, Phil, and myself.

"Cast off the boat from the stern davits," ordered the captain; "stand by there and put him (indi-eating Blarney) in first." In another instant the boat was swept away; how it occurred I did not know, but was told that the painter had parted.

Then came the cry that the brig was filling; at the same time the main deck was level with the water, and was swept by the waves.

The brig was put about and headed for the shore as a last desperate resort.

To the landsman the land seems to be the only place of safety, not so to the seaman; to beach a ship on a surf-beaten shore is the last resort.

The brig sank lower and lower as she ploughed madly through the waves that threatened to engulf her. It seemed a miracle that we were not swept from the deck, or that the brig did not sink.

Another sound now blended with the shriek of the winds, the creaking of the cordage and spars, and the hissing of the water; it was the sound of the surf beating the shore like a continuous cannonade. A long line of white and mountainous breakers foaming in seeming anger was in sight. The brig plunged forward in the increasing seas that indicated shoaling water.

CHAPTER IX.

THE WRECK OF THE "FAVORITE."

LIKE some mad creature the "Favorite" plunged forward, her bow now lifted on the top of the waves and now pitched down into the trough of them. We neared a shore, sea-beaten and seemingly without indentations, when there was a shout from the lookout. In the coast that seemed at first to be but one stretch of sand-bar right and left, there was an opening or inlet, and if we could but reach this, if the brig could not be saved, we at least could beach her in comparatively calm water.

But alas for our hopes! The brig would not answer to the helm. The joyous shout of anticipated safety had hardly left our throats when, with a shock that is indescribable, the "Favorite" struck bottom; then again and again, with awful concussion, making the decks under our feet strain, creak, and groan, and with a harsh grating and pounding sound she was beached within three hundred feet of the surf-beaten shore. The brig, with perhaps all on board, was doomed to destruction!

How shall I describe that scene, as she lay

stranded amid that tumult of shrieking winds and roaring waves? One who has seen the sea only in its fair weather and sunshine moods can know little of its wild fury in a storm.

As the sea struck our doomed craft with terrible blows, like those of gigantic hammers wielded by the demons of the sea and wind, it caused her to groan like some living creature aware of its danger and fearful of its doom.

The shore was not far distant; but the wild and dangerous breakers, like a seething caldron, intervened. The chief mate, in a wild manner, and with a wilder look on his face, exclaimed, "Every man for himself!"

"No, Mr. Harding," said the captain in reply, "we have a duty to perform, both for ourselves and the ship-owners."

The mate, at this reproof, slunk away as a dog does when menaced by its master.

The brig, which at first was head on, had, by the combined action of the tide and the thunderous sea, turned so that her broadside was nearly parallel with the beach, and then heeled over towards the land, farther and farther with every beat of the waves, until the decks were very steep.

"Cut away the masts," shouted the captain.

In anticipation of this order, the second mate had already stationed two of us at the masts with axes. In a few moments the stays and lower rigging were cut, the masts fell with a crash over the side of the brig, and the wreck of them was cleared away.

The craft now righted, and, though she did not keep on level keel, was in a much less dangerous position than before. Meanwhile, such was the fury of the sea that it did not seem that she could hold together for many minutes. But she was stanchly built and though she trembled, groaned, and shrieked at every thunderous wave, as if in distress, she showed no signs of immediate breaking up.

"Who of you men will try to reach the shore with a line?" cried the captain. "It's our only chance of rescue."

"I can swim, sir; I will try," I said.

"But I am the strongest swimmer," said Phil; "besides, Hez's mother would n't like to have him drowned."

"It's a man's work, captain, not a boy's," said Mr. Bell, pushing us rather roughly aside. The captain nodded assent, and Mr. Bell tied around his waist the deep sea line in such a manner that it could easily be detached, and sprung far out into the sea.

We watched him as he came to the surface and struck out for the shore. The line was paid out as the bold swimmer rose and sank with each sweep of the waves.

"The nip is coming," said Phil (who was a magnificent swimmer) anxiously, "when he reaches the breakers; if he don't understand them, he will fail and have to come back, or will" — and here Phil left his conclusion unuttered, for the stout swimmer had reached the surf.

We saw the gallant sailor once after he reached the breakers, then we lost sight of him, and after a moment the line loosened and was pulled back into the brig.

What had become of Mr. Bell?

It was, however, not the time for question but for action.

Both Phil and I now again volunteered to make the attempt. We had had experience in swimming in rough water and in the surf off Rivermouth, and boys are often better swimmers than men because of practice and agility.

It was decided that Phil, who said he had a trick of his own, should make the trial. After stripping to his undershirt and trousers he hung the small forecastle lamp filled with whale oil around him. He had punched in the tin lamp a small hole through which the oil might constantly ooze. The oil he said would keep the seas from breaking in his face and depriving him of his breath.

"Good-by, Hez," said the brave fellow. "Good-by," I said, shaking his hand, and then he climbed out on the jib-boom, and threw himself into the sea.

He came to the surface, rose and fell on the seas like a sea-fowl, and swam with a strong stroke for the shore. We watched him breathlessly as he reached the breakers, and then after a brief struggle got to his feet and went up the beach.

A cheer went up from the brig when it was known that Phil had succeeded in reaching the shore, and that communication with the land was established.

Phil began to pull in the small line, to which was attached a strong cable, but he pulled very slowly, as if he were much exhausted with the effort he had made in swimming.

After a few moments, however, he began to pull more vigorously, until one end of the cable was, after some delay, landed on the beach.

"How will he fasten the cable?" was a query which continually occurred to me, and this proved to be the part most difficult to be achieved, for the land was a sandy beach and no trees were near to which it could be secured. We saw from the shore that he could not do this in any case without help. The brig was meanwhile strained by the sea, that continued to pound and wrench her, and there was danger that she might possibly break up before the cable was fastened. The captain looked at me and I thought I read his wishes.

As there was the cable with Phil at the other end to cling to in an emergency, there was but little danger in my making the attempt to reach the shore.

Our peril, meanwhile, was growing greater and greater. Every sea swept our decks with terrible fury, or lashed the wreck with a force that enveloped it in foam. Whatever was done must be done at once.

I threw off my coat and boots, and, launching myself far out from the brig, struck out for the shore, but as Phil had said, " the nip came" when I reached the breakers. Before I reached them, however, I saw a piece of the main-topmast floating near me, and to this I clung in order to get myself rested for my greater trial of strength which was yet to come. And then it occurred to me that if I could but get this spar on shore it would prove useful. So thinking, I struck out vigorously for the cable, towing the piece of main-topmast by a rope which I had found attached to it.

Reaching the cable, which was but a short distance from me, I swam easily, keeping one hand on the topmast and using the other to swim with, until I reached the breakers, which were furiously chasing each other like wild sea horses with white manes, and roaring with savage fury. I had never swum in such rough water before, and I confess my heart sank as I neared the shore.

It was well that I had saved my strength, for the surf was terrible, and it was fortunate that there was but a slight undertow. The first I understood something of from former experiences while swimming at Rivermouth.

At last, after two waves in succession had hurled me back and forth to and from the shore, I grasped

"LET GO THAT ROPE, HEZ!"

the rope attached to the piece of main-topmast by one hand and the cable for support with the other, and got to my feet; but only to be swept away again by the receding waves. I tried once more with the same result, then made a still weaker effort and failed.

I now caught my breath, summoned all my strength of will, set my teeth, and made a supreme effort, for I realized that my life depended on the issue. The sands gave way beneath my feet, and a wave came with a torrent-like force as if with malice, and engulfed me. I was gasping for breath and slipping away when Phil caught me, at the same time exclaiming, "Let go that rope, Hez!" and dragged me to the beach.

I lay for a moment getting my breath, when Phil said, "What made you hold on to that spar so like time, Hez?"

"Something to lash the cable to, Phil," I said, gasping.

"It's just the thing," said Phil, "but was n't it just like you to think of it?"

Then he gave a look, and seeing that the topmast had gone adrift and was tossing amid the breakers, he watched his chance until it was thrown near him, then rushed into the water and dragged it to the shore.

In a short time we had dug with our hands a deep hole and had fastened the spar into the sand, but not very securely, and braced it by holding on to the rope which I have mentioned as being attached to it. "It won't hold very long." I said to Phil, "but perhaps it will hold until some one can come to make it more secure." This done, we signaled to the brig that the cable was ready, but at first could get no answer. We could see, however, some unusual commotion on board.

At last our signal, after being constantly repeated, was answered, and we perceived that those on the brig were rigging what is known among seamen as a cradle (a sort of boatswain's chair) for the purpose of coming on shore, or for bringing anything they could get for our needs.

In a few moments Bill Tarbox came ashore by means of the cable and cradle, while we held to the guy-rope with all our strength, and we then learned that an awful tragedy had taken place on the brig. (Bill could not swim and was nearly drowned coming through the breakers, as the cable was not very tight.)

Mr. Harding had gone crazy. "He had," said Bill, "been actin' queer f'r some time 'fore and after you come ashore, but when he run at me an' the cap'n with an axe he'd picked up on deck we knowed he was mad 's a March hare. We had some trouble 'n keepin' out 'f his way, 'til he gives a yell, then throwed the axe at Cap'n Zenas, an' with another yell jumped into the water."

"Was the captain hurt?" I inquired.

"Wal," said Bill, "the axe struck th' cap'n's

leg; he limps, but says the hurt is o' no consequence; 't th' same time I don't like the looks 'f his face."

Bill had brought with him the end of a rope one end of which was connected with the ship. He at once began to set the spar more securely into the ground, and brace it with rope to pieces of driftwood driven into the sand higher up on the beach.

"The cap'n wants to know," said Bill, "if there's any inhabitants near here th't we can git t' help us. Whilst we're fixin' this, s'posin' you run up on the high land yender 'n' see how things look, Johnstone."

When I had reached the highest elevation near the shore, I saw two inlets, one south, the other north of us, not, as I then judged, very broad, while west of us there were sand hills with a few straggling trees, and beyond them I could catch glimpses of water.

When I reached the shore again Bill and Phil had completed the work of fixing the spar and the cable. I told them that so far as I could see we were on an island, and that I could see no indications of its being inhabited; in fact, the general appearance would show that there were few inducements for any one to live there, as the land was mostly beach sand.

"Wal," said Bill, "that's what the cap'n thought, that we was on a part of Hat'ras an' that this 's one o' the islands made by th' water breakin' through th' beach. The old man's plan now is to git on shore such stuff 's we want t' make us comf't'bl', an' then 'f she holds t'gether save the cargo if we can. I'm goin' back t' the brig to help th' old man." And the faithful sailor went back to the ship, saying. " The brig 's purty badly racked, an' I shan't stay no longer 'n t' git some stuff f'r keepin' life t'gether till we c'n git help fr'm the mainland."

Faithful to that promise they had begun to send back the cradle to the shore. It was but half way, when the cable parted or slipped from the windlass (just how we did not know) severing all connection with the brig.

We could see all this time hurry and commotion on board, and the sea breaking over the doomed craft with increasing fury. Though the wind had gone down, the sea, as is often the case after a storm, had increased rather than decreased in violence.

"See that," said Phil, " the brig can't stand that long!"

A succession of seas more terrible than any we had witnessed broke over the brig, for an instant shutting her from our sight.

"See!" said Phil excitedly. "See! the "Favorite" is broken in two."

The captain, as near as we could see, was on the quarter-deck when this occurred, while Bill was at the bow.

We saw Bill trying to throw a rope to the captain, but he stood like a statue near the wheel, without seeming to notice the faithful sailor.

In a few moments a smother of foam covered the severed portions of the brig. We could see no one on the wreck. We had seen the last, not only of the "Favorite," but of its captain and the brave sailor.

It was quite dark when this occurred, partly because of a cloudy sky, though it did not rain, and partly because of the approach of night. We strained our eyes for some time in endeavoring to see the wreck, and ran along the coast in the hope that one or both of the men might have reached the shore, but it was so dark that our endeavors were useless.

"It's no use," said Phil. "I've heard Billy say a good many times that he couldn't swim; an' as for the cap'n, I think he didn't care much after the brig was wrecked."

We had no time for grief, and at such times people do not mourn; that comes with freedom from distress and with reflection.

Phil and I munched some wet hardtack we had in our pockets (for until then we had been too busy to think much of hunger), and then as we could not do anything more we lay down and slept as only tired boys can.

CHAPTER X.

ON A BARREN SAND-BAR.

WHEN I awoke in the morning my sleep had been so profound that at first I did not recognize my surroundings, nor remember the occurrences of the previous day. But as I heard the droning of the sea, it came back to me like some terrible dream.

Phil was not in his place by my side, but on getting up I saw him standing on a sand hill near by, taking an observation of the surrounding country.

The wind had gone down, the storm was over, and the sun was shining brightly. I looked seaward, but could see no trace of the "Favorite," and concluded that she had gone to pieces during the night, and drifted seaward with the turn of the tide.

Seeing me awake, Phil came running toward me, exclaiming, "See here, Hez, this is just your style of an island; now you have got it, what are you going to do with it?"

Then I remembered the way Phil and I, while lying in our comfortable bed at home, used to imagine ourselves cast away on a desolate island;

but I felt too serious to answer to him in the same
jocular vein, and replied :

"You may see some fun in this, Phil, but I
confess I can't. All our shipmates are drowned,
and here we are in this terrible place with scarcely
enough clothes to cover us. There seems nothing
to do but to drown ourselves."

"Now, don't growl in that style, Hez," said
Phil, putting his arm over my shoulder. "You
know I always said there was no fun in this kind
of an island, but you always would have your own
way, and now you've got your desolate island!"

The tone in which Phil said this was so ludicrous that, in spite of the seriousness of our situation I had to laugh, and say, "Sure enough, Phil,
what can we do with it?"

"That's what I wanted to hear, Hez," said Phil.
"I learned when I was knocking around in New
York that it was no use for a chap to put on a long
face in a hard pinch, for it only made matters worse
and harder to bear: I was trying to get your
courage up. You've got grit enough, — more than
I ever had, — but I shan't have any if you keep
on looking as you did a few minutes ago. I was
trying to keep up my own courage; you know it
has run down pretty low after looking around in
this desolate place for something to eat, and seeing
nothing but sand."

"Well, Phil," I said, "you are right, there *is*
no use getting down in the mouth. Let's look

around and see what kind of a country it is before we conclude things are hopeless. You remember father used to say: 'A brave man never gives up until everything is tried, and then he keeps on trying.'"

"That's it, Hez," said Phil, with one of his sunny smiles, "and let's try for some breakfast first. I'm hungry! Billy said that he thought this was Hatteras Beach; if that is so, Pamlico Sound is on the other side, not a half-mile to the west of us. I could see water from the top of that sand-hill. Let's go over and see what we can find; there must be clams and oysters, for the water is pretty smooth there."

This being agreed upon, we tightened our belts for breakfast, and set out for exploration westward.

Let the reader imagine, if he can, our deplorable condition. We had on no coats, hats, shoes, or stockings; nothing but thin trousers and under-shirts to cover our nakedness; and this clothing was still damp with sea water.

As we toiled through the sand and over the hillocks we could catch occasional glimpses of the water to the westward, and see the kind of land on which we had been wrecked by the treacherous sea.

On our left, with the exception of our island, as far as the eye could see the beach extended seemingly without a break. Here and there were sand hillocks formed by the drifting of the sand before furious winds; on these were a few clumps of scrub-oaks, while on the lower levels the patches of lowland were covered by coarse marsh grass. The rest was sand, glaring in the sun, drifted by the wind or wet by the sea; except ourselves there was nothing that indicated human life.

As we approached the western shore of this ocean barrier we saw an inland sea, extending north and south as far as the eye could reach. Looking westward we could see land like a blue cloud lying twenty miles or more away.

As we approached the shore a flock of ducks, with a sound like rushing wind, rose in the air and for an instant darkened the sky.

"There's enough to eat if we only had a gun," said Phil, looking hungrily toward them.

"Yes," I replied harshly, "and there, forty miles away, is a settled country that we might reach *if* we only had a boat. If we had a gun, we've got neither a fire nor means of preparing a duck if we shot one."

"Don't be cross," said the dear fellow. "I'm so hungry I really believe I could eat one without cooking; but we won't scold about the cooking till we get the duck;" and Phil made up such a face that I laughed, as he no doubt intended that I should.

The tide was partially out when we reached the shore. I turned up my trousers and waded into the shallow water, while Phil walked and stamped on the sand where the tide had receded, looking for clams or other shell-fish that might have bedded there.

I caught a crab, but soon discovered it was a spider crab and not good to eat. I continued wading back and forth, feeling in the sand with my feet and looking out sharply for anything that was eatable.

"We will try a little farther up," I said; "there don't seem to be any oysters here;" and with this remark I started for the shore, when I trod on something sharp and hard that made me cry out with pain. I did not mind the pain, however, when it flashed upon me that I had often hurt my feet in the same way on oyster shells while wading near Rivermouth.

I plunged my hand into the water and mud and drew out a clump of huge oysters, saying joyfully, "Here's our breakfast, Phil; we shan't starve, that's settled!" And I tossed the oysters to the shore, where Phil got two stones and broke their tough shells before I could reach him. We found the oysters delicious, and after eating them without being satisfied we waded out for more, and soon discovered that those I had already found were on the edge of a large bed of them.

After this we found some round clams, or what are known as quahaugs, on the flats. We soon had eaten all we wished, and then discovered that we were very thirsty, and that we had seen no water except sea-water on this desolate stretch of beach.

Our hopes and prospects, which had looked so rosy but the moment before, were clouded by this discovery.

At last I said, "We have been saved from the sea, and from starvation, only to die of thirst, Phil."

"No," said he, "we shall find water here; when strong men have been drowned we have been saved, and I have faith that we shall in some way get out of this scrape, Hez. Your marm used to tell us we must trust in God. It's a good time to try it now, Hez."

I made no reply, but was ashamed of my doubts, for when I thought of the almost marvelous manner of our preservation, how could I doubt that God had stretched out his hand for our salvation? I was also ashamed that Phil, with less teaching than I, had developed more faith than I had.

We ran around for nearly a half-hour without finding water, when we came to one of the marshes which we had passed and repassed in our anxious search.

"There is water, but of course it is salt," said Phil, throwing a stone towards a little pool in the midst of the marsh. Thinking of a saying of my grandfather, "Never take anything for granted until it is proved," I went to the pool, scooped up a handful of water and put it to my lips. It was fresh! Remembering to have seen some large clam-shells on the beach, such as my mother used for milk-skimmers. I ran and got two of them, and Phil and I drank our fill.

Though the water was tepid and brackish, I do not remember to have ever before drunk anything with such a relish. This pool was no doubt water which in being filtered through the sand from the salt water had become fresh. Truly, as Phil had intimated, God had showed his purpose of preserving our lives!

"Before you got up this morning," said Phil, "I felt so discouraged that it seemed that there was nothing to do but to give up. Then I remembered what marm used to tell me: 'When in trouble, pray.' I had forgotten about it till then, but after this I shall never forget it again. I kneeled down in the sand, tried to pray, but couldn't think of anything to say but 'I'm hungry an' in a tight place; please get me out, Lord,' and it seemed that He heard me, for I felt better as soon as I began to say 'help me.' I never could see any use in praying, but I shall try it now when in a tight spot."

I couldn't keep from smiling at Phil's crude idea of prayer, as something held in reserve until an emergency occurred. But at the same time I thought to myself, "It's the way many grown-up people do. "Truly," I said, finally, "if we draw near to God he will draw near to us."

"We must mark this place," said Phil, "so we will be sure to find it again."

For this purpose I broke off a branch of oak from a tree growing near at hand, and stuck it into the sand on a hillock near the pool; and then, to make assurance doubly sure, we walked toward the ocean in as straight a line as possible, and there set up another mark so that it could be seen from the shore.

We were no longer blue at the outlook, for, besides our hunger being relieved, we both had faith in an overruling Providence, to which the incidents of the morning had given practical force.

We reached the ocean and sat for a few moments watching the breakers as they chased each other to the shore in unceasing succession, and then with mournful echoes receded. That morning they seemed to be saying, "Forevermore! Forevermore!" They had been saying this, I thought, for countless ages; singing a requiem for the ocean's dead.

"What shall we do next?" I said; and we looked into each other's faces.

"It makes me downhearted to hear the sad sound of the sea," said Phil, "and I say, let's get away from it and be doing something."

"Well, what shall we do?" I said.

"I am no authority on desolate islands," he said, smiling; "you go ahead and I'll follow."

I made no response to this sally, for I was intent on thinking.

"The tide is nearly out," I finally said, "and you remember that when we were swimming ashore the tide carried northerly up the coast. Suppose we follow the shore along in that direction, and see if there is anything cast up by the sea that we can use; maybe we shall find a barrel of hardbread, or something of that kind, Phil!"

"It's just the thing!" Phil cried out joyfully, "I wonder I did n't think of it! We might as well begin exploring this place first as last and know all that can be got from it to make us comfortable."

So we set out, walking northward on the hard beach from which the tide had receded.

As we rounded a point of land near the inlet not a quarter of a mile from where we started, we came to a part of the coast that formed a little bay, where, looking northward, we saw a portion of the brig deeply submerged, but with the bow protruding from the water. An object on the flats near the inlet arrested our attention. It looked to us as if it was a log or a huge bundle, but we hoped it might be a barrel of bread.

As we approached it, an unspeakable and nameless chill crept over us.

The same dread was reflected on both our faces. Neither of us spoke, but we drew closer to each other and shuddered. It was a human form; that, doubtless, of one of our former shipmates. We walked slowly and in silence toward this dread object. Both of us stopped a few paces from it and looked once more in each other's faces as if for a renewal of courage.

"It's got to be done, Phil," I at last said, and then, encouraged by the sound of my own voice, I hastened over the few intervening steps and stood beside it.

It was the lifeless body of poor Billy Tarbox!

"Poor Bill!" was all we could say as we gazed at the inanimate form, swollen, and disfigured by the waves' cruel buffets.

"Dear old fellow!" said Phil, "he was such a good, faithful man! Don't you remember his saying that a sailor must be prepared to face everything, and make the best of it?"

"Yes," I said; "and I heard him say he could n't swim, and if he could, he should be drowned just the same if it was so fated. He said he had been shipwrecked four times, and when men who could swim had been drowned he had been saved."

"We must bury the poor fellow," I said; "we can't shirk a plain, but terrible, duty like that."

Before burying him, we took from his feet his shoes and stockings, also took his large silver watch, and his oil jacket, and trousers, removed his belt and sheath knife (which a sailor always wears, but we had removed ours from our persons on preparing to swim ashore). We also felt in his pockets in hope of finding a flint and tinder box. Phil had heard Bill say he always kept by him the means of lighting a fire; and that even should he be cast away on a whale's back he could cut a piece of the blubber and start a fire with it. We found nothing to justify this boast. A fish line, with sinker and hook, and a dull pocket-knife were all that we found there.

After this we scooped with our bare hands a hole in the loose sand far above high-water mark, and to this we carried him, and there we both knelt and I prayed — not very formally, but in a heart-felt manner. Then covering him with sand we turned sadly away.

"It's hard on us, we can't do more," said Phil, "but I know Billy would say we did the best we could."

After this we turned our steps toward the portion of the "Favorite" of which I have before made mention. It proved to be in deeper water than we could reach without swimming, and as the tide ran with great swiftness near the shore we decided that it was dangerous to undertake to reach it.

It was this inlet that caused the current to carry us in this direction when we were swimming ashore, and which afterward carried the wreck to this place.

About a half-mile away there was a continuation of the barren sand-bar. The tide was rising and the water was pouring rapidly through this narrow inlet.

There was no appearance of any human habitation on the other side and so we followed the shore around the inlet to the west.

Here we made two discoveries; on a sand-bar we

found a fragment of an old sail, and at another point a ham, which, as it was covered with thick cloth, we knew to be a part of our cabin stores. After this we found several small things, the most valuable of which was a demijohn covered with wicker-work.

"It's the mate's whiskey bottle," I said.

"Just the thing to keep water in; don't throw it," exclaimed Phil as I made a motion, at the first impulse, to cast it back into the sea.

Later we found a piece of the hatch partly covered by seaweed. This we threw out of the reach of the tide, not knowing what use it might sometime be to us.

We now retraced our steps until we reached the place we had started from in the morning, which was not more than a half a mile away. We were encouraged by the results of our morning's work, for we now had several things to make our life here more endurable.

Phil had begun to whittle from a piece of the topmast which he had split off, with Billy's sheath knife, which was very sharp.

"What are you doing that for?" I said.

"We've *got* to have a fire in some way," he replied, "I don't know exactly how."

"You don't expect to start one by the friction of whittling, do you?" I said derisively; then added, "I wouldn't fret just at present, Phil, for there's no chance for a fire, as I see. I wish we had some kind of a shade, the sun comes as through a burning-glass."

Phil at this jumped to his feet with a yell, exclaiming, "We'll have a fire, Hez, hurrah!"

I looked at Phil thinking he had gone mad, until he took out the crystal of Bill's watch, and said, "Here's a burning-glass!" Phil, with this, tore from the ham some oily paper which was now dry, and then for a half hour sat patiently trying to start a fire. There soon was a smoke in evidence, but no fire. It was impossible to make a blaze with the glass, though the paper was scorched and charred.

At last Phil threw the glass from him in anger saying, "It's all humbug, the things we read in books!"

Afterwards we filled our demijohn with water, got some oysters and clams, and with a piece of raw ham made out quite a supper, — using large clam shells (which we found in abundance) for plates for our oysters. After this we gathered a large quantity of the dried marsh grass and made a bed in a place sheltered from the wind, using the piece of old sail for a bedspread, with poor Bill's oil clothes and pea-jacket underneath to keep us dry.

Then, after our old manner, we began to discuss the events of the day, and, among other matters, how we should get off from this desolate sand-key.

"We have never been far to the southward," said Phil, "and how do we know but there are people living here. People must come here to fish and hunt, anyway."

It was agreed, before we went to sleep, that on the next day we would explore to the southward as far as possible.

Soon after we reached this conclusion we were fast asleep.

CHAPTER XI.

WE MAKE DISCOVERIES.

Early in the morning we began preparations for our journey. We were fully determined not to return until we had made a thorough exploration and learned where this sand-bar terminated, or found its inhabitants if there were any. With these resolutions, we gathered up everything of our property that it was practicable for us to carry, as it was possible we might not return to this place.

At Phil's suggestion we set up the topmast on the bluff near the ocean, with the canvas we had found flying from the top as a signal of distress. We also scratched on the mast a few words, so that any one coming upon it would know of our whereabouts. We filled our bottle with water, as we did not know that we should be able to find a supply on our way. To carry our food, which consisted of ham, oysters, and clams, we cut off the bottom of the legs of Bill's oil trousers and fastened up one end with twine; and as the trousers were very wide they made excellent bags, or haversacks. We carried these bags by straps over our shoulders. The straps were made by cutting Bill's wide belt in two, lengthwise.

The larger portion of the ham, which we had

not sliced, we put into a hole at the foot of the topmast, after carefully wrapping it in dried grass and covering it with stones. Over these we laid the hatch (of which I have elsewhere made mention) and covered the whole with sand. Having made these preparations, and others which are too unimportant to mention here, we started out on our explorations.

As we began our journey the sun rose in unclouded splendor, and such is the elasticity of youth and health that, notwithstanding our environment of hardship and the dreary stretches of sand, we were hopeful, and began our prospecting tour with a certain spice of enjoyment. We determined that, at short intervals, one of us should go to the top of the bluff to make observations of the country, that no important feature of it might escape our attention.

We saw several red foxes, and as they were undisturbed by our presence we felt assured that there were no inhabitants there.

We had not traveled along the hard-beaten shore more than an hour when we came to the limits of the sand-bar. A strait a half-mile or more in width separated us from a continuation of this stretch of desolate barren beach. The whole island we judged to be about two miles and a half long. We went to the top of the sand-hill and gazed on the opposite land, but saw no signs of dwellings or of man's presence there. There was no sound except the screech of sea-gulls and the roar of the breakers.

For a few moments we sat in silence on the bluff, gazing across the strait to the opposite land, oppressed by the dreary outlook that confronted us. We now knew that we were on a sand-bar encompassed by water.

The tears came to Phil's eyes and he blubbered outright, while I felt my heart sink like lead, so oppressed was I by the situation that now was a certainty and not a surmise.

Finally Phil's face cleared, and he said, " Hez, this *is* your kind of an island, and I wash my hands of it, old fellow!"

"Had we better swim across to the other side?" I said. "There may be people living there, and if there are none we are no worse off there than we are here."

"Well, Hez," said Phil, "you *have* got courage, but I feel as gloomy and hopeless as can be. There seems no chance to get away from here."

"I don't feel very hopeful myself, Phil," I said, "but we are no worse off than we were this morning, and we know now just how the land lies. I shouldn't wonder if there were people living on the other side of this strait, after all."

Though I said this to keep up my own courage as well as Phil's, it afterwards proved that in this random remark I had hit somewhere near the truth. There were fishermen's huts beyond land that was in plain sight from where we sat so despondent and gloomy, and we should have found no great difficulty in crossing the strait.

After a moment we began to walk to the westward along the shore. We saw here several shoals of fish, but they were a kind called bony fish, and though Phil was eager to try to get some of them I knew we couldn't cook them if we were so fortunate as to get them.

We skirted the strait and reached the shore of the sound, where we found oysters and clams in profusion, but we had no immediate need of them. We wandered over the entire sand-spit.

It was about twelve o'clock when we came to a little spring in the sand, which we found to be clear, cold, and remarkably pure.

In the vicinity was a number of stones, evidently brought there by some one; on one of them I sat down.

Phil threw off the oil coat which he had been wearing, and as he did this he exclaimed, "What's that?"

I looked up inquiringly, when he explained by saying, "I heard a sound when I threw the coat down — a sort of a clink like a piece of money."

"You imagined it, Phil," I said.

"I don't imagine things, Hez," said Phil. "It is you who hear and see things that never existed!"

I picked up the jacket and began to look it over carefully, for I knew that Phil's imagination never led him astray as mine sometimes did me; but I could find nothing, so threw it on a stone, and then I too heard a metallic clink which awakened my curiosity as it had Phil's.

"There *is* something there," I said; and with that began to search the garment once more.

"It's all moonshine! There's nothing in that old coat but what we see," and with this half-querulous remark I passed the coat to my right hand.

"The coat is haunted, I guess," said Phil jocosely, "for we both can hear something that we can't see."

I, however, was all excitement just then, for my right hand had come in contact with a hard substance that might explain the clink.

Under and just inside the armhole of the right sleeve I found a little pocket, closed by a flap which was sewed down; this I quickly ripped with the knife, but found the pocket also sewed up, and oiled over like the rest of the coat. On cutting the stitches away, I found inside of the little pocket a packet about three inches long, wrapped and stitched in oiled silk, which, when divested of its covering, proved to be a metallic case securely closed, and containing matches that were as dry as on the day they were placed there. Very few people, except those who have been without fire under similar circumstances, can realize our joy at the discovery of these matches.

We quickly gathered some dry grass, and some

dry scrub-oak limbs from a clump of trees which grew near by, and started a fire, at first for the mere novelty of it, but on second thought we concluded to cook something for our dinner.

We sharpened sticks and on them fixed pieces of bacon, and after browning one side of the bacon by holding it over the blaze we put an oyster on it and held the other side over the fire, thus cooking the bacon and warming if not frying the oysters.

We made, as we then thought, a royal dinner; for what was lacking in our cooking was made up by fine appetites, such as I doubt if any king on a throne ever had. If there is any blessing that I then had the loss of which I lament at this day, it was that fine appetite. In looking back to that time I think I never enjoyed food as I did then and there under the blue southern sky, with pure water for our drink. The feast is truly in the palate.

After eating our fill we sat there talking, and laughing, even, for some time. We filled the water-bottle from the spring, and left the fire as regretfully as a miser leaves his gold behind.

"I shall always feel grateful to Bill for these matches," said Phil, "for they seem just like a gift from him."

"Yes," I agreed, "this match-safe and its contents, preserved so marvelously, is the result of Bill's forethought and experience, and justifies his saying that he had the means of kindling a fire always by him."

We had not gone more than a hundred yards from the spring when Phil, pointing ahead of us, exclaimed, "Look: there's a house!"

Sure enough, a short distance ahead there protruded a chimney from behind a sand-hill. We hurried toward it; but found it was only a chimney. Our disappointment was great, for it had not occurred to us that there might be a chimney without a house, or a house without any one living in it.

As we came to it we found that besides the chimney there remained only a few weather-beaten boards and joists, a door, scattered pieces of rusty tin, and a few shingles.

"It was a wreck-house," said Phil; "it was blown down, perhaps, and people who have been here at different times have used the fragments for firewood."

The reason we had not seen it before was that it was hidden between two sandhills, so that looking from the ocean to the sound one could not see it, and so though it was near where we were cast on shore we had not stumbled upon it before.

"More likely they have carried away parts of it," I said. "I have noticed it is the nature of some people to carry off or destroy what they can't use, and very likely that was done in this case."

Phil went to the fireplace and scraped out some

of the ashes and said, "See here!" and with that showed me a lot of nails. "You see by this," said he, "that it is as I said. They have been using it for firewood."

"Yes," I said, "and perhaps they were poor, shipwrecked people like ourselves."

"I'll tell you, Phil, what we had better do," I said, after a moment's thought; "we will build a little shanty right up against this chimney. It is near the spring, and it is convenient to both the ocean and the Sound; it is sheltered from the wind, and there is that clump of scrubs near the spring, — that will be convenient, too."

Phil agreed with me, and said, "Yes, and people will come here for water and wood, and those who 've used the fireplace once may come here again."

Although we had been favored with fair weather since the storm in which we had been cast away, we knew that we could not reckon on it for long. So we agreed to begin the construction of a hut at once.

With this in view we began to clear away a space near the chimney. In doing this work, under the debris we came upon an old rusty fry-pan, which, though broken at one side, was to us like gold, so valuable was it for cooking. "We 're set up in housekeeping now," exclaimed Phil joyfully; "we 've got a place to cook, matches to kindle a fire, and a fry-pan!"

Before dark, so earnestly had we worked, we had not only cleared the space needful for our hut, but had got together all the nails and pieces of joists and boards, and arranged them for our work in the morning.

Not until this did we kindle a fire and cook some oysters and bacon after our old fashion, for the broken fry-pan would need to have a good deal of rust scoured from it before it was fit for use. When we awoke in the morning we were so eager to begin our house that though we had but a few oysters we felt we could not then spend time to gather more.

At first we had planned to build up the sides of our hut with seaweed, but finally decided (as we hoped to be detained but a short time on this island, and as warm weather was near) to build only a temporary shelter that would keep us dry and warm in case of a storm.

For this purpose we sharpened the point of one of the joists, and digging down to the clay set the joist into the ground as solid as possible, opposite and about nine feet from the chimney. This upright stood about seven feet out of the ground, and on this we had planned to put one end of a joist and fasten to it for a ridgepole. It puzzled us for a time, however, how to fix the other end of the ridgepole to the chimney. We could drive another stake, to be sure, but it would be in the way of our fireplace. Finally Phil proposed that we knock out one of the bricks in the centre of the chimney at the desired height, and in the hole thus made insert one end of the joist.

Phil got on my shoulders, and by scratching away the mortar with a nail, and then pounding with a stone, the brick was finally loosened.

It was noon before the ridgepole was fastened, and as we were tired and hungry we set to work to get our dinner.

We scoured out the broken fry-pan, opened some oysters and fried them, and soon had one of the most appetizing meals we had had since we were shipwrecked.

Before night came we had got the piece of sail from the topmast, attached pieces of rope to each side of it, thrown the canvas over the ridgepole and fastened it to the ground by pins, and had a very comfortable tent that would protect us from rain and wind.

During the week that followed, though it rained several times, we fixed up the space left open on each side of our chimney by driving into the ground pieces of board which we split with our knife, and then, using the twigs for wattles, wove them in and out like basket-work (though very roughly) between these stakes, with the long beach-grass for filling. As this did not keep out the wind we gathered seaweed, which lay in abundance on the shore, and, as we were not particular about the looks of our house we filled in the crevices with this and piled it up against the sides. The other end of the tent we built up in the same way, leaving a space so that we could put up the door from the inside. We also banked up the sides of the tent with sand.

There still, however, remained at each end, near the top of our roof, an open space which we could not find means to close except imperfectly; but we consoled ourselves, by saying that holes were needful for ventilation.

After that we built a sleeping-bunk, and also set the hatch upon four stakes for a table, and then we felt that if our surroundings were not very nice or elegant they were at least comfortable.

While engaged in building our hut (and it took us several days), we kept a sharp lookout for fishermen, or for any one who might visit this place.

As we had a fish-hook and line we made several attempts to catch fish, but without success. Phil facetiously declared that the trouble with the hook was, "it was too small for an anchor and too large for fish."

Shortly after we had got the roof to our tent pitched we went to the northern end of the island, with some clams for bait, to try once more for fish. Phil, on the way, had found a small dead fish, which, for fun, he fixed to the hook, unknown to me. When at the strait he threw the hook and fish into the water and exclaimed that he had caught a fish, but I saw by his manner that he was trying to play some kind of a joke on me; but in another moment there was a great whirl, the line tightened, and Phil was red in the face with excitement and exertion.

"It's a big one, Phil!" I said, fully aroused. "Play him as you would a trout, or your line 'll break." Finally, seeing that Phil did not understand what was required, I took the line, and after a struggle of several moments I landed a large striped bass, weighing, I should judge without exaggeration, not far from thirty pounds.

We were very exultant over this big fish, as we carried it to our hut and prepared it for cooking. It was delicious eating when fried with ham fat. The portions we did not eat we prepared for drails with which to catch other bass, or blue-fish, and thenceforth were seldom without this kind of food.

Shortly after this, when we were out on one of our prospecting tramps, we saw a schooner in the Sound; but though we shouted and signaled by swinging our jackets she kept on her course without seeing us.

This incident made us very despondent, instead of encouraging us as I now see it should have done, because it showed that vessels occasionally passed through these waters. At no time since we were cast upon this place were we so doleful as over our failure to attract the attention of the people on board the schooner. I perhaps was the more discouraged for some reason which I did not then understand. I was unaccountably depressed, and lacking in strength and energy.

At another time we came to a place on the shore of the Sound where there were tracks of men's feet in the sand, as if a party had landed there but a short time before. We ran around the island like distracted creatures, shouting and calling, in hopes that some of the men were still there; but all in vain.

At another time, while cooking, we heard the sound of rifles or shot-guns, and rushed out expecting that our deliverance was at hand; but it was foggy on the Sound, and though we shouted and hallooed, no one answered the call.

Thus it came to pass that though we were not suffering from hunger, or thirst, or cold, we were in greater mental distress than we were when suffering all of these ills.

This showed me that truth which has often since been emphasized in my life, that the influence of worry and fret over imaginary hardships, and forebodings of ills that often never come, are to physical hardships as two to one. Later in life I have learned that each moment is complete in itself, and brings only its own ills.

One morning we heard heavy firing in a southerly direction. This excited us very much.

"There are men where that firing is," said Phil, "and I say we've stayed here long enough. Let's leave!"

"Well, what is your plan?" I asked. "We can't swim across the Sound; and we might as well try that as to swim where the tide runs as it does at either the north or the south strait."

"What's the matter with a raft?" said Phil.

"I haven't thought of it before; I believe I should have tried it before this if I had," I humbly confessed.

"We'll try it now, then, if you think it a good plan," said Phil. "Let's start across the south inlet and get out of this at once."

After talking it over we decided to start the next morning early, devoting the intervening time to preparation.

Under this incentive I roused myself to make an effort, but said to Phil: "Philibuster, for some reason I don't feel interested in anything that requires *get-up-ativeness*. I don't seem to have much energy or strength."

CHAPTER XII.

WE GROPE IN DARKNESS.

EARLY in the morning we began to convey to the strait the materials for our raft. In this work we traveled on the ocean side just below high-water mark, where the sand was as hard as a macadamized road.

By the time we had got the door of our hut to the south strait I found myself tired and heated. As I had till then been strong and well, I did not attach to my indisposition any other meaning except fatigue. So I kept at work without mentioning my sensations, other than to say that I was tired.

When at last we had, with great labor, got all our materials for the contemplated raft to the place where we were to embark, on putting them together we found that the raft would not carry even one of us. We were greatly discouraged at this, and I was on the point of advising that we return to the place of our old hut and give up the attempt to get away.

After looking across the narrow strait wistfully at the other shore Phil said, "If you were n't so awful down in the mouth, Hez, I should say our best plan in any case, whether the raft would carry us or not, would be to strip, put our clothes and other stuff on the raft, and swim across, pushing the raft; for don't you see, old fel', we couldn't paddle the awkward thing, even if it would carry us and we had good paddles, and we haven't got anything that is like one."

I recognized the force of Phil's remarks, and mechanically began to take off my clothes, and Phil, understanding my act as a tacit assent to his intimated proposition, followed my example. Without another word we waded into the chilling current and, pushing the raft before us, began to swim.

At first the chill seemed to penetrate to my very marrow, but after swimming a few yards a reaction set in and I was somewhat warmer, but still had to force myself to action. I did not understand that this might mean the beginning of a serious sickness, for I had always been strong and well, and therefore could not understand that I was anything but indolent.

The sky was overcast, and that had, as I thought, some influence in causing me to feel depressed.

"What's the matter?" said Phil, while puffing and blowing and looking very red in the face. "There don't seem to be any git in you, and this raft's going out to sea just as fast as the tide can take it! We've got to put on more steam, Hez, or we won't fetch the other side of this little brook."

I then saw for the first time that a strong current was carrying us oceanward. I put on a spurt, but we still continued to drift toward the mouth of the strait.

"It won't do!" exclaimed Phil, catching his breath and looking scared. "We might as well turn back and get ashore while we can."

"It *must* do," I said, now fully aroused to our danger. "We might as well go to sea with the raft as to go ashore without our clothes."

But though my words expressed confidence and courage, and though they heartened Phil, I was far from feeling anything but a desperate resolution not to turn back.

So without more words we continued battling with the swift tide.

It seemed for a time like working against fate. Phil was out of breath, and my desperation, caused by the knowledge that failure meant death, was all that sustained me.

We were now at the very mouth of the inlet and drifting still farther. I noticed that a short distance ahead the water seemed smoother—almost calm. I thought there might be less tide there and easier swimming. With a few desperate strokes I forged ahead and swam around the raft, clutched and placed between my teeth one end of a rope with which the raft was lashed together, and made a supreme effort, feeling that our lives depended on it.

"HOLD ON," I SAID, "I CAN TOW THE RAFT."

Phil seconded my efforts, while I, seeing that the raft still drifted towards the ocean, became, as it were, frenzied, and put out more and more effort, until at last the raft moved towards the shore without drifting. "By George," exclaimed Phil, "this raft is drifting the other way!"

I soon saw, by sighting objects on the shore, that we had struck a counter-current or eddy, and at the same time found that I could touch bottom, and that the water was scarcely above my waist.

"Hold on," I said; "I can tow the raft."

I heard Phil laughing, and turning, indignantly said, "Where does the laugh come in, Phil?"

"Why," he replied looking back, "here we've been swimming when for the last thirty yards we might have waded."

So it proved; with the exception of a channel about a hundred yards wide we could have waded most of the way, but we had been deceived as to depth by the dark-colored bottom.

After towing the raft for a while we came to another narrow channel across which a few strokes carried us.

We reached the shore, and were pulling the raft above high-water mark so that we might make use of it again if needed, when suddenly everything seemed to whirl around and turn over and over. I staggered and fell: I had fainted for the first time in my life.

When at last I revived Phil was looking very sober and sad.

"I am getting to be a baby — a perfect milksop, I believe, Philibuster," I said.

"I guess not," said Phil; "if you hadn't put on so tearingly for a spell when we were out in the channel we'd have gone out to sea with all our clothes — you swam like mad; I never saw the like of it. It's I that's a baby when it comes to a hard spot, and not you, Hez."

One thing surprised us, and that was that on looking around we saw some of the wreckage of the "Favorite," such as tar-barrels and other things, far above high-water mark.

"What geese we are," exclaimed Phil; "while we've been lying around over yonder the wreckers have been not two miles from us on this coast; otherwise how did this stuff get above high-water mark?"

"Yes," I replied, "but it don't matter now, let's get somewhere where I can get a good rest; I never felt so mean in my life. I can't stand this grub either, it makes me sick."

"Well, you are squeamish," said Phil, cramming his mouth full of food; "this fried fish is awful good."

After this we began our journey up the coast and had not gone far when Phil, who was ahead of me, exclaimed, "Well, here's a go, Hez; we are on another island."

I went to the top of the sand-hill where he stood, and looking off said. "Sure enough, Phil, but what is that down there just above high-water mark? It looks like a boat."

We both started toward it. It proved to be the boat of the "Favorite," in which, it will be remembered, poor Blarney had gone adrift. But we found it to be stove in at the bows and without oars.

"I hope Blarney got ashore alive in it," said Phil, "but it isn't at all likely, for he was no sailor, and he wouldn't have stood much of a chance if he had been."

As the island we were on was nothing but sand there remained nothing for us to do but to get away by swimming.

At first we debated whether we should go back to where we started from in the morning or go ahead.

The island was not over a mile and a half long and we soon reached its southern limit, Phil carrying the door and I the full haversacks, and other useful things. With the exception of a narrow channel, twenty or more feet wide, we were able to wade to the other shore, and found, as Phil said, "When one really gets at a task it never proves as hard as it looks."

By the time we had reached the other shore the clouds that had for some hours overcast the sky gathered increasing darkness; and soon after a furious storm of rain, thunder, and lightning burst upon us. We staggered on in the darkness in hopes to come upon a fisherman's hut.

I was both hot and cold; at times the heat seemed unendurable and at other times I was shivering with cold. I felt indifferent to everything, except a sickening feeling, beginning in my head and extending all over me.

At last I stopped and said, "Philibuster, you can go on, but I am sick and played out; I can't go any farther."

The rain was descending in torrents when we halted between two sand-hills, and Phil covered and sheltered me as best he could with the canvas and the oil jacket.

During the night my sleep was troubled, and I had frequent chills with fever, and found myself continually trying to explain to my mother why I was so wet and comfortless.

"Wake up, old fel'," called Phil.

I threw off the canvas and sat up. The sun was shining; the sky was once more clear. Phil was standing on the hillock above me and pointing, smiling, and saying something which though I heard I could not for some time comprehend; for a stupor seemed to chain my thoughts and perceptions.

"What is it, Phil?" I said; "my head aches so I can't seem to understand you."

I heard Phil say something about houses in sight.

I have but an indistinct remembrance of what occurred after that except that I was soon in a room that seemed very close and ill-smelling, trying to eat food, for which I had an unaccountable loathing.

Then I remember a delicious feeling of being between cool sheets and seeming to hear my mother's voice saying, "Sleep, my boy. You will soon feel better."

When I awoke the kindly face of a young woman greeted me.

"Where am I? Where is mother — and Phil?" I inquired; and then as I dimly remembered how I came there I attempted to get up, when it seemed as if my bones would drop asunder, I was so lame and weak.

"Where's Phil, ma'am?" I asked.

"He's over yon in the boat with my man," she replied, but as she spoke I heard Phil's voice. Then there was a whispering outside of the door. The woman said, "Come in, he's right peart," and Phil was at my bedside.

"I'm awful weak, Philibuster," I said, "but I guess it's time we were going, it must be quite late."

"Don't you know," said Phil, glancing at the woman, "that you have been lying here sick for 'most four weeks, a fever sickness, as John calls it? I guess you're coming 'round all right now. Here, have some clam soup; then turn over and go to sleep again, and we'll have a good talk by and by."

I yielded to the stronger will, turned over with my face to the wall, studied the red flowers on the wall paper, and then fell into a long, restful slumber.

When I awoke Phil still sat by the bed. I yawned and said, "I've had a nap, I believe. What was it you were saying about clam soup?"

"A nap!" exclaimed Phil, laughing; "you've been asleep for twelve hours steady and it has done you no end of good; you don't look like the same person."

"Take down that glass and let me see, will you?" I said. Phil hesitated, then said, "You look a little peaked and thin yet, Hez," and handed me the glass.

I should not have known the thin pale face as mine.

I then learned that I had had what the natives called a "crazy fever." I had been taken in by John Nixon and his wife, who had given me their own bed, and Mrs. Nixon had been nursing me with kindly solicitude for weeks, without which nursing I should doubtless have died. I also learned that we were on that portion of Hatteras known as Chicamocomico, a village of about a hundred families. The men of the little place were, as Phil said, "all fishermen."

"There is one thing," said Phil, "that I don't understand, and that is, that the people around here say there were two people besides you and me saved from the "Favorite." One of them must have been Blarney, but the other said he was a North Carolinian. Now, you know there was no one on board from North Carolina, and this man was, so John says, nearly forty years old."

"What kind of a looking man was he, Phil?" I inquired.

"These are nice, kind-hearted people," said Phil, laughing, "but they are n't much for description. They can say 'howdy,' and chew snuff in any kind of foreign language, but when it comes to telling anything about people they can't tell how they look, so I can understand them. Jane says he was right peart and powerful pleasant like, and that his hair was dark snuff colored, and that he toted off to Fort Hatteras."

"There is one way to account for the man," I said, "and that is he lied to these folks." And with this we dropped the subject, until months afterwards it came up in another shape.

"Where is Fort Hatteras?" I asked, shortly after this conversation.

"Fort Hatteras?" said Phil. "Well, the rebels have had a lot of darkies building it and another fort called Fort Clark 'most all summer down at Hatteras Inlet. They 've got some big guns there, so John says. They are the guns we heard down on that island, I guess.

"One reason we did n't see more people while we

were there was that they were just then busy keeping out of the way of the conscription officer. The people here have been giving more attention to keeping out of sight than they have to visiting or wrecking. A Confederate officer and a lot of men were here this week, and Jane took them up to see you: made them believe you were John and needed medicines; killed two birds with one stone; for the officer sent up some quinine from the fort, and thinking John was sick, hasn't been looking for him since. Wasn't that a joke?"

In two weeks' time I was able to get out in the boat with John, who proved to be a good-natured giant. He had taken a great notion to Phil; and, though not a great talker, was sensible and shrewd.

I began at once talking to John about getting away. He would say but little except that he didn't think it was best for us to be too peart about getting to Fort Hatteras. A few days after this he said he had seen a strange schooner in the Sound which he reckoned was a Yankee schooner that had put in through one of the upper inlets for fear of a storm. That she had that morning signaled for a pilot, and he thought he would go aboard and see what kind of people was on her.

I was not only anxious to be going, but felt that we had burdened these good people too much already.

When I said as much to John and his wife they

both declared that we were no trouble, and that they had had nothing but good luck ever since they took us in. They considered us sort of mascots that had brought them protection.

Finally John said Phil could go off to the schooner with him, and if he liked the looks we could make a bargain with the captain. It was agreed by us all that that would be better than trusting to the Confederates.

CHAPTER XIII.

WE LEAVE CHICAMACOMICO.

THAT day, while Phil and John were off in the boat on the errand mentioned in the preceding chapter, and I was in the kitchen helping Jane mend some fishing-nets, we heard a peculiar call outside. Jane started up, saying:

"The men at the forts are coming; get over yon in the beach grass, and stay away till you see the net hung up back of the house."

I did not wait to question, but started.

Before this I had known that there was a system of signals in use among the villagers to give warning to one another. In all the houses the women, and even the children, were on the lookout, so it would have been almost impossible for any stranger or enemy to approach the place without making his presence known, and giving all persons who wished to conceal themselves an opportunity to do so.

I was quickly hidden behind the sand-hills, where none could approach without my seeing them or receiving warning.

Not five minutes after I left I saw a party of men at the house, and then after some twenty minutes had elapsed, as if they were satisfied that there were no men there whom they could conscript, they took their departure.

I waited, expecting to see the signal displayed, but it did not appear.

After a time I observed two of the neighbors' boys gradually drawing near to me while playing around the sand-hills. I thought nothing of it until they came within a few feet of where I was lying, when I began to comprehend that they were sent to communicate with me.

Without turning his face towards me one of them said, "Missus says you must n't come to the house to-night," and then carelessly, while playing, they made their way back.

It was at ten o'clock at night, or later, when I saw a light in the back window. This was a signal that John and Phil had been at home. In another moment Phil was with me.

"The conscription gang are scattered all through the village, laying for the men to come home from fishing, but they 'll wait till they are old and gray before they catch 'em," said Phil in a suppressed tone, accompanied by a chuckle of amusement.

"I 'm afraid they may catch John, or seize his boat," I said.

"John is not to be caught napping," said Phil; "before we got ashore he seemed to suspect trouble at home, for he suddenly determined to anchor his boat and go ashore in his dory at some other than his usual landing. Then we got word that they were laying for him there. He is at the shore waiting for us now. He says keep a sharp lookout and not be seen."

We went to the place where he had agreed to meet us, and were soon on board of his boat. On our arrival John got up sail at once and stood out into the Sound, so that he might be in the vicinity of the schooner and at the same time keep at a respectful distance from the gang in the town. I now learned that John and Phil had not been on board of the schooner, but had talked to one of the fishermen who had. He told them that it was, as John had thought, a Yankee craft, which, not knowing that the State had seceded, had come in for a harbor.

It was nearly sunrise when we discovered the schooner well off in the bay, and it was ten o'clock when we came near enough to hail her.

In answer to our hail there came an evasive reply, and an invitation to come on board if we wanted any information. We were soon alongside, and Phil and I climbed on deck.

An elderly man stood at the tiller with his feet wide apart, giving at times sharp orders to the only hand on deck besides himself. Without changing his position he cast a scrutinizing glance at John in the boat, then at Phil and me.

"Well," he said to us, "spit it out; what is it?" Then to John he said, "What's the matter? why don't you come aboard?"

We explained to him that we had been cast away and wanted to get home, and if he was going to a Northern port we hoped to get a passage with him.

"No place for land-lubbers, but if you can reef and steer"—and here he gave us another searching glance, and then added, "We are short-handed, or we would n't be in Pamlico Sound." Then, seeing that John was about to cast off his painter, he added, "Come aboard and pilot me out of the upper inlets, and I 'll give these boys a passage; they 'll have to work, though; and I 'll give *you* ten silver dollars to pilot me out of here."

John came on board at once, saying to the captain, "I 'll do my best, but I can't say but the Hatteras Inlet folks ain't right peart after you uns."

"I understand," said the captain, "but if you know the upper inlets we may get the 'Philena' through to-night. I 'm just from the West Indies; got fruit and perishable stuff aboard, and 've got to git to N' York or the cargo 'll be sp'iled. I come through the inlet by them forts in the night, but the thing now is how to git back."

"What made you put in here?" inquired Phil.

"Short-handed and did n't like the looks o' the sky; likely to have a storm 'fore I can make N' York. An' then," continued the old captain in his thunderous bass tones that seemed to make the air vibrate, "I did n't know this State had gone crazy till some of your fishermen told me. I knew that South C'r'liny had gone sort o' wild-- I'arned that 'fore I left N' York. I s'posed the tar-heels 'd stick to the Union!"

And the captain laughed a deep vibrant laugh at his own joke, which at the same time gave me a good opinion of him.

There was almost a dead calm at eleven o'clock, the wind having gone down since we came aboard, and therefore, though headed towards Albemarle Sound, the schooner lay near where we had embarked. At noon the wind freshened, but it was dead ahead.

"I am afraid we've brought bad luck aboard," said Phil to me in a low tone, while I was tending sheets and the schooner was slowly beating up the Sound.

"Don't be an old woman," growled Captain Bangs (this we had learned was the name of the captain), who had overheard the remark, "there's no such thing as luck: we are hemmed in here 'cause we didn't know the tar heels was out o' the Union. The wind's ahead 'cause it blows from the direction we want to go. Luck hain't got the least bit to do with it, my boy. Call it circumstances an' head wind." And the old captain spat over the rail, and then looked up at the trim of his sails.

At sundown it came on calm again, but we had managed meanwhile to get the schooner under cover of the land, where she was not likely to be observed.

It was my watch on deck. The air was still with just a hint of a rising breeze rippling the water. In the east there was a faint flush which betokened the approach of day. Except the measured cadence of the surf not a sound broke the silence.

I was thinking of home, and of the many adventures and hardships I had encountered since I left my dear mother for the uncertain perils of the sea. I was in a deep revery when a faint, sharp sound broke the stillness. I listened intently, and then again heard a measured sound like the distant click of oars. I rushed to the companionway and called to the captain.

Captain Bangs came on deck saying:

"What is it?"

"I hear the sound of oars," I said.

He listened for some time, and then said, "I hear something. I guess your ears are better 'n mine, but it may be the fishermen goin' out in their boats," and then called out, "All hands on deck here!"

When John came on deck he listened, and replied to an inquiry from the captain, "No, cap, I reckon there's more 'n two pair o' oars a-board that boat', an' the stroke o' our folks is diff'rent."

We were soon under way, standing off into the Sound. John had taken the tiller, while the captain was looking through his glass.

"Here they come," he exclaimed, "jist 'round that p'int. It's a hull boatful o' men." And the captain laid down his glass and began to give orders, and at the same time assisted in their execution.

The breeze began to come in little puffs; the schooner answered to the breeze, the water rippled at her bows, and the sails drew tauter on the sheets.

"What d'ye think, sir," said the captain to Nixon; "are we creepin' 'way from 'em?"

Nixon shook his head.

"I'd make no bones o' fightin' 'em," said the captain, "if I had powder an' shot fer that ol' swivel up there for'ard; 't ain't much of a gun, but when I was cap'n of a ship in the Chiny seas I stood off a lot o' pirates a hull day, an' got away in the night; had a good sharp fight; an' I wouldn't mind givin' these folks somethin' to remember me by."

And the old fellow looked as if he would enjoy such a privilege.

"Wet down the sails there, all hands!" shouted the captain; "there comes a little more breeze; there, that's better. Yis, I vow, we're leavin' the lubbers astarn."

After a few moments it was evident to all on board that the captain was right, and that the boat was falling behind in the race.

In an hour's time the boat was no longer in sight, and the captain, who had been intently gazing through his glass, shut it up with a satisfied grunt, exclaiming:

"Well, we've showed 'em our heels, but they'd had us if it hadn't be'n fer the boy. So you see, youngster," said the captain to me, "you brought good luck if you brought any kind of luck aboard. If you'd be'n a-nappin' them fellers 'd ketched us."

We had a good breeze all day. We neared the inlet through which John thought it best to make a passage, and as it was coming on dark, the captain, on John's representation that he needed a little daylight to pilot the schooner through, hove to under the land "so as not to be caught napping."

At daylight we made for the inlet. The breeze was good, and everything seemed to be progressing favorably, when, just as we neared the inlet, a little steam craft was seen poking her nose out from behind the land.

Captain Bangs ordered the schooner about on the other tack with the intention of getting away, saying, "P'raps we can show 'em a trick yit." But even as he spoke a dense smoke began to pour out of the steamer's smoke-stack, and in another moment she was in full pursuit and gaining on the "Philena." I saw a smoke and a flash, and then heard the roar of a gun, and a shot came skipping the water across our bows.

"'T ain't no use," said the captain, "steam beats sail every day; guess we'd better act friendly." And with this he ordered the schooner put about.

In a few moments the "Cotton Plant," such was her name, was alongside and her men swarmed on the schooner's decks, taking possession in the name of the Confederate States. We were ordered on board the "Cotton Plant," which was at once headed for Hatteras Inlet.

In the afternoon we were landed at the inlet, and soon after conducted to the office of the naval commandant, Captain Barron.

He received us with chilling civility; any one could see that he had the habit and manner of command.

"Where does your vessel hail from, captain?" he demanded.

"From the West Indies," replied Captain Bangs, "loaded with fruit an' produce — perishable; sail from N' York, sometimes from Boston."

"A native of New York?" inquired Captain Barron.

"No, sir, a Cape Codder, but 've sailed out o' them ports all my life, ever sence I was ten year old. Be'n four times 'round the world; be'n feri'n v'y'ges all my life; yis, cap'n of a ship f'r near thirty year. Then I thought I'd settle down 't hum; then I had a kind 'f a-hankerin' for the salt water 'g'in. I see you 're a sailor an' know how 't is. Then I put most o' my money in this little craft; thought I'd 'muse myself coastin'. Capt'n, she's a little craft, won't do you no good, an' sence I ain't no designs 'g'inst the Southern folks p'raps y'll let me an' my schooner go. Y' ar' welcome to the cargo; that's fair."

Captain Barron smiled as he replied: "Personally I should like to oblige you; but we are at war with the United States, and your vessel is a prize, and you are a prisoner of the Confederacy."

"But," said Captain Bangs, "you b'long to th 'nited States, don't ye? them are the buttons 'f our common country you've got on y'r coat; 'xcuse me if I offend, but I don't understand things."

"Sir," said the officer haughtily, "I am an officer of the Confederacy and owe no allegiance to the old government;" and then in an insinuating and pleasanter tone he said, "Perhaps we can arrange it, captain, so that you can still command your vessel; we should be glad to give you employment in our way; the Confederacy needs good seamen. It would be preferable, would it not, to still command your own craft to being a prisoner of war? I can promise you letters of marque from our president."

"To do what?" asked the captain, knitting his brow, as if he were trying to comprehend the proposition.

"Why, to capture Yankee vessels; there will be some good pickings, and you will soon get rich."

"An' be hung for piracy, as I sh'd desarve, an' as every one does that raises his hand 'g'inst the flag that's protected him, an' that he's sailed under. No, sir! I'd be sunk in the 'Philena' first an' be damned to all traitors and turncoats!"

There was a look of rage on the officer's face, which the captain perceiving said, "Excuse me, sir. I'm a little heated, but I mean no disrespect to you. Why, I've sailed under that flag when you was in your cradle. I've be'n glad to be protected, an' proud, sir, to stan' under it, an' feel that it was my flag, the flag o' free Americans, that our fathers fought for an' died for; my father fought with Decatur, an' fell dead on the deck of his ship. P'raps you hain't felt 's I hev' all m' life, that ye owed duty to it with y'r life?"

There was a look passing over the face of the Confederate which I could not interpret. Perhaps he was reminded of the time when he swore allegiance to that flag. There was a troubled look on his face, — a look of mingled pain and sorrow, as if every word of the old sailor had cut like a knife; for he had been, but a few weeks before, an officer of the United States Navy, holding its confidence, as well as a position of trust, which he had betrayed and foresworn.

With a white face, almost with a gasp, he turned to the sailor and said, "I do understand, sir," and then turning to an officer he said:

"Take this old man away; see that he is treated kindly and respectfully."

A glance passed between Phil and me, and I

knew that he wanted me to be spokesman, and I also knew that he thought it best to say but little.

"How came you on board of the schooner?" inquired Captain Barron.

"Shipwrecked," I replied, "and were taken on board by Captain Bangs, who offered to take us to New York. This other boy the same," I added, indicating Phil with my hand.

No more questions were asked us, and Phil and I and Nixon were marched through the sand, to the guard quarters, just outside of Fort Clark.

CHAPTER XIV.

LEAVING DIXIE.

The two forts built on the sandy beach of Hatteras were as yet unfinished. Most of the guns were, however, in position, the powder magazines constructed, and the bomb proofs, though they were afterward shown to be unserviceable, were considered finished.

There were about seven hundred men on duty in and around the forts, while a large number of negroes still labored on them under the direction of a graduate of West Point.

A number of rude buildings, which had been built for the accommodation of the soldiers, clustered around these forts or earth-works. The young non-commissioned officer who had us in charge said:

"Captain Barron belongs to the navy, and was some cut up, I reckon, by what your old cap'n said. Why, he played, so they say, a Yankee trick at Washington; he almost got charge of the whole dog-goned Yankee navy when that old Abe stopped it; we should 'ave had a better lot o' ships if it had n't been for that."

This last observation was said in the tone of one who is aggrieved over unfair usage.

"What are these forts for?" I inquired, for I couldn't see any use in defending a sand-bar.

"Well," said, he "I reckon the Yankee ships can't come over the sand beach, an' there ain't water 'nough for 'em to git through over yon," indicating the northern inlets, "an' they can't come through h'yer; if they try it we'll blow 'em out o' th' water."

That my young readers may better comprehend the situation and the purpose of these forts, I will recite a few facts which Phil and I did not then know, and which, in part, may be unfamiliar to the reader.

When the news of the capture of Fort Sumter by the South Carolinians was flashed over the country, President Lincoln at once called an extra session of Congress, to meet on July 4, 1861, and also issued a call for seventy-five thousand volunteers to maintain the laws, and to restore the supremacy of National rule.

These acts of the chief executive were hailed at the North with an outburst of patriotism with a unanimity which never abated in its enthusiasm, and before which party lines were practically obliterated; and the people rushed to arms to sustain the central government.

On the other hand the governors of the slave States utterly refused to coöperate in the National defence; while the secessionists among the people, availing themselves of the call of Mr. Lincoln for volunteers, made a last effort to force the States into rebellion, under the pretext that this call of the Federal government had invaded their rights as sovereign States.

Under these influences one State after another had seceded from the Union, and finally the Confederacy, with Jefferson Davis at its head, issued letters of marque, and invited the rebel States to fit out privateers for the capture or destruction of the merchant vessels of the North.

On the 19th of April, 1861, Mr. Lincoln issued a proclamation declaring a blockade on all the coast from South Carolina to Texas, and on the 29th, Virginia having already seceded, and the secession of North Carolina being imminent, he extended the blockade to the coast of those States. But to establish an effective blockade from Mexico to the Potomac, near Washington, was an immense undertaking.

To understand the value of Hatteras Inlet in connection with this blockade, as well as from a military standpoint, take the maps of North Carolina and Virginia, and you will observe on them a tangled network of internal navigable waters protected by a long barrier of narrow sand islands (of which Hatteras beach, where the "Favorite" had been wrecked, forms the greater part) extending from Currient Sound, near Norfolk, Va., to below Beaufort, S.C.

Through these sand barriers there are, as I have

already instanced, numerous channels or inlets, where vessels of light draft can pass to communicate with the vast inland country, and through which blockaders could not follow on account of shallow water, while the principal or main channels were guarded by the forts at Hatteras Inlet. Once safe within these waters the rebel, foreign, or native trader had the whole country open to his operations.

The English traders and shipbuilders, if not the English government, seemed to have been carefully posted, before the war began, as to all the advantages of our coast line to blockade runners, and also as to the premeditated rebellion, for the ink on the proclamation declaring the rebels belligerents was not dry before they began to fit out at their ship-yards privateers exactly fitted to thread these shallow inlets. In this manner the insurgents were able to receive munitions of war and English goods in exchange for their cotton.

For a time the Confederacy was virtually a province of Great Britain.

Two of the most important points for this inland traffic were Pamlico and Albemarle Sounds.

Neither Phil nor I comprehended at that time the importance of the forts at Hatteras, and I have given these details so that boys who read this narrative may comprehend the part this position played in the affairs of the war.

After our interview with Captain Barron, Phil,

Captain Bangs, Nixon, and I were all confined in a small building used for guard quarters. Our food was very good and our treatment fair, and after about a week we were allowed comparative liberty, after signing a parole of honor not to go beyond certain limits. Under this arrangement John was allowed to go home, only being required to report to the commandant once each week.

At first I was very much interested in my new surroundings. I thought, as Phil said, "It will be something to talk about if we ever get home."

Thus I was very observant and curious regarding the forts. The information I gained was afterwards of advantage to me.

However, I soon tired of Hatteras, and chafed over our forced detention from home and friends. I became tired too of the never-ceasing sound of the surf and the unending calm of the water in Pamlico Sound, as well as of the absurd brag of the Southern soldiers of what they intended to do with the Yankees if they came to Hatteras.

"I want to get away from here, Philibuster," I said one day: "I am tired of it."

"So am I," said Phil, "but what can we do about it? We might as well be a thousand miles from land as to be here, so far as running away is concerned. We have just got to grin and bear it till something turns up."

On the last of July the Confederates were jubilant. When I inquired the cause of their manifestations of joy one of the guard said:

"Our army has just captured the whole durned Yankee army at Manassas, and sent 'em to Richmond."

"What are you going to do with 'em?" I inquired, just to see what their ideas of the uses of the Yankees were.

"Well, I reckon we-uns 'll make you-uns work for we-uns."

Then followed extravagant statements of the performances of the Confederate army, all of which they believed, no doubt, but which we seriously questioned among ourselves.

Up to this time we had been treated with some respect and forbearance, but thereafter the sergeants and officers became overbearing and disagreeable, if not insulting. Even the privates seemed to consider themselves superior persons, and, as Phil said, "put on lugs."

Our rations meanwhile steadily decreased in quantity, and we all grew more and more discontented. This discontent was not the less when the guard began to circulate a rumor that we were all to be sent to Lynchburg.

One day, about the 23d of August I should judge, I was wandering along the ocean shore when I heard a shrill whistle. I turned and saw John Nixon, beckoning to me from a sand-hill.

I knew at once that he had something of importance to communicate, and that he had been on the lookout for me.

"What's the trouble, John?" I inquired; "you look as if"—

"I reckon," said John, interrupting, "that the trouble concerns you-uns as much as it does we-uns. Them people down there are goin' to put me in their army, an' send you-uns off to some big prison up to Lynchburg where they 've got a power more o' Yanks."

"How do you know, John, that this isn't a mere rumor?" I asked. "I've heard the talk about our being sent to some other prison myself."

"This ain't no what-d'-ye-call-it," said John; "my wife's cousin's a clerk 't the cap'n's office an' see the paper 't told the cap what t' do with you-uns, 'n 't the same time Major Anderson come in an' said he was goin' t' hev me put in the squad for drill. I reckon the talk begun 'tween that Cap'n Barron an' the major, 'cause one 'f 'em said 't I 'd make a good man fer th'r navy vessels, an' t' other wanted me in th' army. Now, I reckon I won't take a gun for them folks. Jane won't like it. T'-morrer — so Jane's cousin says — they 'll take away y'r p'role an' send y' t' th' guard-house ag'in. They won't git me. I sh'll be a-fishin'."

"But what's your plan, John?" I said; "I know you 've got one."

"I reckon that guard-house where they keep ye

ain't much to get out'n when I was thar," said John: "the boards t' that lower bunk was loose, an' there's no floor underneath. I dug a right smart hole down ther, m'self, an' I reckon you c'n claw out in a right smart time."

"But what will we do then? We can't get away from this place," I exclaimed impatiently.

"Well," said John with provoking slowness, "I reckon you 'n' Phil 'n' that cap'n man 'd better git out 'n' come over t' th' second crik where I've got my boat an' a lot o' grub fixin's."

And then John outlined a plan by which he agreed to have his boat in a creek about three miles distant. If we did not come sooner he would be there three nights in succession, and longer if we could not get there at that time and he could do so safely.

On returning to the fort I told Phil all this, and more which I have not here given.

The next morning when I started to leave the guard quarters I was told that I had violated my parole by talking to the negro laborers, and the captain was also deprived of his liberty on a similar pretext.

When I had demurred at being restrained, the young officer of the guard showed me his written instructions, that we were not to be allowed thereafter to go beyond guard quarters.

During the day I examined the lower bunk and found, as John had said, that the boards were loose, and that under this there was nothing but sand to obstruct our exit.

On the night of August 25, at about eleven o'clock, Phil, who had been occupying the upper bunk, removed the boards at the bottom of the lower one, and we were ready to try to get out. The second relief had just been sent out, and the guards relieved were soon fast asleep and snoring. Soon after this I saw the sergeant of the guard fasten the door, and then, casting a glance toward his prisoners, he lay down, but apparently not with the intention of sleeping. I saw him making an effort to keep awake, but after starting up and looking around once or twice he sank back in his bunk, and soon his measured breathing assured me that it was safe for us to act.

This was better luck than we had anticipated.

I silently got up, when one of the guard, who slept next to us, looked out of his bunk, and then yawned and lay down again, and was soon fast asleep.

It was a half hour after this when we went to work. It was by no means a hard task to dig away the loose sand.

On starting out we had no trouble in evading the sentinels, who kept but an indifferent outlook, as I had more than once previously observed.

In two hours' time we had reached the rendezvous agreed upon, but at first could find neither John nor his boat. For a time I thought some disaster had overtaken him; then thought I would try a signal which he had taught us. It was at once answered, and in another moment John came ashore in a dory from his sail-boat which he had secured off-shore, where she could not be easily seen.

To our surprise we found not only John's wife, but also Captain Bangs on board. I had told the captain of John's plan and had described the situation of his boat, and he had made his way to the place early in the evening by evading the guard and slipping out of the door.

John Nixon's boat was twenty feet long, sharp at both ends, half-decked forward, and, as he often said, was the best boat on Pamlico Sound, and fit to make an ocean voyage in.

By Captain Bangs's advice he had formed the plan of passing through one of the northern inlets, and then of making his way up the coast of Delaware and New Jersey, but was in hopes that before going so far we should fall in with some northern-bound vessel and be taken on board.

A gentle southern breeze was blowing when we got up sail and steered to the northward.

"I hope we shan't see that or'nery 'Cotton Plant' anywhere," said John anxiously; "one o' ye 'd better go for'ard an' keep a lookout."

We kept from six to ten miles from the shore during the next day, and when night came steered nearer the shore.

"I s'pose," said John, "we might git through at the Ocracoke Inlet, but mebbe the Hat'ras cusses 've got a boat there."

It was about twelve o'clock that night when we tacked sheets and stood for one of the northern inlets, where John said the channel was very narrow and intricate, and where none but those familiar with its constant changes ever ventured.

As we neared it we found the tide going out like a mill-race, and calling for all of John's attention to keep the boat from grounding.

Suddenly there came an ominous call: "Boat ahoy! What boat is that?" John made no response at first, but said to us on board, "Keep down in the boat so they won't see ye."

When the call was repeated in a peremptory manner, John cried out in a tone of great alarm, "A fishin' boat; the blamed tide's toting me out to sea, an' I want to get in shore; throw me a rope, or give me a tow."

John's tones seemed so genuine that the people on board the hostile craft seemed thoroughly deceived.

"No steam up," came the laughing reply. "Let down y'r sail and row in."

"Throw a line, I say, or I reckon I'll go on to these doggoned flats; I dar' n't let go the tiller, an' I'm jest a-gittin' out to sea right fast,—an' my wife's expectin' me t' hum 'fore this."

A hoarse laugh was the only answer, as we were swept by the strong current out into the ocean.

"I reckon 't was that or'nery 'Cotton Plant'; they did n't have up steam, an' if they fire their durned ol' gun now they can't hit the boat."

In another moment the steamer could not be seen for the darkness, and then we trimmed our sails so as to lay our way up the coast.

"That was an all-fired good trick y' played on them fellers," said Captain Bangs. "I almost thought y' *was* scared."

"I was n't 'feared they 'd ketch me; the'd got stuck on th' flats 'f the'd started after us; but I *war* 'feared the'd fire that big gun an' sink 'er, or I would n't 'a' made such a durnation yelpin' 'bout it," said John in his high-pitched drawling tones.

"They won't put chase; should n't wonder if they thought the joke was on their side," said the gruff captain in a tone of satisfaction.

We were some fifteen miles up the coast when a glorious day broke, and under a full press of sail, with the wind abeam, we went on our way. During the day we held our course without sighting a single sail, all on board, with the exception of John's wife, taking turns at standing watch.

About ten o'clock the next morning Captain Bangs, who was on the lookout at the bow, as he stood snuffing the air, and looking at the sky said: "We sh'll hev a change o' weather in course of twenty-four hours; it's comin' on t' blow."

Just then he stopped suddenly in his weather

prophecy, and pointing in a north-east direction excitedly exclaimed:

"What's that over there?"

We all declared we could n't see anything except some dark clouds.

"Clouds," said the captain derisively, "that's the smoke 'f a steamer, but she makes a lot o' smoke, or there must be a lot of 'em together."

John made no remark, but stood off shore that he might intercept the craft.

"What are you up to, John?" said Phil; "they may be rebel craft for all you know."

"Naw," said John contemptuously, "the rebs ain't got only a powerful po' lot o' vessels,—not 'nough to make all that smoke."

"Yis," agreed the captain, "an' then if I ain't a landlubber they burn hard coal, an' most o' these folks (making a motion with his hands toward Hatteras) burn pitch pine or soft coal."

"I wish't I'd a glass, but I am pooty sure there's a fleet o' vessels out there," said Captain Bangs.

"Perhaps they are English ships," I said, "coming to help these rebs. The rebs, when I was at the fort, said they expected the Johnny Bulls to help 'em."

"No," said the captain, shaking his head decidedly, "not at this stage o' the game. If the English help in any way it'll be by sellin' somethin'; they won't help either side till they're certain which is comin' out on top in the fight."

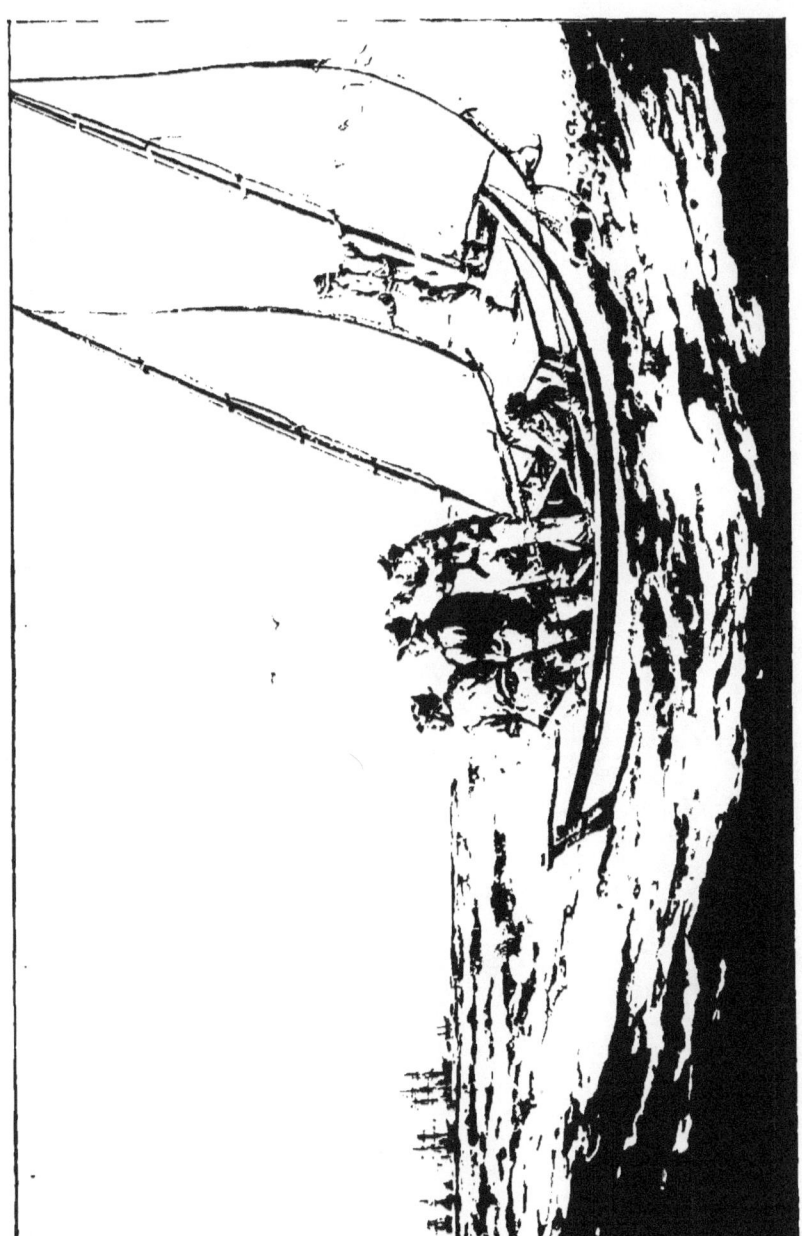

"YES, THEY 'RE UNCLE SAM'S BARKERS, AN' NO MISTAKE."

As we neared the ships, or rather steamers, Captain Bangs declared that they were war steamers. "If there ain't the stars and stripes," said he, "my name ain't Bangs. Yes, they're Uncle Sam's barkers an' no mistake; 'n' I may be a fool, but I think they're on their way t' call them blasted sinners to repentance down there t' Hat'ras."

In course of a quarter of an hour it became certain that it was a squadron of war vessels.

CHAPTER XV.

THE BOOT IS ON THE OTHER LEG.

As we neared the fleet which we had seen in the distance, it proved to be, as the old captain had surmised, a squadron of United States war vessels, accompanied by chartered steamers.

"Boat ahoy!" came the call from the nearest steamer. "What boat is that?"

John answered in a feeble, high-pitched tone; but the old captain, disregarding his answer, replied by shouting out in a more seaman-like style through his hands hollowed for a trumpet,

"The boat 'Jane,' from Hatteras, with escaping prisoners from the forts. What steamer is that?"

And then in an aside he said, "That'll fetch 'em; they'll want to know all we know."

"The United States war-steamer 'Monticello,'" came the answer. "Will you come on board?"

On receiving an affirmative reply, the steamer slowed up and took us on board and our boat in tow.

Until the moment of my arrival there I had never been on the deck of a war-vessel, and I was amazed at the dazzling white decks, the neatness and brightness of the uniforms of the officers and sailors, and the polished metal and taut rigging of this ship. To my eyes she looked more like a craft for a holiday show than for serviceable action; but mine was the mistake of a novice in naval affairs.

"Good deal o' gingerbread work here," said Bangs in his suppressed bass, and then, with an approving look at the orderly seamen and the white decks and taut rigging, added, "Everything ship-shape to a marlin-spike, though."

"You are wanted at the office," said a spruce-looking young gentleman. We were conducted to a spacious cabin, where seated at a table, on which were charts and writing materials, were two officers of the ship. The older of these addressed John, saying:

"You are a native of Hatteras, we understand?"

"Yes," responded John, "my wife and I war both born there."

"What are you leaving the island for?"

John responded by telling the circumstances, which the reader already knows, and added:

"'Most all we-uns' folks — 'most all the men folks, I mean — have be'n druv off by these crazy folks who ain't satisfied with this country an' want t' fight."

"You are a Union man, I take it, Mr. Nixon?" said the officer pleasantly.

"Yes, I reckon th' United States ar' good 'nough f'r me," said John. "I had rights 'nough 'thout fightin' th' Yankees; I ain't got no niggers, an' don't want any that kind o' truck, neither."

"I suppose you are a pilot in these parts; most fishermen are."

John shook his head, saying, "I know th' channels an' Pamlico, I reckon, but a small craft an' a big ship are diff'rent."

After putting a few general questions about the island and its people, the officer began to inquire what we knew about the forts.

"I think this young feller has a pictur' he made o' the forts," said Captain Bangs.

I hung my head, for I knew the drawing I had made was anything but a good one, though I had drawn a better one from it for one of the non-commissioned officers of the garrison. I, however, took it, crumpled and soiled, from my pocket, and at his request both Phil and I stepped to the table or desk, and in reply to his questions soon gave him all the information we possessed, which afterward proved to be of considerable value. The officer also brought out, by a few questions, the story of our shipwreck on Hatteras.

After the interview we were assigned to quarters with the petty officers, and in half an hour felt ourselves very much at home among them.

One of the sailors said to me, "Blast my eyes, youngster, you 're sailin' under close reef. I've got some togs that b'longed to Bill Barnacles, a young chap that died."

Then he showed me a suit of sailor's clothes that were just about my size. These, after some bargaining, I bought, giving him Bill's watch and a promise to pay him five dollars some other time.

I put the clothes on at once after the bargain was concluded, and the sailor who sold them said he would have thought they were made for me.

We learned that the squadron consisted of seven war-vessels: the "Minnesota" (the flagship of the squadron), the "Wabash," the "Monticello," the "Susquehanna," the "Pawnee," the "Harriet Lane," and the "Cumberland"; carrying altogether one hundred and fifty-eight guns, many of them of heavy calibre.

In addition to these war-vessels, there were the "Adelaide," the "George Peabody," and the tug "Fanny," which were chartered steamers and transports; there were also two or three schooners without masts, and a large number of iron surf-boats. We learned that on board of the transports was a body of nine hundred troops, under the command of General Benjamin F. Butler, while the naval expedition was commanded by Flag Officer Stringham, U.S.N.

As Bangs had surmised, this formidable array of battleships was on its way to attack the Confederate stronghold standing at the entrance of Pamlico and Albemarle Sounds.

As we came on deck, Captain Bangs said, "'Tween me an' th' mainm'st, shipmates, I think the boot 'll be on t' other leg with them blasted rebels that was so high an' mighty with us t' Hat'ras; I'll git my schooner back, an' they'll git a lesson, true 's my name 's Bangs!"

And the old sea-dog, with a grim smile, bit into a huge plug of "navy," as if to emphasize his satisfaction.

"It'll take a powerful lot o' lessons t' learn them thar folks, I reckon," said John very earnestly. "You c'n learn a stupid or a fool, but I reckon our folks over thar' are plumb crazy."

Early on Tuesday morning Hatteras light was in sight. When we rounded the outer shoals there was a heavy ground swell, and as we neared the shore the beach, as far as the eye could see, presented an unbroken line of surf. By five o'clock in the afternoon the whole squadron had come to anchor at the southward of the cape.

During the night busy preparations were made for the landing of troops in the morning. The surf boats were hoisted, and signals were exchanged between the ships of the squadron and the flagship. These and other preparations showed that a drama of naval battle was to open with the dawn of the coming day.

John was sent to the flag-ship, where it was thought he might be of use, as he was familiar with the inlet and other features of the island.

As early as four o'clock the next morning the crew of the "Monticello" was summoned to break-

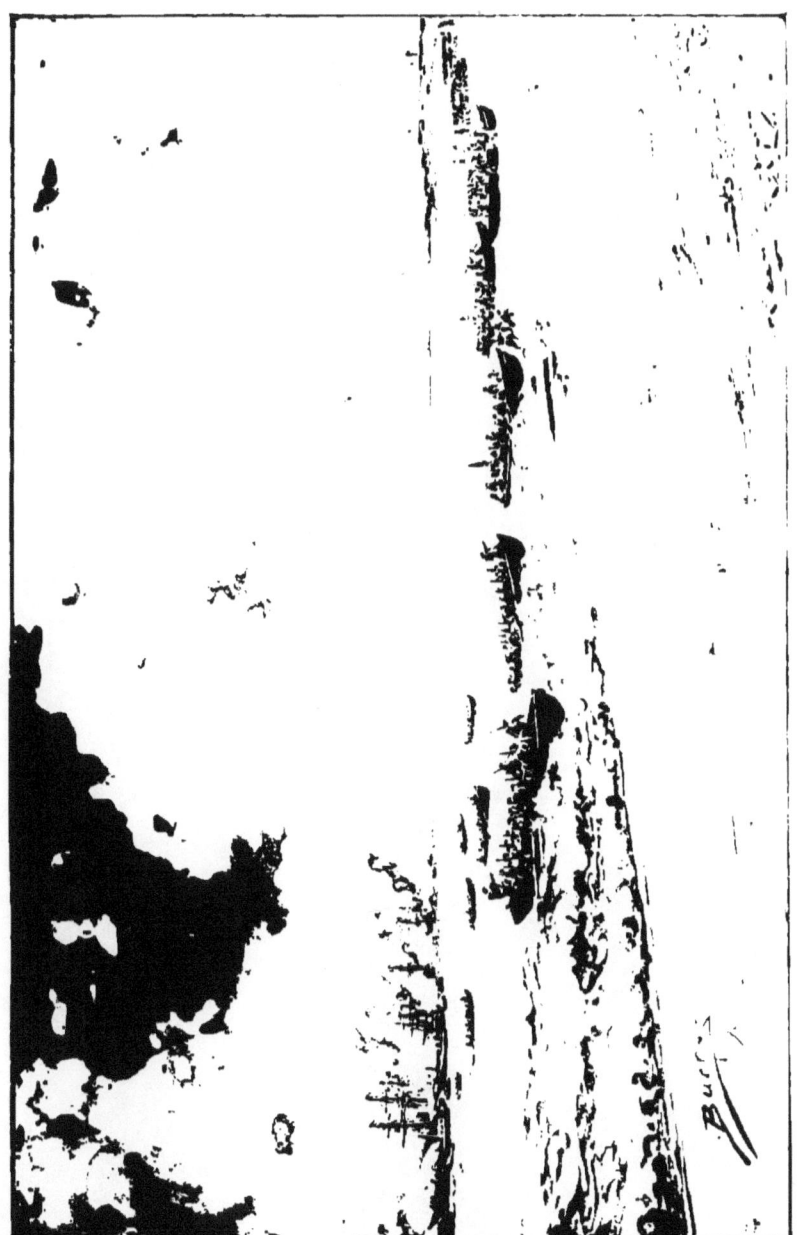

LANDING OF THE U.S. TROOPS AT HATTERAS.

fast, and by seven, with the "Pawnee" and the "Harriet Lane," the steamer was ordered to assist in covering, or protecting, the landing of the troops.

The place selected for the landing was about three miles from the forts, where there was a slight bend in the shore, and less undertow than at any other portion of that part of the beach. Shell were fired from our ship to protect the troops when landed.

The dismasted schooners were anchored near the shore, and then allowed to drift near the breakers, after which each of the iron surf boats took from them fifty or more soldiers to the shore.

Phil, at his request, was allowed to accompany an officer in one of these boats, but I did not get the chance, in which, as will be seen, I was fortunate.

A boat from the "Pawnee" made a successful landing, but some of the boats that followed were swamped, and most of them, when they entered the surf were, with the greatest difficulty, kept from capsizing. Some of them I saw hurled on the beach with the waves sweeping over them, while the half-drowned soldiers struggled through the water to the shore. The surf boats were so badly crushed by the heavy breakers that they could not return to the vessels; and after some three hundred men had been taken to the shore no attempts were made to land any more.

Those on shore were left in a very perilous and

uncomfortable position, without provisions, unable to return, with their ammunition wet, and liable to be captured by a superior force which might easily be sent against them.

In the distance, on the forts, the enemy's flags could be seen defiantly floating.

All this time I had been interested in watching the gunners, and the shell that were occasionally thrown over the troops towards the enemy.

My attention was, however, soon drawn to still more exciting scenes.

At about ten o'clock in the forenoon there was a movement among the remaining vessels of the fleet.

"Blast my timbers," said Captain Bangs, "if I don't think they're goin' to give them forts a lesson from the Ten C'mman'ments, sech as, 'Thou shalt not steal,' or somethin' of a moral natur' f'r th'r good! What craft 's that?"

"That," said the sailor addressed, "is the 'Wabash,' towing the 'Cumberland,' and that craft following them is the flag-ship 'Minnesota.'"

"I s'pose they're prooty well fixed f'r shootin'?" said the old captain inquiringly.

"Yes, sir," said a petty officer, whose acquaintance I was cultivating, "the 'Wabash' carries forty-five heavy guns, the 'Minnesota' forty-six, the 'Cumberland' twenty-four, and the 'Susquehanna' out there getting under way carries seventeen guns."

"One hundred and thirty-two bull-dogs barkin' in one fight!" exclaimed the old captain. "Why, they c'n blow them forts out o' the sand into Pamlico Sound!"

The vessels went forward into position southeasterly from the forts. As they showed their sides to us we saw a jet of flame and smoke leap from their ports, followed by a thunderous roar and concussion that echoed over the water; and then from the forts there came an angry flash and roar, as if in acceptance of the challenge to combat.

The first battle between earthworks and ships, in the Civil War, had begun.

In from ten to twenty minutes the "Minnesota" and the "Susquehanna" added their guns to the clamor and were belching flame and smoke, and filling the air with terrible explosions, the sounds of which came rolling and vibrating over the waters.

"That's a pretty good play of the commodores!" exclaimed an officer who stood looking off at the ships in conflict. "By Jove, they can't get *his* range while *our* ships plump almost every shot into their sand-heaps. Just see the shell burst above them!"

Sure enough, we could see the sand thrown up as the shot struck the parapet outside of Fort Clark, and little clouds of smoke above the forts showed the bursting of shell there, while the shots from the guns of the forts either fell short or threw up jets of water beyond the ships, as they struck.

The reason for this was that the ships instead of remaining stationary constantly passed and repassed the enemy's forts in narrowing or widening circles, delivering their fire as they came in range. By these tactics of the admiral the artillerists at the forts were constantly baffled in their attempts to get range of the ships. If by good luck they nearly got the range they would lose the advantage so gained at the next bout, for the ships did not pass twice at the same distance. Thus every shot made by the enemy was in the nature of an experiment, and during that part of the action not a ship was struck.

I watched the red tongues of fire and jets of white sulphur smoke that leaped in constant succession from our ships, while the concussions shook the deck on which I stood, and seemed even to rock the earth beneath the sea.

The squadron moved majestically without halt, delivering fire and throwing death and destruction among our enemies.

The bursting shell, and other evidences of distruction, impressed me as something terrible; or perhaps sympathy with my father's people gave me this feeling.

"It's awful," I said, "for those poor fellows in the forts."

Meanwhile the "Monticello," having performed her mission in landing and covering the troops, turned her bows toward the fleet and steamed down the coast, firing shot into the forts as she advanced.

We then noticed that the flag of Fort Clark was down, that its guns were silent, and that the men were running from it like chickens from the swoop of a hawk.

"I guess," said Captain Bangs, standing seaman-like, with his feet wide apart and with the sarcastic smile of an injured man avenged, "that them rebel landlubbers won't steal any more schooners from honest men ag'in right away."

When we arrived at the mouth of the inlet the fire of our ships had slackened, and Fort Hatteras did not return the fire.

I heard an officer say, "The fight is all out of them; they've got enough of it."

We had just begun to make our way into the inlet when a signal came from the flagship for the "Monticello" to return and go to the "Minnesota."

As we lay near the huge flagship, John and another person came on board the "Monticello" as pilots.

We then went forward and entered the breakers, the lead being often thrown so as to keep the craft in the deepest water; but, as we advanced, notwithstanding this precaution, the ship more than once struck bottom, making everything on board rattle.

As we turned the point of land at the inlet we found the water more and more shallow; and the vessel pounded the bottom constantly.

Orders were given to turn and work the vessel out again, when there was seen a flash and smoke from Fort Hatteras, followed by the bellowing of its guns, and their shot shrieked and howled over our heads and around us.

I was standing abaft near the two pivot guns when I heard a quick order, and the guns were manned and began to make sharp replies to the rebel battery.

Meanwhile the ship, though pounding the bottom as we backed and filled, turned her head seaward, and by aid of full steam, and taking advantage of the swell, made her way out again.

But the rebel guns meanwhile did ample execution. One shot struck the ship on the port side, carrying away the davits, drove fragments of the boat through the galley, from whence I saw the cooks coming slowly, but, as Captain Bangs said, "very quick for cooks."

Still later another shot carried away the foretopsail yard, and the sail on the port yard-arm, stove in the gig, and carried away the bottom of the whaleboat.

The "Minnesota" and her sister ships had meanwhile promptly opened on the forts. This caused them to slacken fire and soon to cease altogether.

If I had thought the fight terrible at a distance, how shall I describe my emotions when actually under fire?

I assisted in simple matters at the pivot guns,

such as picking up the swabs or handspikes when they fell from the hands of the men, and assisting the powder-monkeys, as the boys who passed the powder were called.

My flesh prickled, and a feverish sweat broke out at the roots of my hair, and then coursing downward seemed to settle in a kind of weakness and trembling around my knees, where it lingered, making them at times so weak they could hardly carry me around the deck.

I was frightened as well as excited, but owing to my somewhat stolid temperament I did not show as much fright as the two powder-monkeys at the guns.

After what seemed to be a long time (though I learned afterwards that it was less than fifteen minutes) we were afloat again, and then stood off shore heading towards the flagship, on reaching which we took on board carpenters to plug the shot holes and to make other temporary repairs. Then we stood toward the forts once more, firing as we went. But the forts had had enough fighting for that day, and made no reply. We saw, however, indications that they were making preparations to resume the fight the next day.

As the roar of battle died away one after another of the ships drew out of range, except the "Monticello," the "Pawnee," and the "Harriet Lane," which went in shore to protect the troops.

Above the clamor of the carpenters' hammers

and mallets we could again hear the surf rolling in on the shore, and a seaward murmur that told of a rising storm.

As darkness came on it began to rain, and we could see dark forms around the fires kindled on shore by the troops, which showed that there was but little sleep there that stormy night.

With the morning's dawn the storm had subsided, the sun was shining, and the water was less rough.

From our position we could see the stars and stripes flying from Fort Clark, and the rebel flag from Fort Hatteras.

When I got on deck Captain Baugs said:

"Them pirates that stole the 'Philena' seem t' want 'nother dose o' punishment, an' there comes them old barkers t' give it to 'em!"

I looked and saw the whole squadron standing in toward the shore, with the side-wheeler "Susquehanna" in advance.

The firing from the ships soon began, and was full as fierce as that of the day before, and the aim seemed more accurate, every shell apparently bursting in or above the fort, enshrouding it in smoke and throwing up clouds of dust.

It was but little wonder that, as we learned later, the garrison was driven from the guns and took refuge in the bomb-proofs. For an hour and a half of the latter part of the conflict the shell landed in the centre of the fort, and finally demoralized its officers and men by smashing through the bombproof where a crowd of them had gathered for protection.

At eleven o'clock we saw a white flag on the staff at the rebel fort, and knew that the defence was abandoned.

Fifteen hundred prisoners surrendered, the chief officer of whom was Captain Barron, who but a few months previous had been holding a position of trust under President Lincoln in the United States navy.

The result of the capture of Hatteras Inlet was of great importance, for it not only gave to the national government possession of the key to the inland waters of North Carolina, but afforded a point of support for our blockading squadrons, and stopped, in part, the fitting out of piratical expeditions on these interior waters.

CHAPTER XVI.

ON SHORE AFTER THE BATTLE.

Just before the battle was over I got permission to accompany a midshipman, who was going to the shore in one of the boats.

I had not seen Phil since the day before, and wanted to talk with him about getting home on one of the ships, as it was thought that the "Monticello" would remain on duty in these waters after the rest of the squadron had left.

The soldiers whom I found on shore had had a hard time since they were landed there, nearly thirty-six hours before. They were without a proper supply of food, water, or shelter. The utmost good-nature, however, seemed to prevail.

There was a line of stacked muskets, near which were fires, at which the men were drying their clothes, and cooking. Most of the soldiers wore a strange-looking dress, consisting of a red cap, a short jacket open at the front, and baggy trousers terminating at the knees, below which were canvas leggings and shoes. The men wearing this dress I was told belonged to Hawkins's regiment of zouaves.

"Say, cully," said one of a group to whom I

addressed an inquiry, "hev y' got anythin' dry 'bout ye t' lend? I ain't seen noth'n' dry 'cept m' throat sence th' pitched us on t' this sand-heap."

The individual who thus addressed me was a blond young fellow with a slouching gait, a solemn-looking countenance, and a voice which ranged from a thin treble to a squeak like the filing of a saw, and, as I afterwards perceived, whose nearest approach to a laugh was a still shriller shriek and a spasm-like contortion of his sallow face.

"Plenty of water last night," I said suggestively.

"Yas, an' plenty in these bags o' our clo'es," said the blond, for illustration wringing his wet, baggy trousers-knee.

I asked if any of them had seen Phil, and accompanied my question with a description of him.

"Yis, I see that chump hang'n' 'round here. Ain't seen 'm lately, dough," said another.

"Dat feller? Yas, I 'member him. He's no slouch. No more chump t'n yous are. He told s'm' tough yarns 'bout be'n' shipwrecked," said the first speaker, whom they called Blenders, and who, addressing me, continued: "Yas, he went up t'r th' fo't with us; was th'r w'en th'r ships begun t' plump some iron things 's big 's nail-kags. Th'y come rid'n' in t'r that sand-heap like fun, an' druv us out a-fly'n'.

"Y'r th' feller dat's wid him when he's shipwrecked? Den 't's true? A'r jist tor't he was jist givin' us guff — jist chinnin' t'r us. But 't was tough 'n' we got slop'n' 'roun' las' night. Jist wait 'll yo', while I pile some o' dis stuff 'n' in an' I g' long wid yous. My cap'n 's up ther'."

"Don't trouble," I said, "I know the way; I was a prisoner up there, and know all about the fort. So you saw my chum there?" I continued.

"Well, I sh'd smile! I lit out, tho', when them nail-kags com' a roar'n' an' shout'n', ridin' int' th' fo't. An' don't yous forgit it."

By this time Blenders had finished his meal. This consisted of part of a goose, which I was told was one of a flock that had hissed at the zouave uniform. It had been killed for showing disrespect to Hawkins's zouaves. On our way up to Fort Clark Blenders still continued to talk. He did not scruple to say that if he ever got home he'd never take a gun and knapsack again.

"This sleep'n' out 'n th' rain don't suit me worth a Bowery lamp-post, cully," and then with a desolate groan with which he constantly interspersed his remarks he said, "Yous sailors gits th' best 'f us, y'r carry yous house wid yer, or rader yous house carries yous, cully; jist a-rid'n' 'round wid it. If 't had n't bin f'r d' ol' blazer — th' what-d'-y'r-caller?"—

"The 'Monticello,'" I suggested.

"Y's; if 't had n't bin fer her jest throwin' nail-kags at dem de'r rebs, dey 'd lit on us like a thousan' o' Hav'stra' brick."

On arriving at the fort I found Phil in a full suit of rebel gray which he had found in the officers' quarters; it didn't fit very well, but it was an improvement on the ragged dress he had cast away.

The sound of the guns of the Federal fleet still continued, and the rushing sound of the shell traversing the air was terrifying to sensitive nerves.

"Just hear d'm talk'n'," said Blenders. "jaw'n' away 't de fort; th'y'll knock everythin' to p'ec's so th'r' won't be no stuff'n' left in 'em."

"I b'lieve they've stopped firin' up t' th' fo't th' rebs 're in," said Blenders's captain. "Say, can't some o' you boys kind o' sneak 'round there an' see what's c'm' over the sp'rit o' the dreams o' Johnnie reb?"

"A'r now, cap'n, don't give ut t' us so high flown," said Blenders, with one of his piercing tones which I had learned to regard as a laugh. "I'll take m' shoot'n'-stick an' g' up an' see w'at 't means."

"Guess we'd better go too, Phil," I said; "we might as well see all that's going on."

So we went with Blenders, who meantime continued to talk, clipping his "ings" in a most lawless manner, and, as Phil said, speaking as if it was too much work to wag his jaw to pronounce his words.

When we came in sight of the fort we saw a new flag flying.

"They've surrendered," said Phil; "the white flag says they've got enough of fighting."

As we advanced toward the fort, we saw their men on the parapet, and then began to meet soldiers in gray, who were as a general thing willing to give descriptions of their part of the fight. Every one of them seemed to think he had escaped death by a miracle. I don't remember about the details they gave us, but got the impression that they had been badly frightened, and I also noticed that they spoke more respectfully of the "Yanks" than I had ever heard them before.

Phil cast a significant glance at me, saying:

"They have had what your grandfather would call 'a change of heart.'"

Blenders went back to report, while Phil and I went forward to the fort, where we found that it was indeed true that the garrison had capitulated. That the bombardment had been a terrible one the barracks around the fort gave evidence. When we entered the fort, we found that everything that could be destroyed by heavy shot was in a condition of dilapidation and wreck.

At one place there was a hole in the centre of the sand parapet, which, I was told, was produced by exploding shell; while on the exterior slope there were holes made in the same manner. I was told that during the last part of the bombardment a shell passed through the ventilator of the bomb-proof, and though it did not explode it kicked up such a dust and smoke that the utmost consternation prevailed among the crowd of officers and men who had sought shelter there: they thought the magazine had caught fire.

From the description that a sergeant (the same young fellow who had taken charge of me when I was first marched to the guard quarters by order of Captain Barron) gave me of the effects of the shell that struck thick and fast in the interior of the fort, it must have been something terrible.

"What do you think," I said, "of being able to blow the Yankee ships out of water now?"

His answer dazed me.

"T wa'n't fair f'r you 'n Yanks t' take all the ships; I reckon if we uns had our share we'd make it right hot fo' you uns."

"Before this war is over," I said, "I think your people will find they made a mistake in supposing the Yankees wouldn't fight. I have always noticed that people who are slow in getting angry are more to be feared than any others."

"You-uns can subdue we-uns, but you-uns can't conquer we-uns," said the young sergeant, in his high-pitched Southern tones, and with tears in his eyes.

A feeling of melancholy came over me when I reflected on the terrible strife of brother with brother, and the blood that must be spilt and the suffering endured, before these people of a common language and kindred could arrive at such an understanding of their differences as to make a settlement of them possible. Yet how little did I, or any one else at that time, comprehend the magnitude to which the strife was yet to grow. Perhaps it was because I was equally of Southern and Northern lineage that the strife seemed more terrible to me than to others. And then I thought of my dear father among these mistaken but brave people who were his kindred and friends, and wondered how he regarded this fratricidal strife.

This feeling was, however, transient, and soon gave place to satisfaction at seeing these people, who had treated me with but little consideration, and even with insolence, beaten and humbled. Ah! had I known, could I have seen into the future, I should have felt less satisfaction, and perhaps a degree of consternation at what it held for me and for those who were dear and near to me.

We could see steamers in the Sound black with troops sent to reënforce the forts. These soldiers were evidently curious observers of the fight.

Their curiosity seemed to abate when the tug "Fanny," from the fleet, came to the landing, for they hurriedly left.

"You see," said the young rebel sergeant, in the tone of one who was grieved, "that we-uns 've got a right smart o' men, but you-uns 've got all the ships, and half 'f 'em b'long to us, I reckon."

When the "Fanny" came in I went with Phil to see who was on board.

Among the passengers I noticed a thick-set, florid-faced man in the uniform of an officer in the United States army.

"That ol' feller with a cock eye 's Ben Butler," said Blenders, who had come to the wharf with us.

I had often heard my grandfather speak of lawyer Ben Butler, and from what I had heard I knew this to be the same person, and hence regarded him with some curiosity.

There was in his face and bearing a look of power and audacity. One of his eyelids drooped over the eye, and when he spoke he threw back his head as if to see the better from under the half-closed lid, and at the same time to emphasize a remark. Young as I was, he impressed me as one who was capable of undertaking anything difficult, and who delighted in attempting it. His face, as well as his manner, told that he was one who could give and take terrible blows, and rejoice in a trial of strength and wits that would daunt other men.

"So that is Ben Butler," I said.

"Y's," said Blenders, "an' y' don't want t' be leanin' on t' him f'r a lamp-post neither, cully. Ol' Cock-eye nearly ate up our colonel t' other day. What did he say? Well, I did n't hear, but I heard ol' Ben thump th' table, an' our colonel jist a-litin' out 's if th' hook an' ladder 'd struck him."

"What was it about?" I inquired.

"Don't 'zac'ly know, but 't was somethin' 'bout

that he didn't like 't 'cause our of'cers 'd strung some 'f the men up by th' thumbs."

When the general had been to the fort, he came down with several of his staff, and stood for a time on the deck of the "Fanny."

"I am going to speak to him," I said.

"Better keep away from him," said Phil; "he looks to me like a feller that would eat a chap at one gulp."

But disregarding both Phil's and Blender's cautions, I went up to him and taking off my hat said, "Can I speak to you, general?"

He gave me a rapid and stern glance, and looking down into my face said sharply, "What is it?" and then added, "I don't command the navy."

"I don't belong to the navy, general," I said. "I was shipwrecked on Hatteras and was made a prisoner, and made my escape in a boat to the squadron. I want to get home."

"Where do you belong?" inquired the general in a modified tone.

"In Connecticut, sir," I replied; "I am the grandson of Hezekiah Perkins, of Wichnor. I've heard him mention you — you were his lawyer in a big land case."

The general eyed me sternly for an instant, but I met his eye unflinchingly.

"Yes, yes," he finally said; "I remember him. What can I do for you?"

"I want to get home first, and then I want to get an appointment in the navy to fight for my country, general. I've been a sailor, but I've had a good education."

"Well," said the general, making a few rapid scratches in a note-book, "I will see what I can do. You and your friend can go to the flag-ship with me when we go; we shall be going soon now."

In a few minutes a group of Confederate officers came to the "Fanny" to visit the flag-ship, and tender their surrender to the flag-officer, Commodore Stringham.

As I left the "Fanny" I found Phil and Blenders ready to congratulate me on having, as Phil said, "interviewed Ben Butler and escaped with my life to tell the story."

"Le's look at you," said Phil laughingly; "are you much bit up?"

I told Phil of my interview, in a few words, and said, "We are to go to the flag-ship on this boat, the 'Fanny.'"

"You 've got cheek 'nough f'r a double row 'f teeth an' a high collar," said Blenders admiringly. "So you 'r' kitin' home, are you? Well, I wish I was goin' t' N' Yo'k."

The last we saw of Blenders he was resting one shoulder on the spile of the landing, with both hands in his pockets, and with one leg thrown over the other in the very attitude of a Bowery boy with the blues.

We were soon on the deck of the huge "Minnesota," which we found to be a magnified edition of the "Monticello" in cleanliness and neatness.

And here I found myself face to face with General Butler. He gave me a severe look, and then, without a word to me, turned and looked Phil over from head to foot, and said:

"What position do you hold in the rebel army, and how came you here?"

"This is my chum, general," I said. "He is n't a rebel; he exchanged his ragged suit for that one, which he found at the fort."

"You'll do," said the general, with a grim smile, "you've begun reprisals already," and with this remark he went to the commodore's cabin.

After standing around on the deck for a while admiring the neatness and order that prevailed everywhere, we were conducted by a petty officer to our temporary quarters.

The next morning early we were on deck, and at about ten o'clock were summoned to the commodore's office, where we found General Butler and Flag-officer Stringham. And here also, to my surprise, I found John Nixon, just leaving the cabin.

The commodore was a stately, elderly man with the manner of one accustomed to command, but at the same time very gentlemanly. The commodore nodded to the general, as much as to say, Go on; and the general proceeded to put a few sharp inquiries about John Nixon, and made me tell my story of being cast away, and also our escape from the rebels. I inferred that some doubts had been entertained of John's reliability and loyalty, for one of the questions asked was:

"What was the occupation of John Nixon while you were with him?"

"Fishing," said Phil, "and dodging around to keep out of the way of the rebs."

Phil's reply provoked a smile, and then the general gave him a stare from under his drooping eyelids, and proceeded to cross-examine him and me, occasionally turning his face to the commodore as if to call his attention to some answer of ours. His questions were so sharp, and at times savage, that I felt, as Phil said when we got out of the cabin, "If I'd had anything on my conscience I'd been scared." As we came on deck we met John again, and were told by him that he was just going to see General Butler once more.

In a short time we met John in a highly elated mood.

"That Ben Butler is a right good man, give me these," said John, showing us two golden half-eagles; "said I earned 'em yesterday; an' he give me this letter to Colonel Hawkins, an' says he'll give me regular pay to pilot an' t' find what th' rebs 's doin'."

We shook hands with the dear fellow and sent our respects to his wife, and our thanks for all she had done for us.

Our voyage to Hampton Roads was uneventful, except that in observing the drill and seamanship on board we became infatuated with life on a man-of-war.

On our arrival at Fort Monroe we were, through the kindness of General Butler, given transportation papers for Wichnor, by the way of Washington.

CHAPTER XVII.

HOME, SWEET HOME.

The trip to Washington was made by night, and we passed through the city the next morning so quickly that we saw but little of it, except the mud through which we wallowed, and some of its sharp contrasts of squalid suburbs, and classic and immense public buildings.

Nothing that concerns our story occurred until we reached Baltimore, where, after having crossed the city from one station to another, we found ourselves obliged to wait for a train before proceeding to New York. While here an incident occurred which came near placing Phil and me under lock and key.

It will be remembered that Phil was dressed in Confederate uniform, while I wore the uniform of the United States navy, and that we wore these because we had no other clothing or money to purchase any.

While Phil and I sat in the waiting-room chatting and reading a newspaper, a thick-set, roughly-dressed man came up to us, and grasping both Phil and me by the collar, said in sharp, peremptory tones, "Here, come with me, I want you," and with this began to drag us away.

"Will you please tell us what we have done, sir?" I said as respectfully as I could. To this reasonable inquiry he gave a rough rejoinder, whereupon I began to resist, when he snapped a pair of handcuffs on my wrists, and Phil, who up to that time had made no resistance, wrenched himself loose and ran away.

"We are on our way home, our transportation papers are here," I said, indicating where. He thrust his hand into my pocket and seized the papers, and without looking at them transferred them to his own.

"Will you please look at those papers, and let me know your authority for arresting me?" I said.

"I'll show you my authority," he said, with a savage pull at my handcuffed wrists, at which I cried out and began to resist with all my stubbornness and strength.

The scene by this time had caused quite a number of persons to gather around, and to them I appealed, when the brute struck me a staggering blow with his fist.

Two men in the uniform of the navy had by this time come up, and one of them said, in very quiet but decided tones, "What is all this about?"

"I am a detective, this man is a deserter, that's what's the matter," said my captor sarcastically, facing with me the men who wore the navy blue. As my face was turned to them I at once recognized the officer.

"TAKE THOSE HANDCUFFS OFF THAT YOUNG MAN'S WRISTS!"

"Mr. Bell! Mr. Bell!" I cried out, "you know me. That man has taken away the transportation papers given us; we are just going home!"

The detective was just about to strike me again, when Mr. Bell said:

"No more of that, sir! I am a naval officer, and if you have any warrant for his arrest I would like to see it."

"I am on the lookout for such men," said the detective, "and don't have a warrant; don't need one."

"I know this man," said Mr. Bell, "and will be responsible for him."

"I don't know you," said the self-styled detective, "and for all I know you may be a deserter yourself."

"I think you know me, though," said Mr. Bell's companion, now pushing himself in front of the detective.

The ruffian's face fell as he abjectly stammered out, "I did n't know you, sir, I — I"—

"Take those handcuffs off that young man's wrists; restore those papers; now apologize to this officer."

This was uttered in a tone of stern authority, and the detective, whose manner at once had become changed, said:

"There's been so many deserters since the battle of Bull Run that we've had to be a little rough, and arrest men on suspicion; there was no offence intended to your friend, and I hope he will pass by my roughness. Perhaps I am a little too zealous."

"Now you have apologized, take yourself off; and if I do catch you at anything like this work again, I will make it my duty to see you taken care of," said the officer.

The brute slunk away like a whipped cur. I thanked the officer for his timely interference, and also thanked Mr. Bell.

"We thought you were dead," said Phil, who had been standing in the crowd, but who now came up to shake hands with Mr. Bell. This was the first that he had seen of Phil (at this time), and he was at a loss to know who he was; but when he recognized him he shook hands with him very heartily, and said:

"I would as soon have expected to see a ghost as to see either of you. As you said to me, I thought you were both drowned."

We told our story in brief, and explained how it was that we were not in citizen's dress.

It turned out that Mr. Bell was waiting for the same train to New York that we were, and that his friend had come to the station with him to see him off.

Mr. Bell's friend spoke very kindly to us before leaving, and to my surprise addressed Mr. Bell as lieutenant.

We were so delighted to get out of our scrape, and at the same time to meet our former second mate, that our joy more than counterbalanced our former chagrin.

On our way to New York we sat together.

"We thought you were drowned," I again said to him, "though we heard at Chicamacomico that one man was saved from the wreck, and that another man had come ashore in a boat, and we thought that man may have been the Irishman we called Blarney."

"The one that was saved from the wreck was I," said Mr. Bell, "and the other man I think was Blarney. He enlisted in the Confederate service, and as I was acquainted with one of the officers at the forts I was allowed to ship on board an English vessel bound for Halifax, and from there got back to the States. Through the influence of the friend you saw with me at Baltimore, I have been appointed a volunteer officer in the navy."

"How was it that you got ashore?" I inquired. "We saw you reach the breakers, but that was the last we saw of you."

He told us that he had been stunned and dazed by being dashed against a piece of timber just before reaching the surf, but had instinctively kept himself afloat while being swept here and there at the mercy of the waves, and when just about to give up, a piece of plank that had floated from the brig struck against him; this he grasped with the tenacity of a drowning man, and finally threw himself across it. After this he remembered but little until some men with a boat rescued him at the inlet, where the tide, he was told, had probably carried him. The men who had rescued him assured him that the brig had gone to pieces, and that none on board had been saved; they took him to Chicamacomico, and from thence to Hatteras Inlet.

On our arrival in New York, Mr. Bell insisted on lending each of us money enough to purchase a good suit of clothes. I said, "We have friends at home who are not poor, and we shall be with them to-morrow."

"It is because you will be among friends soon that I insist on lending you enough money for that purpose," said Mr. Bell. "You surely won't refuse to accept a small favor from your shipmate. If a man ever needs to appear in good dress it is among friends."

So he went with us to a clothing-house and spent a half-hour in fitting each of us with a neat citizen's suit.

After this he accompanied us to the Wichmor boat, and upon my remarking that he seemed very familiar with the city he replied:

"Yes; I used to live here. Some of the pleasantest and some of the saddest hours of my life have been spent here; and I am here now to make inquiries regarding people very dear to me."

He shook hands with us in a very pleasant manner, and wished us all kinds of good fortune. "I am glad to have met you again," he said, "and if I can be of any use to you hereafter, let me know."

The steamer had started when it occurred to us that we had neglected to get our former mate's address, in order to repay him the money loaned us. We were vexed at ourselves for our thoughtless neglect, and Phil exclaimed:

"That's just our luck, as soon as we got track of him to lose sight of him again. I never saw a man I liked so well except your father, and Mr. Bell has some ways that are just like his."

When we awoke in the morning and went on deck we found the boat opposite Rivermouth, not many miles from our home. As we came in sight of Wichnor, its houses nestling among the foliage far upon the heights, or on a level with the river, and its churches and public buildings gilded by the rays of the morning sun, made a scene more beautiful than words can express. I tried to say something of this to Phil, but my words choked me, and the tears started to my eyes unbidden. I then saw that there were tears in his eyes, and I knew he understood me.

And then (my heart sank at the thought) suppose something has happened to mother during these months since I last heard from home. But this thought I did not long retain, for, youth-like, I thought that what I wished must be.

As we neared the wharf Phil said:

"Hez, there's the place where I pulled you out of the water years ago, and there's your grandpa's house,—and, by George, we are almost in! It seems a thousand years since we left the dear place."

We landed and made our way through the streets. It was early morning and but few of the people were yet moving.

We were not more than half-way up the street — I say "up" advisedly, for the ascent of the street was as steep as the roof of a house — when we saw Vag nosing around in a neighboring yard.

I put my fingers to my mouth and gave a sharp and peculiar whistle with which I was accustomed to call him. He stopped and looked around in a surprised and thoughtful manner, as if he could not believe his ears, and then resumed his nosing.

"Here, Vag," I called, and he came like a shot out of the yard and looked up and down the street, snuffed the air with a foolish, suspicious look, as if to say:

"That sounds like Hez Johnstone, but most likely I am being fooled."

Phil and I both burst into laughter at Vag's look of comical suspicion and amazement, at hearing which, as if it dispelled all doubts, he came bounding upon us, whining and yelping with the greatest delight, and then ran in circles around us, barking in the most extravagant manner.

He had not ceased these antics when we reached

the stone steps that led to grandfather's house, and my mother came to the open door to see what was the matter. She ran down the steps to greet us. For the time her cool New England reserve was thoroughly thawed, and she cried and laughed in the same breath.

She had received the evening before a letter that I mailed to her at Fort Monroe. She had also seen an account of the wreck of the "Favorite," in which it was said that all on board perished except two persons.

The months that passed until she heard from me had been sorrowful ones for my poor mother, though she had insisted that I was still alive.

My grandfather, whose icy exterior very seldom showed emotions, was quite demonstrative for him.

He held out both hands, which trembled as he said:

"My dear boy, it does me more good to see you than — than — ten thousand dollars; yes, and I 'm glad to see you too, Philip."

While at breakfast we told the outlines of our story, and especially dwelt upon that part of our experience which related to the battle at Hatteras Inlet, and our interview with General Butler and the admiral of the war squadron.

"You were pretty bright to get out of it alive," said grandfather. "Yes, I call it pretty smart. Hez, you 've got some of the Perkins push in ye I guess, and will make your way in life."

"Quite a thaw," said Phil, winking at me after grandfather had gone out. "If some of the folks around here could have heard him they would have thought him crazy."

Even my mother, who overheard this remark, laughed and said:

"Your grandfather has got feelings, but he don't show them often; he felt pretty bad when he thought you were drowned."

It was certainly a recompense for my hardships and sufferings to receive such a welcome home, and it was all the more appreciated because it was in contrast with the treatment we had often received while absent. It enabled me to see the difference between those who were actuated by real affection for me and those who were indifferent.

After breakfast grandfather and Phil went downtown, and my mother and I had a long, affectionate, and confidential talk.

I mentioned that I had heard about my father at Newberne, when she, to my surprise, said she had received several letters from him while I had been absent. The first of these was dated shortly after I left home, and in it he said, "I have written several letters to which I have received no answer," and then mentioned sending a draft on New York for a hundred dollars; he said that the people were distrustful of those who had Northern correspondents, and he sometimes thought the mails were tampered with. In another letter he spoke of the growing bad feeling against the North, which was being fostered for political purposes, and incidentally spoke of the secession sentiment as "a craze of an hour which will soon die out." He further mentioned the bitter feeling against Northern sympathizers, as those were styled who said a word in defence of Northern people, and said that he had been obliged to be careful in order not to be placed in a position of antagonism to those around him. In another letter he said that at his father's earnest wish he had accepted the captaincy of a military company that had been formed in the county. The next letter was dated after the attack on Sumter, and in it he deplored the growing sentiment in favor of secession, in North Carolina. In this letter was enclosed a draft on New York.

The next letter had been written just after the secession of the State. In it he said there was talk of calling the regiment to which he belonged into the service for active duty; but he was confident the better sense of the people would prevail, and that there would be no bloodshed, and added, "If there is fighting I must go with my people."

This was the last letter received from my dear father. There had never been any explanation of what had become of the letters written by him that my mother had failed to receive.

After reading these letters I said: "I am afraid there has been a conspiracy to draw father into a position where he cannot retreat without dishonor, and that the reason for intercepting his letters was to further that plan, and possibly to bring about a breach between him and you."

The next day, while Phil and I were down-town, a tall fellow in a shockingly ill-fitting suit of Union blue blocked our way on the sidewalk, saying as he extended his hand, "How be ye?" and then we knew by the voice that it was Jim Bisbee. "Wal," said he, "they du tell me that you an' Phil Gurley 'v' hed perils by land an' sea. An' I see by th' mornin' paper that y' think o' goin' int' th' navy. Wal, I don't blame ye f'r bein' a patriot, — I'm one, tu, but then I could n't stan' it t' be killed an' hev my stomach turned topside-turvy all 't the same time. Had n't y' better sort o' reconsider the motion, as they say in taoun meetin'? Naow we've got a bang-up rigimint, an' maybe ye'd git t' be a corporal 'f y' jined us."

The thing that interested me in Jim's conversation was that he intimated that we had got into the papers.

"How did the newspaper know anything about us, Jim?" I asked.

"Why, the hull taoun's talkin' 'baout ye. P'rhaps Gurley c'n tell ye haow th' papers got hold on 't," said Jim, as he winked at Phil and walked off.

"Well," confessed Phil, "I did n't know that I was talking for print, but a fellow talked to me at the store, and they told me afterwards that he was a reporter on the 'Messenger.'"

When I had got the paper I found a column of matter under a big scare-head, giving an account of our adventures, and especially detailing our connection with the fight at Hatteras Inlet.

On reading it I said to Phil: "That newspaper man seems to have pumped you pretty dry."

"Yes," said Phil sheepishly, "and he did it as slick as pulling a cork from a bottle. I had n't any idea that I was being interviewed. He did n't say much, but he seemed so awfully interested that I let myself go."

Phil, at this, looked so distressed that I laughed in spite of my disposition to be provoked and annoyed.

On our way about the town we met the Hon. Whitcome Cute, who shook hands with us as if we were his dearest friends.

I was much pleased at the notice of so distinguished a man, and told grandfather of it.

"That's just like Whit Cute," said he. "Ten chances to one he did n't know you, though. I was talking with him a day or two since, when a chap with a load of wood from Bean Valley stopped to say 'How do ye do' to him. Well, to see Whit shake hands with him you would certainly have thought they were the dearest friends. And then Whit said, 'I'm busy just now, but call around to my office and we'll talk over old times.' After the man had left he said to me, 'Perkins, who was that old chap?'"

"You see," sarcastically chuckled grandfather, "that's part of a public man's stock in trade: he has to pretend to know everybody.

"The piece in the paper," said he, "won't do you any harm and may do you more good than you think for. Public men like to help those who have been noticed in the papers."

After this I detected him mailing to different persons copies of the paper that contained this reference to Phil and me.

CHAPTER XVIII.

IN THE NAVY.

At the time of which I write, the attention of the country was directed to the Army of the Potomac, then being organized by General George B. McClellan. It was expected that it would soon wipe out the disgrace and retrieve the disaster of the defeat at Bull Run, which had humiliated Northern pride and correspondingly encouraged the insurgent South. But little public attention was given to our navy, and while our young and adventurous men crowded to enlist in our armies there was not a corresponding enthusiasm to serve on the sea.

On the other hand, a large number of trained officers of Southern birth had left our service to cast their lot with the Confederacy, while those seamen who had returned from stations abroad, and whose terms of enlistment had expired, were impatient to be discharged to enjoy that shore liberty — and to spend their money in a manner dear to a sailor's heart. Owing to these reasons there was an unusual opportunity for well-educated young men to rise in the naval service, and Grandfather Perkins, foreseeing this, exhibited unusual interest in endeavoring to get Phil and me in a position to be advanced therein. The Hon. Whitcome Cute had advised that we should endeavor to pass an examination in order to enter an advanced class at the Annapolis Naval School, where, if we were able to pass such an examination, we should, after remaining a year or more, doubtless receive appointments as midshipmen, and also start with the advantage of a technical education in naval affairs. But this sound advice received but little attention from two headstrong boys, and Grandfather Perkins was not a great believer in what he scornfully called book-learning; he believed that practice is superior to theory, and, as he termed it, "one month in the navy, in time of war, would be better schooling for young men than all the naval academies in the world."

While this view accorded well with the desires of both Phil and myself, it was not by any means a correct one. The theory taught by professors in schools is, after all, but the result of the knowledge which others have gained by practical experience and often by "hard knocks." After acquiring the theory through books, practice quickly transmutes it into the gold of real practical knowledge.

I do not remember (if I ever knew) just how it came about, but in December, by advice of grandfather, who no doubt had been advised by some one else, Phil and I took the boat for New York, and on the day of our arrival went over to the Brooklyn Navy Yard and enlisted in the navy.

From thence, after remaining on board the receiving-ship for a short time, we were drafted and sent to the "Congress," then lying at Newport News, Va., guarding the mouth of the James River.

We arrived there the first of January in 1862, and were sent at once on board the "Congress."

On arriving on board, we reported to the executive officer, Lieut. Joseph B. Smith.

We were dressed in the becoming blue uniform of United States sailors, and as we saluted he looked up pleasantly and said, in his deep mellow tones:

"So you have come to be sailors, have you?"

I replied that I was hoping to become something besides a common sailor.

"Well," he replied gravely, "if you did n't expect to become anything better, I would advise you to jump overboard at once."

He was dressed in navy blue, his face was dark with the tan of the tropics, and he had the bluff, cheery manner of a sailor, to which were added the manners of a gentleman. His high brow and firm-set mouth, though the latter was concealed in part by a full beard, showed him to be a man of determined character as well as of good intelligence. He had a manner of mingled firmness and good-nature which made me like him at once, and I thought him an ideal sailor and gentleman.

He questioned us as to where we had been at sea,

and asked us a few other questions about our schooling, and then assigned us to duty.

I had not been long on the "Congress" before I learned that, though there was a large number of men there, there were but few sailors among them.

One of the old sailors whom I met had been on board this vessel for several years, having reënlisted after three years' service in her on the Brazilian station. He was a man of more than ordinary intelligence, and for a wonder, as I afterwards learned it to be among sailors, did not drink spirituous liquors.

"I should have thought," I said interrogatively, "you would have stayed on shore awhile to see your folks."

"Well, youngster," said Josiah Leech, for such was his name, "I haven't got father, mother, or sisters living, though I have got a brother somewhere drifting around the world like myself, an' as I'm an American and we're likely to have some work in the navy, I stuck by the old 'Congress.' I know her from truck to keel;" and the old salt smiled good-naturedly and stowed a large quid of tobacco in his cheek. "Yes, youngster, I stood by this craft when, as you might say, the rats left her."

"What do you mean by rats, sir?" I inquired.

"Well, youngster," said Josiah, turning over his quid to the other cheek, "I ain't callin' my old shipmates names by any means, but it's a sayin' 'mong sailors, an' a fact as well, that if a ship is goin' to meet with misfortune, them gents, the rats, 'll leave beforehand. Well, ever sence we come from the Brazilian station, my old shipmate, Jim Knowles, said the rats 've been leavin' this ship; saw some goin' ashore at Charleston myself."

"You don't believe that stuff?" I said interrogatively.

"Well," said Josiah, spitting over the rail contemplatively, "not 'nless they went in droves. Rats are good sailors, an' I guess some of 'em want a day or two on shore, like the res' of us."

"You don't mean to say the crew left because the rats did?" I inquired.

"Well, no; I don't mean that 'zactly. You see we 'd been most three years on the Brazilian station, an' when we got to Charleston, our term 'f enlistment was about up. The men was wild for liberty ashore. Jack, you know, earns his money like a horse, an' spends it like a jackass, an' 'f they 'd just given Jack his liberty for a few days, with a little inducement to join the ship again, they 'd 'ave come back like a lot o' school-boys to their homes after school. When Jack's money 's all gone you c'n handle him as easy as you c'n furl sails in a calm after a storm. The crew was promised their discharge if they 'd come down here where they would all be discharged as soon as a ship could be got ready to relieve 'em. But the

Naval Department did n't keep their promise, an' the men was sulky; then, after waitin' six months, they got so sore-headed an' dissatisfied that they broke into open mutiny. One night they threw overboard the locks an' sight-covers; cut some o' the trainin' tackle to the guns, an' some of the gun breeching. *Then* the order come to discharge them whose time 'd expired. An' after that you could n't git one of 'em aboard agin with a derrick."

"Well," I said, "it seems to me the Naval Department should keep its agreements with sailors, if it expects them to work willingly."

"Sailors," said Josiah, "have no rights that captains feel bound to respect, an' here we are with a few sailors drafted from the other ships, an' a lot of greenhorns; what kind 'f a chance do we stand if them Southern folks send out some craft to fight us? Of course we 'll lick 'em some way, but we ain't in ship-shape to do it.

"Here 's about two hundred men aboard that 'd be seasick in a calm; them fellers from Fort Ellsworth are nice boys enough, but they don't know the flying jib-boom from a marlin-spike. We 've got some good officers as there is in the service, and that 's the reason I 've stuck to the ship after the rats have had the intelligence to leave."

And Josiah gave a hitch to his trousers and went to work polishing with beeswax the huge gun number 12 on the starboard side of the ship, so one could see his face in the shine of it, "good enough," as Josiah said, "to shave by."

Phil and I, and a young fellow named Wilson, were selected with others to serve as a gun's crew to a thirty-two pounder on the gun-deck. Leech was first captain, Wilson second captain, I was first loader, Phil second loader, while two raw-boned fellows of what was called the Fort Ellsworth men were first and second spongers, while the side tacklemen were of the same crowd: in all, thirteen men, including the powder-men, or, as the sailors call them, "powder-monkeys."

On the gun-deck there were fourteen of these guns each on the port and starboard sides, and two at the stern on the same deck, while on the upper deck, which is usually called the spar-deck, were fourteen short thirty-two pounders. I soon became proficient in the gun-drill, and Phil with his usual quickness "took to it," as Josiah said, "like a baby to its mother's milk." Leech took much pains when at leisure to teach us points in gunnery and seamanship. On my part I was not only observant, but gave all my spare time to the study of the "Ordnance Instructions," a copy of which I borrowed of Josiah, so that though not as quick at learning as Phil I made up in attention and study for it, and in a month's time very few things in serving a gun were unfamiliar to me.

One circumstance occurred which brought me into favor with the captain. I was called to his cabin in the absence of his clerk, to do some writing, and, as I have before intimated in these pages, I prided myself on writing a rapid and legible hand, as well as being quick and correct at figures. The captain was pleased to notice this, and asked me some questions about my experience as a sailor, and this incident, as it will be seen, afterwards bore fruit.

I was telling Phil of the notice I received in the captain's cabin, when he said laughingly:

"Well, old boy, we ain't getting promotion very fast; but first captain on a gun here seems more of an office than an ensign's appointment did on shore at home. It don't seem that we will have any fighting, either."

"I guess," said I, "we've got as high positions as our knowledge will entitle us to at present, and as for fighting I ain't hankering after it."

"For my part," said Phil, "I am considering myself lucky they didn't make me a powder-monkey."

"We are likely to have some fighting," I said. "I heard the captain talking with Lieutenant Smith about an iron vessel the Southerners are building at Norfolk. The captain seemed to think that any kind of a craft that they might build would not amount to much; but the lieutenant said that he knew Brooks (who is said to have contrived the iron-clad), and that he is a hard-headed, sensible officer, though just a little cranky on the subject of iron-clads. He also said he had heard that old Frank Buchanan is to command the iron-clad that they have made from the old 'Merrimack,' and if this is true there will be some hot work cut out for us (that is, if the iron-clad idea is good for anything), for there is n't a more determined or capable officer afloat, so Smith said, than Buchanan."

There had been some talk about an iron-clad among the men, for whatever is talked of in the cabin finds its way to the sailors of a ship.

When I spoke to Leech about the iron-clad he exclaimed:

"Avast there, you lubber! Iron ain't the stuff to carry much aboveboard on the water; it's all well enough on land, but blast my eyes, 'tween me and the mainmast, I'd rather have a plank o' good oak, afloat, than a ton of iron!"

And in this opinion Josiah voiced the general opinion of the ship's company, or its sailors at least.

It is well to say here that the authorities at Washington were aware that an iron-clad was building at Norfolk, and the secretary of the navy had before that time contracted for every form of an iron craft then known to naval men, and one, as will be seen, that was never known of before in naval architecture.

We heard nothing more about our appointment to some better position than that of common sailors, and the only letter I received from grandfather simply counseled me to be patient and learn all I could.

There soon occurred an event that not only broke the monotony of sea-life, but which gave us fighting enough to last most boys a lifetime; an event that will not only be immortal in story for all time, but which also in a single day revolutionized naval warfare, and made the wooden vessels of all the navies of the world impotent.

CHAPTER XIX.

THE ADVENT OF THE "MERRIMACK."

The morning of the 8th of March was calm and beautiful. The sun shone in a sky of unclouded splendor, lighting up with golden flashes the gently undulating waters of Hampton Roads.

Our good ship lay at anchor not five hundred yards from the shore of Newport News, where we could hear the beat of the drums and the shrill music of the fifes that roused soldiers in the camp on the bluff opposite to us. On that morning I remember the merry clack of voices that followed the breakfast call on shore, the grateful fragrance of the pines wafted to us on the morning breeze, and the indescribable smell of land that comes to the sailor on the sea.

As soon as the sun was well up, our sails (that had been wet by a shower during the night) were loosened, that they might dry. This was preceded by the usual scrubbing of the decks, and other duties that begin the day on board a man-of-war.

Up-stream, a few hundred yards from us, and a little farther off shore than the "Congress," lay the "Cumberland," swinging lazily at anchor on the incoming tide, with her boats hanging to her lower booms, and the washing of her sailors in the rigging. Her lofty sides and her taut rigging outlined on the water and sky made her look like "a painted ship upon a painted ocean."

Seven miles or more away towards Fort Monroe were the "Minnesota," the "Roanoke," and the "St. Lawrence," besides several gun-boats.

In the hazy distance across the channel was to be seen the low land of Craney Island and Sewell's Point, at the mouth of the Elizabeth River.

All the time we had lain here, there had been, as I have elsewhere said, rumors of a dangerous iron-clad craft that was building at Norfolk to destroy our fleet at Hampton Roads — not that any one on board was alarmed thereat, for the old sailors scoffed at any such "horse-marine contrivance" being able to stand a broadside from one of our ships, much less that of our whole fleet.

It was eight o'clock or past, while I was on the spar deck, when I heard the officer of the deck say that there were two steamers in the James River about twelve miles distant. I did not learn his conclusions regarding them, and the remark was of so little interest to me at the time that I doubt if I should have recalled it but for the terrible and tragic occurrences that followed.

The captain had been detached from the ship, leaving the executive officer in command.

At about ten o'clock there was observed from

our decks long lines of black smoke in the direction of Norfolk, indicating that steamers were coming down the Elizabeth River. The black smudge of smoke constantly increased in volume, when, at about one o'clock, three steamers rounded Sewell's Point, and were visible from the deck of the "Congress." Then our crew became aware (how, I do not remember) that the iron craft of which we had heard was one of these vessels.

This, however, did not alarm us. I remember that old Josiah said, as he rolled his quid in his mouth with a half smile of evident contempt, when I asked him what he thought about her, "She'd better give us a wide berth, youngster, or we'll give her a broadside that 'll send her to Davy Jones's locker like a shot."

"But," I replied anxiously, "they say she is all iron, Josiah."

"Avast there, you land-lubber!" said he; "she'll sink all the quicker for it."

And such was the general sentiment of the old sailors on board — one of contempt, rather than of doubt of the result in a battle between us.

Between one and two o'clock these hostile steamers were seen descending with the tide, and in their midst was a strange structure, or a portion of it, protruding like the roof of a house from the water, surmounted by a smoke-stack.

As they were apparently coming toward us, there was a bustle of preparation on board our ship.

The sails were quickly furled, the drums beat to quarters, the men took their stations. The guns were shotted, the magazines opened with the gunners at their posts. Shot, shell, and cartridge were all in place, swords, pistols, and boarding-pikes in the rack, while the surgeons' table gleamed with knives and saws, in terrible but needful readiness.

As the iron-clad slowly neared us, young Wilson, who, though but twenty years of age, was an old man-of-war's man, said:

"She moves awful slow; we'll get a lick at her and sink her the first broadside!"

Little did we then realize that so many of our brave men would be sleeping their last sleep before the sun went down that night!

At half-past two the strange craft was but a quarter of a mile from us. We still awaited orders, and, with our guns trained at a proper elevation, silently viewed her approach, I, on my part, with strange tremors of expectation and nervous apprehension, while awaiting the order to fire.

Before this, however, we had seen the "Minnesota," the "Roanoke," and the "St. Lawrence" hurrying towards us to take part in the fight, so did not in any way fear the general result of the conflict.

The shore batteries had already opened fire with prodigious noise, if not with much result. Then the "Cumberland" opened with her heavy pivot guns, and we were astonished that the strange nondescript was still coming on without reply. Suddenly a flash amid smoke came from her bows, and then a roar as the shot struck our sides and rattled on our decks.

Then the long-expected order came for us to open fire. The lanyards were pulled, and when the smoke cleared we expected to see her sinking. What was our surprise to see her apparently uninjured, moving from us. Her starboard ports flew open and her terrible broadside smote us with a tearing, crashing sound impossible to describe. Then, without taking further notice of us for the time being, she slowly passed us within three hundred yards, making towards the "Cumberland," which, with the shore batteries, was firing every gun that would bear on her. But never did brave men make a more hopeless battle. To our dismay we saw the shot glance from the sides of the iron craft, apparently making no more impression on her than if they had been foot-balls filled with wind, instead of solid shot.

After the "Merrimack" had steered for the "Cumberland," a shot from one of our stern guns carried away the flag of the iron-clad, and the green Fort Ellsworth men thought she had surrendered, and began to cheer. Lieutenant Prendergrast, on the gun-deck, said:

"Don't cheer, men, the fight is n't over yet."

Shot meanwhile smote us, as it seemed, from every

direction; there was a fire on our gun-deck, and terrible cries came from our wounded as they were carried to the cock-pit, with mangled forms, and with their blood pouring to the decks, while the dead still lay among the guns.

It was awful! But worse soon came. I, with others, ran to the spar-deck in my excitement, and there saw that some of our men were loosening the sails. I was soon reminded that my station was on the gun-deck below. At that time the scene on the gun-deck baffles description.

On nearing the "Cumberland" the rebel captain called out, "Will you surrender?"

"No," was the reply; "I'll sink alongside first!"

The rebel craft then struck the "Cumberland" with her iron prow, with a crash; and while shouts and dreadful cries came to us on the still air she wriggled back from the doomed ship, leaving a great gash in her sides. With a roar from her guns the "Cumberland" listed to port, and then with her dead and wounded and many living she went down head-first (as if disdaining even in her last struggle to make a backward move), with her colors still flying. This I saw in a mere glimpse through our port-holes during the surrounding confusion.

The gun-boat "Zouave" had meanwhile come alongside of us; she was a tug with but two guns. She made fast on our port side and passed her tow-line through one of our scuppers amidship. It seemed an age while this was being done. Then the bow of our ship was brought around towards the shore, in order to run her aground. But it was, as it proved, a disastrous move. As we were headed for shore we heard simultaneously a roar of guns and the ripping and tearing of plank and timber. The whole stern of our ship was shot away.

The meaning of this, as I soon learned, was that the "Merrimack" had got astern, within a few hundred yards of us, and was raking us fore and aft with her heavy broadside guns. The two guns at the stern were disabled by the breech fastenings being torn away; and most of their crews lay killed or wounded around the guns.

Broadside after broadside followed until the deck was slippery with blood, the guns were wrecked, and, worst of all, we could not bring one of them to bear on our enemy to make reply. The captain of our gun lay dead with the lanyard grasped in his brawny hands; young Wilson was impaled with a splinter through his lungs; Phil had his left arm wounded, the first port tackleman and two others were killed, the second wounded, and the whole deck was one scene of appalling distress and wreck. The very remembrance of that scene after all the years that have since passed freezes my blood.

Amid all the confusion and distress, the shrieks of the wounded and their moans and cries of anguish and calls for help, I got kaleidoscope-like glimpses of the lesser scenes taking place. I saw Acting Captain Smith come down the afterhatchway and, while one foot was on the ladder, put his hand to his mouth to give an order, and fall dead in the act. I noticed also at this time a stream of blood pouring through our scuppers (like water while washing down decks) on the decks of the "Zouave," and I remember wondering if my blood too would soon join in swelling that sanguine stream.

We had meanwhile grounded, and after what seemed an hour, though I learned afterwards that it was but a few minutes, the rebel iron-clad having finished her work, Lieutenant Prendergrast (in command since the death of Lieutenant Smith) caused the white flag to be hoisted in token of the surrender of our ship.

To escape the terrible scene below decks I went to the spar-deck, followed by Phil, who dripped blood as he walked, and got him in a position back of the mainmast where he was in part sheltered from the shot that now struck us from the riflemen on shore.

It was while I was doing this that a small rebel steamer came alongside, to secure such arms as were possible, and also, as I afterwards learned, to order the crew out of the "Congress" preliminary to burning her.

Having bound up poor Phil's arm with my handkerchief, and given him and young Wilson (who was in rear of the mainmast) a drink of water, I walked aft and saw a young fellow, apparently an officer, step from the paddle-box of the little rebel steamer to the hammock netting of the "Congress" (it being just level with the paddle-box), then go aft and seize the colors which were trailing from our stern. While winding them around him he was struck by a rifle-shot from the shore and fell dead on our deck.

I am thus particular in narrating this incident, as it was afterward claimed that he was shot while rescuing the wounded of the "Congress."

The ship was now on fire in several places; the enemy finding the fire too severe for their liking hauled off, with a few of our officers for prisoners, and opened fire on the "Congress."

As there was no further duty to perform, and as the fire that was raging on board was likely to reach the magazine soon, those of our crew remaining on board, not disabled, devoted their attention to rescuing the wounded and saving themselves.

The boats, which were attached to the ship by a line from the jib-boom, with a boat-keeper on board with instructions to allow no one to get on them, were now brought alongside and filled with our men. Phil, Wilson, and other wounded, as well as some who were not, were put in one of these boats, while I took to the water and swam ashore.

It was fortunate that I did so, for the fire soon after reached the magazine, and the fragments of the dead, and the bloody and mangled ship, were scattered over the waters.

This ended my participation in this most memorable conflict.

Thus in little more than two hours the "Merrimack" had destroyed a heavy frigate and a large sloop of war, mounting together seventy-four guns, and had killed in battle and drowned two hundred and fifty of their crew, — a destruction hardly matched in naval warfare.

Yet the work of the "Merrimack" was not yet finished. After the events narrated she steamed into Hampton Roads (leaving our burning frigate and the sunken "Cumberland" and their crews to their fate), heading towards the "Minnesota," accompanied by her consorts, the "Patrick Henry" and the "Jamestown."

The "Minnesota," in attempting to reach the scene of the fight, had run aground about half-way between Fort Monroe and where the "Congress" lay. This, instead of being a misfortune as it then seemed, proved to be her salvation; for the iron-clad drawing twenty-two or more feet of water (and as the tide was then almost out) could not get within a mile of her. Only a single shot from the iron-clad ship struck the "Minnesota." The fire from the rifle guns of her consorts was, however, more destructive; but when the "Minnesota" finally brought one of her heavy guns to bear on them they turned tail, while the

"Merrimack," not being able to reach her, steamed away in the direction of Norfolk, accompanied by the smaller and less dangerous crafts.

This was about sundown on that eventful 8th of March.

And thus ended the first fight of iron-clad against wooden ships in the history of naval warfare.

Little remains to be said, except that the heroism of those on board of the "Cumberland," which I have not attempted to tell (only as I saw it with one of those glimpses which a man catches in a fight, while surrounded by danger and confusion), as well as that of my shipmates on the "Congress," was as grand as anything that ever took place on the sea.

That evening, after I had got on shore and was drying myself at a fire kindled by our sailors, I heard some further details of the "Cumberland's" heroic fight and fate. One of her sailors, with a simple pathos, told me that the captain of his gun would not leave it, but, throwing his arms around it as if it was his sweetheart, and thus clasping it, went down with the ship. And then was told to me how the guns were fought from gun-deck to spar-deck, and only abandoned when the muzzles were under water. And all this occurred amid the shots and shrieks, and the crashing and creaking of timber, broken by the tremendous broadside of the "Merrimack."

The old sailors were broken-hearted over their defeat.

Some mourned the loss of shipmates; but one of the most pathetic figures that I recall was the captain of one of the guns on board the "Cumberland" mourning the loss of his gun.

Later in the evening I, with others, under direction of Lieutenant Prendergrast, walked to Fort Monroe, where was gathered a most melancholy crowd of landsmen and sailors. It was one of the darkest periods in our national history; none knew what the morrow would bring forth; one thing was, however, deemed certain, and that was that the "Merrimack" would come out from her lair and complete the destruction she had begun.

But while we thus despaired, Providence held in store a surprise, not only for us, but for the exulting rebels, who were confident of our humiliation and defeat with the coming of another day.

I had had nothing to eat since morning, and strange to relate had not remembered that I was hungry, so intense had been my excitement. But on coming in sight of the sutlers at Fort Monroe, and seeing some of the sailors eating there, it suddenly occurred to me that I too was famished. I mention this as showing how emotions or powerful excitement will sometimes make one forget even hunger.

After I had finished a good meal of sutler's pies I turned to leave, when I almost ran into an officer. I saluted and was about to pass when he called me by name. It was Mr. Bell, the former second officer of the "Favorite."

"How came you here, Johnstone?" he inquired in a tone of surprise.

I explained to him that I had been one of the crew of the ill-fated "Congress." Then followed an explanation of how Phil and I had enlisted in the navy with the expectation of an appointment of some kind, which had not come.

Mr. Bell smiled as he said: "They wind red tape rather slow in the navy, — but where is your friend Phil?"

I replied that Phil had been wounded, and was then under the surgeon's care at Newport News; that his wound was not very serious, and that after I had swam ashore, without telling him for fear he would desire to accompany me, I had walked down to the fort, thinking my services might be required in the morning.

"That speaks pretty well for your nerve," said Mr. Bell, "after such a shaking up as you've had! It is just as well, perhaps, that the 'Minnesota,' got aground, or she too might now be at the bottom of the Roads."

"Are you," I inquired, "on board of her?"

"No," he replied, "I'm a volunteer officer on the gun-boat 'Terror.'"

"What do you intend to do if the rebel ironclad comes out to-morrow?" I said.

"There is not any *if* in it, my lad; she will come

as sure as the sun rises, and God knows what we shall do, or where we shall be before the sun sets on Sunday."

"I'd like to go on board with you," I said; "perhaps I might be of use."

"Well, I'll take you, but I do not know that it is a friendly act. I tell you plainly that I see no hope of anything but disaster before us. It is simply the intention of all on board to fight and go down with the ship—there seems nothing else to do; but if you want to go, come along."

"My father used to tell me," I replied, "that 'a man could die but once, and the time to die was when he could die doing his duty.'"

Mr. Bell looked at me for a moment with an expression on his face which I could not interpret, but after a moment said in a low tone as if to himself, "Your father must have been a gentleman."

"He was," I replied, in much the same tone as that in which he had spoken.

Before I could get leave to accompany him, however, I was ordered to embark on a boat for the "Minnesota," then aground, as I have said, not far from Newport News.

The night was calm and the moon was not yet up, but the burning "Congress" threw a lurid glare across the water, to me a grand but depressing sight, for I recalled the brave men, so full of hope but that morning, who lay in death on board.

Long after I arrived I watched the fine but

melancholy sight, her shrouds and rigging illuminated with fire and her open ports lurid with flame, when between one and two o'clock she blew up in a succession of explosions throwing towards the stars fountain-like showers of sparks, each rivalling the others in height.

Then I " turned in," as sailors call going to bed, and slept soundly until aroused by the shrill music of the boatswain's whistle.

CHAPTER XX.

IRON MEETS IRON.

It was a beautiful Sunday morning; the air was balmy, and scarce a breeze stirred the waters of beautiful Hampton Roads. I went on deck at an early hour with one of the petty officers, whose acquaintance I had made while I was on board of the "Minnesota" at Hatteras Inlet. The sun was up and the decks were being scrubbed, for not even impending battle is allowed to interfere with the routine on board of a man-of-war.

"Have you seen that queer craft alongside?" inquired my friend.

"No," I replied, "I have n't heard anything about her; where is she?"

"Why, right here," he replied, looking over the side of the ship toward Fort Monroe.

I looked and saw a diminutive dark-looking craft, sharp at both ends, with a round structure about ten feet high in the centre, and a square box-looking structure at her bow. Her deck was nearly level with the water, there was no side railing, and she was indeed a queer-appearing craft; looking, as my friend said, "like a shingle sharpened at both ends, with a tin can set in the centre."

"What is she for?" I inquired.

"They say," he replied with sarcastic emphasis, "that they are going to fight the rebel iron-clad with her, when she comes out."

"Fight!" I echoed in astonishment; "I can't see anything on board that she has got to fight with. Where are her guns?"

As we spoke there came towards us a sailor on her deck, and to him we addressed the same inquiry.

"Guns?" he replied, with a gesture towards the round structure. "In the turret there, and between you and I and the mainmast, mates, they'll give that rebel craft that raised the devil here yesterday (and that you seem so scared about) all she wants and change to boot."

"I guess you have n't seen the 'Merrimack,'" I replied.

"She'll see us if she comes out here into Hampton Roads again; and she may think herself lucky if she ever gets back," and he spat contemptuously over the side.

"What makes her go? I don't see any sails or smoke-stacks."

"Well, there's our smoke-stack," he said, pointing to two slit-like openings in the deck abaft the turret. "They 're made of good plain air and can't be shot away."

"This is a sort of a sub-marine craft," said another; "blast my eyes if she did n't come most of the way from Brooklyn Navy Yard under water."

"Come away from there," said an old sailor; "that chap takes you for a horse marine; he's codding you."

I thought the same, and in any case had but little interest in her, as all I had heard and seen gave me little faith in her ability to cope successfully with the rebel iron-clad.

"They 've got confidence," said my friend.

"Yes, and we too had confidence on board the 'Congress' yesterday morning, but she sank the 'Cumberland' and destroyed the 'Congress' notwithstanding all of it," I said bitterly; for I remembered the brave men now dead, who on the morning before had gone into the fight so confident of their ability to defend themselves and the honor of the flag.

"There is some one on board that has given these men confidence," said my friend, "and let us hope for the best; but to me it seems that it would have been just as well for them Washington folks to have sent us a sardine box as that thing."

The craft we had been thus contemptuously discussing was the "Monitor." She had arrived from New York at nine o'clock on the evening before, and at two o'clock that morning had anchored alongside the "Minnesota." By a coincidence that looks like the interposition of Providence, she had been finished the same day as the "Merrimack." She was at once sent to open the Potomac (then obstructed by rebel earthworks) to the navigation of our shipping. The Naval Department, in these orders to her commander, also gave orders "that the 'Monitor' was to make no stop on her passage except at Fort Monroe."

On the afternoon of the 8th, when her brave commander heard the sound of the fight at Hampton Roads, he hurried forward, in hopes to arrive in season to take a hand in the conflict. On his arrival he reported to Captain Marston, of the "Roanoke," who "suggested that he should go to the assistance of the 'Minnesota,' though as the officer in command in the absence of Flag-officer Goldsborough, he had received peremptory orders to send the 'Monitor' to Washington without delay."

Had she arrived the morning previous, no doubt this order would have been obeyed, but her arrival after the disaster of Saturday determined the brave Marston to disobey and retain the "Monitor" to protect the fleet.

Thus it was, by a series of accidents, that the little "Monitor" was present that day to meet the "Merrimack," and dispute with her the supremacy of the sea, although at that time she had not been accepted by the naval authorities, and was the property, technically at least, of private individuals.

At about eight o'clock we saw the enemy's vessels (that had been lying at anchor near Sewell's Point since the previous night) coming in our direction.

The drums of the "Minnesota" gloomily beat to quarters; the men took their stations with despondency, mingled with grim determination, on their rugged faces. There was cause for their gloom. The situation was such as to justify distrust if not hopelessness: the "Minnesota" had been badly cut up in the fight of Saturday; the "Roanoke" was unmanageable from breaking her machinery; the "St. Lawrence" was a sailing vessel, and could do but little in calm weather. What better could we expect than the fate of the "Cumberland" and the "Congress"? There was but little confidence that the "Monitor" would be able to cope successfully with the "Merrimack;" and yet this queer, insignificant-looking thing was all there was between our wooden ships and destruction.

The rebel iron-clad, instead of taking the course she had taken on Saturday, after steaming down the Rip Raps, turned into the channel by which the "Minnesota" had reached her position, and then rapidly approached us.

When she was within a mile of our ship, the men, who had meanwhile had their breakfast, were again summoned to the guns, and opened fire upon her with their stern guns.

And now ensued a scene the mere remembrance of which (after the lapse of more than a quarter of a century) again makes my blood tingle in my veins.

The "Monitor," hitherto concealed from her antagonist behind the "Minnesota," darted out and placed herself between the rebel craft and our ship, and steered directly for the rebel frigate.

We saw the " Merrimack " slow up as if in astonishment that so insignificant a craft should dare to approach her; then, while her wooden consorts scattered, the huge " Merrimack " trained her forward guns, aimed, and missed their mark, for the " Monitor " presented to the guns of her antagonist only her turret (as the largest mark), a cross-section of scarcely twenty feet by nine. Then our little craft answered with a solid eleven-inch shot, which was indeed a *monitorial* one. It smote the huge frigate, and made her tremble with the blow!

" By heavens," exclaimed the captain at our gun, " but our little one can speak for herself!"

Then the " Merrimack " turned, and fired every gun of her terrible broadside at the little champion. The shot mostly went over the " Monitor " (which in comparison with her huge antagonist seemed but a toy), and those that struck her glanced off harmlessly into the sea.

There was a murmur of applause among our men, who were, however, not yet convinced of our defender's invulnerability.

" That's a good one for the big one!" said one of the men; " hit 'em again, little one!"

And then, as if in answer, the rebel craft at close range fired broadside after broadside, in rapid succession, to which the " Monitor " replied, until the contestants were enshrouded in smoke.

When the smoke cleared and the little "Monitor" was seen apparently unhurt, while the armor of the rebel craft was reported to be bent and loosened, confidence began to take the place of doubt and uncertainty.

The excitement on board was so great that it almost broke beyond the bounds of discipline. When the "Monitor" finally lay alongside the huge "Merrimack" (as it seemed to us almost touching her) an old sailor at our gun said: "Blast my eyes, but I believe the little one will lick her, after all!"

After fighting at this close range for a while we saw our little champion still uninjured, darting around the big iron-clad as if in search of some weak place, and at the same time firing as she moved.

Her every motion was watched and commented on; we were in a tremor of expectation, not knowing what was going to happen next. It was like a fight between two knights of old, selected to represent opposing forces; not only our fate but the fate of empire, perhaps, depended on the issue. It seemed that if the "Merrimack" should triumph it meant not only the destruction of the war-ships at Hampton Roads but the establishment of a Southern empire that would control the continent, the ruin of the Republic, and the failure of a government by and for all the people.

The "Merrimack" carried ten guns to the "Monitor's" one; she fired at least two shots to every one fired by the Union iron-clad, but many of her shots missed their mark and struck the sea beyond, throwing up fountain-like jets of water.

We had at first expected so little from the "Monitor," she was so apparently inferior to her antagonist, that any success from her seemed wonderful. But when broadside after broadside, at such close range that the vessels seemed to touch each other, had time and again been received, and the little craft was not only afloat, but as the old sailors said " making spunky replies to all that the big fellow could say," and playing at will around her gigantic and frowning antagonist, then exclamations of wonder and admiration broke from the lips of all on board.

At last, after this strange contest had lasted three hours or more (every hour seeming a day, so great was the suspense), and the "Merrimack" having vainly endeavored to ram the "Monitor" (which had been able to avoid the blow on account of her superior quickness), as if despairing of success against her lively antagonist, turned and steered once more for our ship. As she came in point-blank range of our guns we gave her a broadside that would have blown out of water any wooden ship in the world. But it was like throwing pebbles against a solid rock. She returned fire with her bow gun, sending a shell crashing into us that spread destruction through our ship, set it on fire, and tore four rooms into one. The second shell that struck us passed through our hull, and with a terrific explosion blew up a little tug lying alongside, producing the wildest confusion on board our ship. We believed we were about to meet the fate of the "Congress."

Another shell was fired into us, when the little "Monitor," by throwing herself between the two, compelled the "Merrimack" to change her position, and saved us from destruction. Just then, however, the rebel iron-clad grounded.

When I looked from the port again it was to see the "Monitor" apparently retired from the fight, and we then thought she had received a mortal wound. We learned later that this was occasioned by a hurt received by the brave commander of the "Monitor." He was standing in the pilot-house directing the fight when a shell struck and exploded directly in the sight-hole (or slit) through which he was looking. He received in his face the force of the blow, which stunned him and filled his eyes with powder, blinding and confusing him. Thinking the pilot-house had been destroyed, he gave orders to withdraw from the fight. Young Lieutenant Green took command and steered once more for the enemy, which had meanwhile taken advantage of the "Monitor's" temporary withdrawal from the fight to turn tail for Norfolk.

The "Monitor" fired a few shots at the retiring craft, but the "Merrimack" continued on, accompanied by her wooden consorts, reminding me of a big school-boy bully being helped off from the field after an unexpected check made by a smaller boy. Then the old sailors began to say that it was as plain as the nose on your face that the "Merrimack" was glad of an excuse to turn tail.

Thus was ended the most remarkable naval battle ever fought (all things considered), for in this fight a verdict was rendered against wooden ships. In substance, they were all destroyed on that eighth and ninth of March, 1862; for after this, one of our "Monitors" would have been competent to sink all the wooden ships of the navies of the world.

CHAPTER XXI.

AFTER THE CONFLICT.

The little "Monitor," after driving her formidable antagonist from Hampton Roads, anchored alongside the "Minnesota," as fit for service as when she went into the fight. Beyond a crack in the iron logs of her pilot-house and a few dints in her turret, made by the huge shot from the rifled guns of the "Merrimack," she was comparatively uninjured.

Whether or not the "Monitor" was a victor has, I am well aware, been discussed, affirmed, and denied; yet it has never been questioned that the Confederate Goliath left the field of the fight to our David, and was at once put into the dry docks for repairs at Norfolk.

The interest among us in the "Monitor" was great. Those who had viewed her with contempt were now enthusiastic in their admiration of her.

"Blast me, but she's a kind of a Mother Cary's chicken of a craft," said Bill Knowles, an old man-of-war's man of my acquaintance, while we were looking over the sides of the "Minnesota" down on the deck of the little craft. "See how the waves go right over her! Blame my eyes, but that feller was right when he said she was a kind of a submarine craft. I would n't be astonished if she should dive and come up a mile from us."

"What I don't understand," said another, "is where she keeps all of her guns."

"Guns!" ejaculated Knowles. "She don't carry but two, but them 's regular thunderbolts!"

"What I seed with my own eyes I seed, and you nor no other horse-marine jackass can't make me see dif'rent. Did n't these two eyes of mine see 'em shooting from that queer round house they call a tarret, from twelve to twenty places in it? And now, though, ye can't see that many ports, but it stands to reason that the guns is there, and th' portholes too, if y' can't see 'em; but what gits the weather gauge of me is where they keeps them stowed when they ain't a-firing."

"Keep 'em stowed! Why, you wolverine," said Jim Knowles, "while they 're firin' one they 're loadin' the rest of 'em down in the hold; they act as ballast there, or she 'd be top heavy with all that iron above decks."

And with this Jim winked a prolonged wink on one side of his face and looked wise on the other.

"Well, shipmates," said another, "between me and the mainmast, what gits down to the roots of my hair is, how they anchor her without a chain, windlass, or anchor."

"I know where her smoke-stacks are," said

another old salt; "I see the smoke come out of them two slits in her deck."

"Belay there!" said another; "her smoke-stacks are on the bottom side of her, and by a sort of economy o' forces they discharge it in th' water!"

"Likely," assented another; "'t would n't be no more strange than the rest of this craft that can't be hurt, and goes around heavens knows how, and fights a big lumbering craft that smashed everything to flinders till this little craft come along and larned her better manners. Now jest look at her crew settin' 'round on her deck. Not one of them, they say, was hurt, and was as comfortable all the time as if that rebel iron craft was j'st throwin' b'iled 'taters at 'em 'stid 'f big shot."

"Well, shipmates," said Knowles, who was an oracle on board, "whatever is or is n't, one thing is true, that little craft out thar' preached a sermon on Sunday that the Confederates won't forgit in one while, and that beat all the sky-pilots of the navy."

We were not alone in our wonder and enthusiasm for the little craft, for, with the flashing by telegraph of the tidings of this fight, there was excitement in every town and village of the land.

Thus it was that the gloom and uncertainty of Monday, March the 8th, gave place to rejoicing and confidence. No wonder that many of our people felt that in the opportune appearance of the "Monitor" God had reached forth his hand for our nation's protection.

Almost before the fight between the iron-clads was over, measures were taken for the abandonment of the "Minnesota." This was soon accomplished, and I was once more at Fort Monroe, where I obtained leave to visit Phil and our other wounded shipmates at Newport News.

I found Phil sitting in front of a hospital tent. He was quite cross because I had left Newport News without seeing him.

"I was under Lieutenant Prendergrast's orders just as much as I was when on shipboard," I said. "Besides, you know you would have wanted to go, and that was n't best. The surgeon told me you'd got to keep still awhile or you was likely to have trouble with your arm."

"That old saw-bones," ejaculated Phil crossly, "makes a mountain of this molehill of a scratch. Why look a-here," said Phil, suiting the action to his words, "I can use this arm"— But here his remarks on the subject ended, for a decided pallor and an expression of pain came to his face, which seemed to illustrate to him, as well as to myself, that he had a very sore arm.

"You must stop that kind of fooling, Phil," I said, as I assisted him in replacing his wounded limb carefully in its sling, "or you will give the sky-pilot a last job for yourself!"

"Well, maybe you are right, Hez," said Phil, with a twinge of pain still evident in the expression of his face. "I guess I'll have to keep this arm in its hammock for a while longer. But say, speaking of the sky-pilot reminds me that the chaplain said, when he was in to see me a little while ago, that there is a Connecticut regiment about a half mile from here in camp. The chaplain is from the Nutmeg State, and is a fine old man. Now, what say? Supposing we go down and see if there is any one from Wichnor there?"

I assented, and Phil went to see the hospital steward, and soon returned, saying: "It's all right: the steward says 't will do me good!"

When we arrived at the camp of the —th Connecticut we found several persons whom we knew, and after chatting awhile with them started off to see others from our town who we had been told were in camp. We had arrived at the end of one of the company streets, near a large overgrown tent, when some one called out to us:

"Hullo, broad-britches, where be ye goin'?"

It was Jim Bisbee. He was eating sutler's pies, "with an energy," as Phil said, "worthy of better pies."

"Hullo," I said, "have you got a contract to eat all that stuff?"

"Gosh! no," said Jim, grinning: "wish I had, though," and then, as he bit into the pie, extended his hand for a shake, and greeted us (between bites) very heartily, saying:

"I snum, how be y'? It seems kinder like hum t' see your faces: it does, I vow! Ain't it awful

"HULLO," I SAID, "HAVE YOU GOT A CONTRACT TO EAT ALL THAT STUFF?"

getting 'nough t' eat daown here in rebellion? That is, som'thin' that goes t' the spot? I get daown t' this sutler's shop 'baout this time o' day, 'cause 't is jest 'fore drill time. Wife sent me a big box o' nice provisions last week, an' a lot of greenbacks; an' I 'v' e't up the fust an' begun on the second; which is t' say, I 'v' jist begun to convert greenbacks int' stuff t' eat."

"Should think you 'd use up your wages pretty fast at the rate you are going on, Mr. Bisbee," said Phil.

"Git aout!" said Jim; "my wages don't 'maount t' shucks; f'r this sutler's stuff 's j'st like fog; it don't stick by y' or fill up wuth a cent; I can eat a cord on it an' not git full. Tell y'! I 've be'n drefful hungry sometimes. But talkin' of myself makes me forgit that you 've had hard times tu. Have a pie?" and Jim handed us one apiece.

"Well, as you are a man of property," I said, "I suppose they are glad to trust you when you get out of money."

"'Fore this money come," said Jim, "I'd used up all my pay, and I ast 'em t' trust for a few doughnuts and crackers an' cheese and sich. This dummed sutler said he would n't do it. I told him I owned tew farms an' a lot o' truck, an' he said, darn him, 'Bring on y'r truck an' we 'll trade;' so y' see, I 've be'n losin' flesh."

"You ain't losing your appetite, though," said Phil, with a sly grin, for he liked to hear Jim talk.

"No," said Jim, with a dubious smile, "I snum, that sticks tu me closer than my skin. 'Less the war ends drefful quick, I'm feared 'twill be th' ruination of me. I've eat up tew cows an' a hoss already, plague if I hain't!"

"It's awful!" said Phil, winking at me. "I've got a pretty good appetite myself."

"Here, have some more pie," said Jim, and then continuing said: "But where was y' when that awful big fight was a-goin' on o' Saturday?"

"We were on board the 'Congress,'" I said, "and Phil was wounded; have n't you noticed that his arm is in a sling?"

Jim stopped eating, and, facing us for the first time since he had hailed us, dropped his pie and ejaculated:

"I'm a selfish lunkhead not t' 'ave seen it! Say, Phil, du y' feel bad any ways? If there's anythin' y' see 'round here that y' want, say the word an' th' fur flies!"

And the tears started to the generous fellow's eyes, at the thought that Phil was wounded and he had taken no notice of the fact before.

"Oh, I am all right, Jim," said Phil; "the old doctor down here makes a big fuss over nothing."

"L't me jist look at that sore arm, f'r when I write ham I want t' tell 'bout it."

"No, you don't!" said Phil; "one *regular* sawbones is enough."

"Gosh, I wonder y' 're livin' t' tell on 't!" said Jim, after we had told him about our experience in the battle of Saturday. "I just tuck a part in that gosh-danged fight myself; an' I don' know what I sh'd 'a' done if I 'd been exposed tu th' perils of the deep, besides them shot bigger 'n hogsheads that come a-howlin' round here! I j'st fired an' loaded; an' fired so fast that I found five charges o' cartridges in that musket th' next day that had forgot t' go out o' that gun; snum if I did n't! Wal, 's I was a-sayin' when I stopped t' tell you 'bout the way that ole gun acted: we loaded an' fired an' kep' advancin' on th' enemy, an' shuttin' up our eyes an' firin', an' dressin' on th' colors: an' 't was lively times, an' that 's what makes me so dummed hungry, I du b'lieve!"

"If the enemy had been the sutler," said Phil, "they 'd been totally destroyed, would n't they?"

Jim smiled as he said, "Naow, Phil Gurley, that 's the truth; but honor bright, we just banged away at 'em like all p'sessed! But say, Phil Gurley, ain't y' goin' t' let me have a peek at that sore arm?"

"Stop your nonsense!" said Phil: "it 's nothing but a scratch, an' I don't want you fooling with it."

"Wal, Phil," said Jim, "I did n't mean anythin' but well by ye, ye know I don't, an' I don't know as I blame ye. I never like t' be fussed over m'self. So y' was reely aout there on th' deep?

Wal, did n't it beat all natur'? — that old iron roof of a Noah's ark! I wonder there 's a grease-spot of any of us left. I calculated I was th' only Wichmor feller that 'd live t' carry back th' news. By gum! some o' our fellers was awful scat; 't was 'baout all the cap'n an' me could du t' keep 'em in line."

"What did you keep 'em in line with? or did n't you keep them in line, but only tried?" said Phil.

"Of course," said Jim, with a droll twinkle in his eyes, "we had a sight o' trouble 'baout it. Every time our fellers fell back th' cap'n an' me'd go back an' rally 'em an' dress 'em on th' hindmost one. We just had a turrible tussle here! Th' cap'n lost his hat, an' he drawed his sword an' went t' find it, an' got lost in th' swamp; by gum if he did n't! Then I said t' our boys, 'Forra'd! We'll rescue the cap'n an' his hat, or die on the field o' glory an' mud!' And just then one o' them big shot come up the hill, sayin' 'Sssccattt!' An' dummed 'f every last one o' them men did n't dig f'r that swamp like all p'sessed; they 'beyed orders t' the letter — an' I in advance tu, 'cause I had t' dress 'em on the colors. I should n't like t' be on board of a ship," continued Jim, "f'r ther' ain't no field thar' f'r fine manœuvrin'."

"Promotion is n't so rapid in the navy as in the army, but there is all the fighting any one could desire," I said; "at least we 've found it so."

"Wal, say, y' know I 'm a corp'ral?" said Jim.

"You 've got up pretty well," said Phil. "I suppose a corporal is quite a fellow, ain't he?"

"A feller!" said Jim; "guess not; he 's 'n of'cer! You know when I fust got t' be a corporal I thought I'd stop wantin' t' be higher, but it did n't seem t' satisfy; I know naow haow Napoleon felt, an' kep' feelin' till he just wanted t' gobble th' whole airth."

"That would include sutlers' shops and all, I suppose?" said Phil.

"Yes," said Jim, "th' whole boodle of 'em. Say, hev' a doughnut? They ain't much tu 'em; kind o' sweetened rainbows; yer can eat a peck on 'em an' not know it."

In this way Jim continued drolling on, making us laugh, and enjoying the fun himself, while seeming to be in earnest. He made many inquiries about our prospects, and gave us, in his inimitable manner, some shrewd advice.

When I told him I was on the "Minnesota" on Sunday, and saw the fight between the "Merrimack" and the "Monitor," Jim was greatly interested, and said solemnly:

"I feel turribul 'sponsible 'baout you, Hez, f'r I fust put it in y'r mother's head t' let y' hav' a try at the sea. My exper'nce did n't seem t' du a speck o' good in keepin' y' ashore; an' naow y' stand a chance o' gittin' drounded an' killed both."

Just then a drum sounded, and Jim said, "There's that pesky drum callin' me t' arms ag'in! Fust its revilee, then it's guard-mount, or dress-parade, 'r some dummed thing all the time—now that's drill. Su'pose I 'v' got t' train my gizzard aout, 'fore I'm haf full tu!"

And shaking hands with us, Jim started for his tent, and soon reappeared trying to buckle on his belt and eat pie at the same time.

"Duty calls!" said Jim with a wink, and having adjusted his belt and bolted his pie, he marched to duty at right shoulder shift in a very soldierly manner.

"Jim is a good one," said Phil, "and it did me lots of good to hear him run 'so like a saw-mill,' as he calls it; he talked most of that non-sense just to make us laugh; for you and every one that knows him knows that he's got a lot of good sense."

After remaining with Phil for the day, I returned to the fort and found that a mail had come for our ship's crew. I received two letters from home; one of these was from my mother, and the other from grandfather. The last related to getting appointments for Phil and me in the navy.

The cause of delay, as grandfather said, he had ascertained to be that the rules prevented our being appointed to the positions of either master's mates or ensigns until we were eighteen years of age. "We will stretch a point and say you are seventeen now, so in another year you'll get your appointments. Meanwhile apply yourselves to learning everything that will be of use to you in those positions."

I felt rather blue over it, for, boy-like, I was impatient and did not recognize that, as grandfather often had said, "The world was n't made in a day."

The letter from mother enclosed a letter she had received from father. As shown by the post-mark, he had found some way of having it mailed in Washington, and so the letter had reached her sealed. In the letter I noticed that father's sentiments had changed, for he spoke of the South as "my country," and there were mingled in his utterances little touches — such as speaking of the Northern people as "the enemy," its government as "the abolition government," and Mr. Lincoln as "your president." I could not understand how so fair-minded a man could so change. This was all the more wonderful when I considered that originally he had been opposed to secession, and had been at heart a Union man. But I did not then understand how the constant misrepresentations of the Confederacy, of its press and of its government, made every act of our people seem wrong, and embittered the Southern heart. Civil war cannot be carried on long without producing that effect. Neither did I at that time understand the power of public sentiment, wrought to frenzy in a desperate struggle like that on which the Southern people had embarked. The politicians, having brought on the war, must succeed or be ruined, and they promoted the feeling of rage and bitterness among the people.

Thus the blows, first reluctantly given by most of the Southern people, grew more and more violent, until to kill Yankees seemed a glorious act among this naturally chivalrous and kindly people. Then, besides this, I did not realize the fact that my father was by education and training a Southern man, and that when among his own people once more his moderate sentiments might prove only skin deep.

Still, in my mind he was above ordinary men, and could never be capable of an act that was personally mean or dishonorable.

Yet the fact remained that I was of intensely Union sentiments, and my father, whom I loved above all men, was a rebel, and seemed to believe himself right in fighting on the other side. It was "father against son."

CHAPTER XXII.

ON THE "SPITFIRE."

On the 29th of April, 1862, Phil and I were assigned to duty on the "Spitfire," a gun-boat of light draft intended for inland waters and river service. She was what at that time was known as a double ender — sharp at both ends so that she could back out where she could not turn around.

Grandfather had written to me, saying: "I have brought so much influence to bear on the authorities at the Naval Department at Washington that, if it don't move them, I think it may agitate them some."

We had little doubt that our being assigned to duty on the "Spitfire" was one of the symptoms of this agitation, in order that we might stand a better chance for promotion.

When I learned that the steamer was to be placed in service on the inland waters of North Carolina, I had a vague hope, foolish as it may here seem, that I might be able to get tidings of, or perhaps have an interview with, my father. To do this I felt that I was willing to risk much, and undergo almost any hardship. Though an interview of this nature occurred, yet had I known the conditions under which this wish of mine was to be granted, I confess I should have shrunk from the ordeal. It is fortunate that we cannot forecast the future, otherwise how many would shrink from a plain course of duty!

We joined the "Spitfire" at the Brooklyn Navy Yard, where she was undergoing repairs in the dry dock. On reporting we were surprised to find that the lieutenant commanding was a beardless youth scarcely twenty-three years of age, and looking even younger than his age would imply. He was a graduate of the Annapolis Academy, and had won the position he then occupied, over older and more experienced officers than himself, by coolness, bravery, and good judgment. One would scarcely believe, to see this beardless, spindle-shanked, tow-headed, boyish-looking person, that he had already distinguished himself in some of the most daring deeds of our naval warfare.

When Phil and I reported for duty, seeing Lieutenant Dashway on deck, and thinking he was one of the midshipmen, we entered into conversation with him and talked much more freely than we should have done had we known that he was our commanding officer. He asked us a great many questions, and, as sailors would phrase it expressively, "pumped us dry." We were not a little taken back when, on asking, "What kind of a captain have we got here?" his manner changed from familiarity to sternness, as he replied:

"I am in command here; you will report yourself to the executive officer for duty at once."

The "Spitfire" was schooner-rigged, and carried two pivot-guns and eight thirty-pounders on her sides. The next day being Sunday and the "Spitfire" being ready for sea, we hauled out into the stream and steamed down the harbor, out beyond Sandy Hook, and down the coast.

Among the men on board there were two whom I had previously known on the "Congress:" one of them was Bill Knowles and the other a young sailor named Winslow, a Cape Cod man, well up in seamanship, though with small education.

We steamed along the coast without events worthy of note, until off Hatteras, when on rounding the cape the wind gradually rose, the sea became very rough, and the sky had a dull, leaden look that betokened a so'-easter.

At about two o'clock the wind was still rising, and the sea was so rough that we had our hands full. Our craft was kept on the port tack, hove-to under close-reefed foresail and mainsail. In the driving mist and rain it soon grew dark. It was my watch; the decks of the little craft were drenched with spray which was charged with phosphoric glare that added to the wildness of the storm.

About three o'clock in the morning an arch of light rising in the west told us of a sudden change of wind. The mainsail was quickly lowered, and when the storm struck us the fore-sheet was shifted over. When our craft would sink down in the trough of the sea I could see the phosphorescent water high above the level of our decks, and at times it seemed as if it would be impossible for us to ride out the storm.

When I turned in the storm was raging with increasing fury; but when in the morning it was my watch on deck, I found to my astonishment that the sun was shining, the wind had abated, and our little craft was steaming once more along the coast under full sail.

"Why is it," I said to Knowles, "that there are so many sudden changes off Hatteras?"

"I don't know, an' I doubt if any one else does," growled Knowles. "I only know it is the most changeable here of any place on our coast, an' as to the whys and wherefores you might 's well try to account for your mother-in-law's temper six months after marriage."

"Mr. Bell once told me," said Phil, "that these sudden changes are thought to be caused by the gulf stream being so much nearer the coast here than at any other point; and that, with the fact that the water deepens very rapidly from the shore to one hundred fathoms and then falls abruptly to over two thousand five hundred, is thought to have something to do with the sudden and capricious weather here."

"I guess that is a new-fangled reason," said Knowles, "for I never heard of it before; but I've heard the Hatteras fishermen say that lightning can be seen from the light-house there at any time of the year."

"Yes," said Phil, "I have heard John Nixon say almost the same thing."

That day we passed through Hatteras Inlet, and signaled the flag-ship that afternoon.

The next morning, having received orders, we steamed up Pamlico Sound, where we were to watch at the mouth of one of the rivers for vessels that were attempting to run the blockade. For, the general coast being clear, it was only at such points that they could load with cotton and turpentine, and attempt to evade our vigilance by emerging from the interior by the passage of these rivers in the night.

It was a very monotonous and tiresome service, and the old sailors were inclined to growl, especially those who, like Knowles, had seen more exciting and remunerative service in blockading duty on the coast.

"We might just as well be on wheels," said Knowles, "as to be foolin' 'round here! I like a little prize money in mine, and blue water instead of these dirty rivers, where you can't turn 'round without danger o' gettin' aground and stirrin' up the mud. About all we can expect to get here is the shakes and fever. There's the master's mate sick with it, and the whole ship's company will have to go into dry dock to get these malarial barnacles off of 'em by and by."

"Belay there!" said an old sailor that had sailed with the lieutenant longer than the rest of the ship's crew. "If you are thinkin' there ain't goin' to be any lively times on board this here craft, y' don't know much about the chap that's in command! Why, shipmates, he's more in love with trouble than the most of us is with our bread baskets. If he don't cut out some work to shake the barnacles off of y', and the fever out of y', too, then y' may call me a lubber!"

"An' y' make a mistake in supposin' there's no danger here," chimed in another old shellback, "for when y' get up one of these rivers a little ways, y'll find masked batteries, an' sharp-shooters, an' that, too, at p'ints where y' can't go 'round, go ahead, or git back."

"An' misquitoes an' torpedoes, to kill an' bite y', an' blow y' higher'n the mainmast, an' annoy y' generally," said another, giving a hitch to his trousers for emphasis.

The men laughed to hear torpedoes classified with mosquitoes, but I have no doubt they thought the latter as great an evil as the first, for it was one that was ever present with us when up the river, where, as Phil said, these pests presented their bills after business hours.

"Well, our little lieutenant will go where any one will follow; he's just a-hankering f'r trouble, only them 's are above him are holdin' him in," said the old sailor.

It proved true that our lieutenant commanding only lacked permission to enter upon more hazardous undertakings. Quite a number of the men were sick with malarial fever, and among these the captain's clerk; so I was requested to take his place for a time.

Though it was a place that I had no liking for, I did my duty while I occupied it, and received the hearty commendation of the lieutenant for the rapidity, neatness, and correctness of my writing. Although I did not, I trust, try to parade my accomplishments, yet I was not averse to showing that I was well educated, and was not only quick in figures, but well up in higher mathematics.

I think it was partly owing to this fact that when, shortly after, one of the master's mates was, as Knowles termed it, "dry-docked," by being sent to the hospital at Brooklyn, I was put to the duty of acting master's mate.

After being in this position for several months an order from the Secretary of the Navy was received, with my appointment as ensign. I was not displeased that I was to do duty in that office on board the "Spitfire." No order came for Phil's promotion, but I am sure he deserved it more than I did. He generously declared that he would rather I should get the position than have it himself, and seemed to rejoice at my good fortune more than if it had come to him. This did not surprise me, for it was in keeping with the manly and unselfish nature of one who had not one particle of envy in his soul.

It was in February, '63, while I was on duty as officer of the deck that I first learned that Mr. Bell, now lieutenant United States navy, was on duty in these waters. He came on board to visit our lieutenant, with whom he was acquainted. Before he left the steamer I was off duty, and paid my respects to him.

He inquired for Phil, and he was sent for, and, as he had always been a great favorite with Mr. Bell, I was not surprised at the hearty greeting he received.

"I am glad, young gentlemen, to hear a good report of you from your commanding officer, and that one of you has received promotion."

"Yes," I replied, "mine came at last, but Phil has n't got his yet, and you know he is a better sailor than I am; my promotion was simply good luck."

"There is no luck or accidents, everything is ordered or directed by some power higher than ourselves," said Lieutenant Bell. "No one who has observed the course of this terrible war can doubt that. If this war had been closed a year ago we should have left the cause of all this bitterness between brothers untouched, and should have it all to fight over again some other time. I have been taught, too, in my own life that there is a directing power higher than man. I was raised at the South and taught to consider work as unworthy of a gentleman. I got married, quarreled or disagreed with my father, and without profession or trade tried to support myself and family. I was overtaken by what we call misfortune. I was compelled to go to sea as a common sailor. Under the name I now go by I worked my way up. My experience has proved a blessing to me, and while there is much that is very bitter and hard to bear as a consequence, I have no doubt that it has been so ordered, and that I shall find it is for the highest good. It has developed self-reliance and manhood in me, and I thank God every day that I know how a man before the mast feels. But for the Providential direction of my life, I should be fighting against my country like some of my kindred and friends."

A look passed between Phil and myself when Lieutenant Bell referred to his being of Southern birth, and I knew that Phil would like to have me tell him of my father. It had always been hard for me to talk of father with those who did not know him and the circumstances under which he had left home; they might misunderstand him, and besides it could do no good.

One of the duties of our ship was to watch the mouth of the river that communicated with the interior of the country, to intercept and capture vessels coming from the enemy with cotton and other cargoes, in an attempt to run the blockade. So at times while on this duty we penetrated these rivers for miles, but we were generally received by the people with more energy than courtesy.

In April, taking advantage of the high tides prevailing, we steamed up one of these rivers for several miles in an attempt to capture some schooners said to be loaded with cotton, waiting for a favorable chance to get out. We had gone up the river some ten miles without falling in with these crafts, when a battery on the river bluff opened fire on us. While steaming ahead to get out of range we began to make reply with shell. Phil was in charge of the pivot gun abaft, and was making some fine shots. In the midst of this exciting fire an ignited shell cartridge fell out of the gun to the deck and rolled sputtering and hissing to starboard, when Phil seized a bucket of water and threw it upon the dangerous intruder, thus preventing a disastrous explosion on our deck. Our commander, who saw the act, afterwards complimented Phil on his coolness, when Phil simply remarked:

"The charge must have been damp, captain, or it would have exploded."

The lieutenant, however, made mention of this heroic conduct in his report, and after a while, on his recommendation, Phil was appointed by the Secretary of the Navy a master's mate on the "Spitfire" as a reward for gallant conduct.

So Phil had the good fortune to win his promotion, and it was the general feeling on board that no one ever more richly deserved it.

That night, not seeing anything of the vessels we were looking for, after some sharp exchanges of shell and shot, and after we had succeeded in making the position of the enemy untenable, we retired, fearing the enemy would barricade the river below us.

Early the next morning we started up the river once more, when we found that the enemy had taken a position for their battery on a high bluff, where we could not give our guns sufficient elevation to shell them out.

Seeing this, we backed down stream, at a bend in the river, out of sight. Here I was ordered by the lieutenant to take a boat with a party of men and make a reconnaissance on shore, for the purpose of ascertaining the strength of the enemy.

We landed in a swampy thicket, where, leaving our boat in charge of one man, we moved towards the enemy. We had not got out of the thicket when we came upon four of the rebel boats, and though we only surmised the purpose of their being there (because of the shovels and picks we found on board of them), we pushed them into the stream. After this we advanced along the river bank until we came near to the bluff where the enemy had established their battery.

Here, after cautioning my men to make as little noise as possible, we made a wide circuit around the bluff and came up in the rear, for the purpose of spying out the situation.

We halted in a thick undergrowth of black jack, pine, and tangled vines. Here, leaving the men, I crept forward to where I was able to look out on a cleared spot on the brow of the bluff, where the battery was stationed. But just as I was about to look out I heard a sound that made my heart jump. It was the measured tramp of a body of marching men coming towards me. I flattened myself to the ground and waited. They were moving along a path which ran so near to where I was lying that it was astonishing they did not see me; but they passed on, and I had the satisfaction of hearing the sound of their footsteps grow less and less distinct, and finally die away in the distance.

I inferred from the few words I had heard them utter that they were on their way to sink the very scows we had set adrift in the river for the purpose of barricading it. When I looked out in the rear of the enemy's position I saw some twenty men with their muskets stacked lounging around the guns, laughing and making uncomplimentary remarks about the Yankee gunnery.

Between the battery, which consisted of three brass field-pieces and a light ship's-gun, and the woods were stacked their muskets.

I crept back to my party, and ordered them forward. The whole party of twenty-five men was soon in position. Then, with a rush, we were on our foes, between them and their stacked muskets, calling upon them to surrender.

Those that attempted to run we shot down, and the others surrendered. After rolling the light guns down the bluff and spiking the larger ship-gun we made our way back to where we had left our boat; it was gone. From the sound of musketry down stream that broke out at just that time, we concluded that the steamer was having a dispute with those who were attempting to barricade the river.

We were in a quandary what to do, when Knowles's sharp eyes saw one of the scows of the enemy we had set adrift, caught in the projecting limb of a tree. It was but the work of an instant to reach it and bring it to the shore, put our prisoners on board, and, using the shovels for paddles (for there were no others), cross to the opposite side of the river, and go with the current down to our steamer, in hope thus to reach her on the side from the enemy.

Before we reached her, however, I discovered that they were on both sides of the stream, for when lower down there came a crackling of muskets, and several of our men and prisoners were wounded. I do not know how it would have fared with us if one of our prisoners had not exclaimed, " You are firing on your friends!"

They ceased firing, and while they were hesitating and in doubt we shot out of range of their fire.

In a few moments I was safely on board the "Spitfire" with my prisoners.

It was not long before we had cleaned out the riflemen and were left undisturbed.

The lieutenant commanding complimented me on the manner I had performed my part in this affair.

CHAPTER XXIII.

ATTACK ON SECESSIONVILLE.

When I reported to Lieutenant Dashway, he at once resolved to make an attack on quite an important town on the river, some thirty miles above. His plan was to sweep the river, destroy salt-works, vessels, and any munitions of war that might be found. The success of this plan depended upon surprising the enemy by a quick dash, and then fighting our way out again.

I remember, even now while I write, the look of brave confidence on our youthful commander's face, and the determined resolution expressed in his firm-set jaw and in his steel-blue eyes, as he made this decision.

As we passed the bluff down which we had rolled the guns and thrown the muskets we had broken, he said:

"We'll get those guns on board when we return."

We had steamed up stream about fifteen miles without encountering the enemy, when we saw two schooners coming down on the tide. One of them, that was loaded with turpentine and cotton, was set on fire by her crew to prevent her falling into our hands, and the other was run ashore in the mud.

We ran alongside of the one which had been fired, but finding that it was impossible to save her we continued on our course. The pilot assured our commander that it was important that he should have daylight as well as high tide to pilot the steamer back through the crooked river-channel. We stopped just long enough to destroy some salt-works on the banks of the river, and then dashed forward toward the town at a speed as great as the crooked and narrowing river would permit.

On our arrival at the little town we found the people totally unprepared for our reception. We quickly landed in our boats, but not quickly enough to prevent the escape of several officers by the dirt road, to a still larger town some twenty miles from there.

We threw out pickets to prevent a surprise; we then took possession of the court-house and other public buildings (for it was the county seat), and seized a number of small arms, and a large mail at the post-office, where I had been sent for this purpose. The postmaster had modestly secluded himself, but the mistress, either braver than her husband, or having more confidence in Yankee sailors than he had, remained behind. I first secured the mail and sent it to the boat, and then confiscated the negro servants at the office and sent them to the steamer. While I was performing this duty the good woman of the house was bravely storming at me, with all the epithets at her command. I allowed none of the men under me to make reply, and personally I treated her as courteously as if she were showering upon us compliments instead of unsavory abuse.

While I was at the post-office, few men were visible, as I have intimated; but I had one very pleasant visitor, whom I shall not easily forget. It was a beautiful young lady with the brightest eyes I ever saw, who, not knowing that the office had changed hands, had driven to the door, seated gracefully on a pony.

As she drove up I stepped to the sidewalk and lifted my hat. With her beautiful blue eyes she gave an inquiring flash at me, from the gold braid on my hat to the boots on my feet. I confess that glance made me feel very insignificant. She had not understood who or what I was until she alighted and stood at the door, when the shower of abuse from the wife of the postmaster enlightened her. Then with one more flash from her eyes, she turned as if to remount her horse; but that animal, as if it had become infected with the sentiments of the town, had walked away from Yankee contagion.

"Knowles," I said, for he was one of my party, "bring that horse here for the young lady."

After some difficulty the pony was secured and brought to the doorway, where the young lady accepted my assistance in mounting.

Before starting her horse into a canter, she turned, bowed, and gave me a smile that for the instant completely turned my head; then she clattered down the street. All this took place in less time than it has taken me to tell it.

The recall having been sounded shortly after, I said good-day to the scolding mistress and started for the boat. Knowles and the rest of my crew were just ahead of me, leading the way. He turned back to urge me to hurry, when in an instant the party had gone from our view. At the same time we caught sight of some of the townspeople skulking and lying in wait, and for fear that they might open fire from the houses I turned into another street.

This caused some delay, and when I arrived at the landing I was chagrined, not only at finding that my boat was gone, but that some men had got two guns in position on the left bank of the river and were about to open fire on the steamer.

There was no time for question or delay. I hastily glanced along the shore to see if there was some kind of a boat in which I could get back to the steamer, but there was none in sight. I then dodged around some old warehouses, and from thence down to the river-side, where thick, low foliage concealed me. Knowles had gone in some other direction, where I did not concern myself, having enough trouble of my own, and I was left to my unpleasant reflections, and to work out my own salvation as best I could.

I was in a bad fix, so much was sure. Here I was in an enemy's country, and that too after taking a prominent part in depredations of a character likely to wound the pride and aggravate the temper of much more humble and better-natured people than I ever gave these the credit of being.

I sat down in the thicket to think out a plan of escape to the Union lines. I came to the conclusion that I had better keep as near the river as possible, as in case of pursuit I could swim to the opposite bank, and also by this route I possibly might find a skiff or some other kind of boat to get down the river in. This disposition to keep near water is almost an instinct with sailors. I once asked an old sailor what he would do if he was ever compelled to beg, and he replied that if he ever got wrecked like that on shore, the first thing he would beg was a boat to get away from land in. Though, as the reader knows, I had had some experience on land, I was thoroughly imbued with this feeling so common to sailors, and felt safer for being near the water.

I was dressed in uniform; had on my belt, with sword and revolver, which an officer of my rank wore when on duty. Thinking that the gilt buttons and gold braid of my coat and hat might betray me if seen even at a distance, I turned my coat wrong side out and thrust my cap into one of its pockets, and placed on my head a gray silk handkerchief wound turban-like. I then replaced my belt and started down the river, keeping to the wooded fringe that skirted its shores.

This was late in the afternoon, and night soon came on. Under its concealing veil I felt that my chances for escape were increased; but I had not gone more than a mile when I was stopped by a creek which I must cross or go around. The latter was not to be thought of; so, in hope that by daylight I might find a boat in this little stream (it was so near to the town), I concluded to wait and make a search for this purpose.

I found a sheltered nook, got some dry leaves together for my bed, and munching some ship's bread which I had in my pocket (to say nothing of chewing the bitter cud of reflection), I fell asleep as sound as if in my hammock on board ship. I was awakened, it seemed to me only a few moments later, by the morning sun shining in my face. I was a little stiff and lame in my legs; for a sailor unaccustomed to walking on anything but plank is soon wearied in his legs while on land.

The sky was clear, and my mind was as clear as the sky; I felt equal to anything. The air was balmy, with just enough of the cool crispness of spring in it to make exercise inviting. I at once began to scan the shores of the creek for a boat to cross in, and to pursue my travels under more easy circumstances. I was following a river path when

I heard the tramp of horses, and in my modest desire not to attract attention, I stepped from the path to the concealing foliage. Two horsemen walked their horses past me. I heard the word "Yanks," and then one of them said, "Their steamer is shut in so they can't get away."

I inferred from this that the "Spitfire" had been detained in the river over night by barricades or other obstructions. I did not trouble myself about that, for I had learned that one can best attend to duty who attends to that which is before him, and who does not fret over things that are not present to his senses.

I was now more cautious, for I knew I must be near houses, or a house at least, and I also knew that if I fell in with any one but a field negro I was likely to find an enemy.

I went nearer to the water, and began to scan every nook along the shore near me, to find a boat. I was not long in finding a small skiff tied to a tree; there were no oars in her, and believing them to be hidden near the boat I began to look for them. I was just about to give up the search when I was confronted by an old and very black negro, with a pair of oars on his shoulder and a basket in his hand. I had found the oars, but with them an unpleasant incumbrance that was likely to upset my plans.

We both halted in surprise, in a sort of "Who'd 'a' thought of seeing you?" manner. I, however, recovered my wits and self-possession first and said, "I want to borrow your boat and oars awhile, boy."

I had learned that assurance and cheek go a good way with ordinary men, and that the blacks of the South were no exception to this rule.

"Can't len' dis boat, sar," said the black man; "got to go fish'n'."

"No one will know anything about it," I said, "so let me take the oars."

But though he hesitated he apparently did not fall in with my mode of looking at things. Seeing this, I changed my tactics by saying, "What have you got in that basket?"

"Got a pone, sar, fo' m' dinner."

"Here," I said, "I will give you this silver half-dollar for your dinner."

I offered this, partly because I wanted the dinner, and partly to get him to commit himself so he must do more. Seeing him hesitate, I said, "Keep the basket, I want only the food."

He reached out his hand for the silver, and then handed me the food. It was fried chicken, corn cake, and sweet potatoes. I ate a portion and put aside the rest for future use, and between bites said to the old darkey:

"Sam, I'm a Yankee; when we get these rebs licked, Uncle Abe's going to give you all your freedom. Now, if you'll just row me down to our steamer to-night I'll give you a hundred dollars in greenbacks; besides you'll get your freedom without waiting for it."

"I knows y' was a Yank — one o' them dat was up to de co't-house dar, an' de pos'-offis; I see ye dar, sar, an' I knows yo' fust t'ing, but I reckon I cann't go, sar; I's got a wife an' chil'n, sar, an' a right good ma's'r."

"Well, then," I said, "set me across here and then go on with your fishing, and I'll give you this greenback."

The old man's eyes glistened, and after looking cautiously in every direction, he consented to row me across the creek.

After he had landed me on the shore I handed him the greenback and then said, "Is n't there a Johnstone family living here, or near somewhere?"

"No, sar, but ole Mass'r Rufus Johnstone libs 'bout twenty mile' from yere on de dirt road, sar."

I reflected, "So I am among my father's people as well as among enemies."

"Where is the young Master Johnstone?"

"He's to de war in Richmond, I reckon, sar." And the old man peered curiously into my face, as if he would understand why I asked such questions.

"Where's his boy Andrew now?"

"Golly, sar, I reckon he to d' war wid Ma's'r Rufus, sar; he's pow'ful fon' ob him; mighty proud boy, sar." And the old man gave me another questioning look, as if he would like to know how I knew anything of the "quality people" of that locality.

He told me that in less than three miles I would come upon another creek. I tried to get him to promise that he would go down to that creek and set me across; or, better still, help me down the river several miles. He finally promised me he would if he could do so without danger of being found out.

I did not think he would betray me, nor did I have much confidence in ever seeing him again. Self-interest would, I argued, keep him from betraying me, for he was likely to be punished if it was known that he had been holding conversation with, and taking money from, a Yankee. I afterwards learned that the friendliness shown to distressed Union soldiers so uniformly during the war, was largely prompted by that feeling the poor ever have for those who are more unfortunate than themselves.

I traveled along the river-side without incident of note until I came to the creek which the old negro had mentioned.

On arriving there I seated myself in the sunshine near the creek. Back of me ran a cart-path or road but little used. I had not been there long when the sound of voices arrested my attention. I looked through the mass of foliage and saw two men leisurely walking along the path. One was elderly, the other young, tall, and good-looking, but with a sinister expression on his face that gave me an instinctive dislike, similar to the repulsion that people feel towards a serpent. The younger was saying:

"If I succeed I shall expect your influence, or something more, with your ward." At this the elder man said proudly:

"I won't interfere, understand that, John Ferold; an old man whose sympathies are blunted has no right to interfere in a young girl's choice of a husband."

I had noticed that near the river was a house of the liberal Southern pattern of the better people, and inferred that these gentlemen belonged there. After they had passed I went up the bank of the river to get a better outlook, and then, having seen but the one house with its cluster of negro cabins, I turned back and went down the bluff in another direction; here I again began to scan the shores for some kind of a boat with which to cross.

I had about given up the thought of finding one, and had seated myself among the foliage but a little way from the water, and had begun to remove my clothes in order to swim the stream. I had taken off my coat and belt and was glancing around for something to float them on, when I heard a splashing in the water. I looked out through the bushes, and a tiny, narrow boat in which was seated a young and graceful woman drifted into view. It was almost like a shock when she turned her head towards me and I saw the same beautiful face I had seen at the post-office.

She was hanging over the side of the little craft, splashing the water playfully with her hands. I began to admire her unconscious and graceful pose, as with her sleeves rolled back she caught at a floating lily leaf or paddled the water with her hands. I thought that I had never seen so beautiful a sight. A strand of her long braid of hair had become detached and almost swept the water, while a few tiny curls played at her ears and on her white neck. The sight brought a strange regret that I was a stranger and an enemy. Ashamed of my vagrant, traitorous thoughts, I turned to shut them from my mind.

I was about to resume my outer clothing when there was a splash and a little scream. I turned and saw the girl in the water, where she had been precipitated by the partial upsetting of her boat. I rushed to her rescue, for how, even when in danger myself, could I hesitate to respond to a call of humanity?

A few strokes brought me to her just as she was coming up from under water a second time. I had soon brought her to the shore, where she lay like a dead person, while I danced around like a frantic lunatic rather than like a sensible young

I TOOK HER UP AGAIN AND STRODE RESOLUTELY TO THE HOUSE.

man. I filled my cap with water and deluged her face, when the poor girl was suffering already from a surfeit of that element.

Then my presence of mind returned with the thought of my own peril, and remembering the formula for restoring the drowning I applied it, and soon had the satisfaction of seeing her open her eyes. I waited no longer, but putting on my coat right side out I adjusted my belt, put on my cap, and taking her in my arms hurried up the bank to the house I had seen. As I was rushing on, with her dripping form clasped in my arms, she regained consciousness and gave a little shriek as if her heart was in the cry. Then grasping my neck with one small, beautiful hand, she said imperiously, "Put me down, sir."

I obeyed, for I was piqued and cool enough then. "You fell into the river; excuse me if I couldn't see you drown. I must help you to the house."

As if to emphasize this view of the situation, she once more fainted. I took her up again and strode resolutely, and I confess somewhat angrily, to the house.

She had meanwhile become conscious, and without more ado allowed me to carry her up on the broad veranda, where I laid her down on a couch or seat, and was confronted by the elderly gentleman I had seen earlier in the day.

"What does this mean, sir?" he said, haughtily

glancing at my uniform. "I have n't the pleasure of your acquaintance."

"The girl had fallen into the water; I did n't think an introduction was necessary to save her from drowning, sir," I said in tones as frigid as his own. "Excuse me, sir, for saying she has received a severe shock and needs immediate attention."

The old gentleman, who had evidently been almost paralyzed by the apparition of a Yankee officer before him under such circumstances, now came to his senses and began giving to the stupid servants rapid and intelligent orders.

I said "Good-day" and was about to withdraw, when the old gentleman said:

"A moment, sir; to whom am I indebted?"

"Ensign Johnstone, of the United States navy, sir," I replied stiffly.

The old gentleman extended his hand and grasped mine heartily, saying:

"Excuse me if I was somewhat shaken. I assure you no offence was intended. My name is Henderson, sir. The young lady you saved from the water is my ward, Miss Dora Henderson. I am deeply your debtor. Please step into the room with me."

I rather reluctantly complied, for though I was anxious to know if Miss Dora had recovered, I felt I must be looking out for myself or go to a rebel prison.

Miss Henderson was in an adjoining room and

was, so the old negress who had taken charge of her said, "fast recovering."

Having learned this, I turned to Mr. Henderson, saying:

"I am here, as you must understand, under conditions of some peril, and will bid you good-day."

Then I lifted my hat and was about to go, when he grasped my hand, saying:

"I see — hum — haw — yes: very handsome of you, and the circumstances don't lessen my obligations in the least," and then significantly added:

"Remember I know nothing beyond that. You are safe here if you will remain. I am under great obligations to you, I am sure."

He accompanied me to the door and I walked down through the grove.

CHAPTER XXIV.

DOWN THE RIVER.

As I walked down the avenue leading through the grove I met face to face the young gentleman whom I have already mentioned having seen with the older man. He stopped and made a quick motion to his hip pocket. I did not hesitate, but placed my hand significantly to my belt.

"Miss Henderson," I said, "has met with an accident."

Without waiting to hear more he started up the avenue as if he had been shot out of a gun. I smiled to myself to see how quickly I had turned the current of the young man's thoughts.

Ever since I had plunged into the water, and especially since I had taken the young lady in my arms, my nerves had been invigorated so that now my feet seemed scarcely to touch the ground. I had no sense of danger, and my mind was then as clear as if doing duty on shipboard.

I found the little boat from which the young lady had been precipitated, drifting in the creek; I stripped, swam out, and brought it to the shore, tipped the water from it, and viewed with much satisfaction the light and graceful proportions of the craft which I had determined, without any compunctions of conscience, to take possession of as an act of war.

After dressing and turning my coat once more, so as not to attract too much attention, I took the oars and rowed away down the creek, out into the broader river, hoping to reach our lines.

I was forty miles and more from Pamlico Sound, and how many from my ship I did not know; I was encompassed by dangers, without provisions or any means that I knew of of obtaining any. I recognized, however, that I must not hesitate on that account. I decided, also, that time was of the greatest consequence in this attempt; that while I could not do wholly without food, I could at a pinch go forty-eight hours with the little that I had on hand, and must bear hunger resolutely if need be, rather than give over my attempt to reach my ship.

While thus busy with my thoughts I was rowing with a long, steady pull, and at the same time admiring the boat as she shot through the water in answer to my strokes. In glancing her over, I saw a blue ribbon which I had no doubt belonged to the young lady; I stopped, picked it up, and wet as it was placed it in my breast pocket. As I did so I smiled, and felt myself blushing at so sentimental an act.

I rowed along near the left bank of the river, in order to keep out of sight. I was not a little elated at the manner in which, so far, I had escaped from the complications of the morning, and also at the decided brightening of my prospects. My undergarments were wet but I did not mind that, for a sailor gets accustomed to it as one of the inseparable conditions of his life on the sea. The weather was mild, and the exercise of rowing kept me warm.

Though, as a whole, I was not dissatisfied with my conduct in rescuing the young lady I found myself reviewing the occurrence, and wishing I had said this or that, and left unuttered the things I had said.

In about three hours I reached a part of the river where I saw that the enemy had attempted to construct a barricade. I also saw an opening where it looked as if the "Spitfire" had broken through this obstruction under a full head of steam. Glancing high up on the river-banks above, I saw that the enemy had a battery in position there. Just as I made this discovery, "bang" came a report from one of the guns, and a shot threw up a jet of water beyond me. I did not increase my stroke, for I knew it was hard to hit a movable target; besides, if I showed haste in trying to get away it would confirm their suspicion that I was an enemy, and lead them to pay more energetic attention to me than if they were in doubt; while if I rowed quietly it would leave them uncertain, and I should get the benefit of it. With this I rowed deliberately to the side on which the battery was planted, as if I was about to land there.

When I had got under the shelter of the shore, and out of sight, I clung close to the wooded margin and rowed with all my might, for fear of an unpleasant challenge. Circumstances favored me, and I neither saw nor heard anything more from the Confederates at that time.

I had meanwhile made such speed that I was soon a half-mile from where I had seen the battery.

It was quite late in the afternoon when I hove in sight of the schooner that had been run on shore by the enemy, and the blackened timbers of the one that they had set on fire to prevent it falling into our hands. As I saw no one, I rowed up under the stern of the grounded craft, fastened my boat, and went hand over hand up to her deck by means of her davit-ropes that hung dangling at her stern.

On reaching the deck I gave another glance in every direction without seeing an enemy, and then went down the companionway into her cabin.

She had evidently been well ransacked before my arrival, and for a time I could find nothing to eat to reward my search.

I had about given over the attempt, when I perceived in an obscure corner what I thought was a cupboard. I soon was satisfied that it was, and as it was locked, after some trouble in finding the means for doing so, I smashed in the panels.

I was delighted to find what I have no doubt was the captain's private store of food. There were some very nice ship biscuit of a superior quality, some candles, also sardines and other canned goods, as well as jams, cigars, and other goodies, such as cheese and soda crackers. I filled my pockets with food, and ate as I went around the schooner on my errand of examination.

After this I sat down at a little table and satisfied my appetite with canned preserves, and other things, which tasted so good that I could have shaken hands with the captain and complimented him on his good taste in selecting these provisions for me. A full stomach made me feel well contented with my quarters, and I decided to remain on board until dark, have a nap, and then with darkness resume my journey down the river, in hopes with the dawn of the next day to find myself with still better prospects of reaching my ship.

Having made this decision, I lay down on the transom in the cabin, dosing and thinking over the occurrences of the day. In spite of the danger that encompassed me, I had not been able to get the beautiful face of Miss Dora Henderson out of my mind. I confess I did not like the idea of a little rebel taking so much space on the walls of my fancy, and tried to shut her out. But try as I might her face obtruded itself.

I couldn't understand it, for I was not (or at

least up to that time had never been) susceptible
to the charms of woman or girl. Finally, I
explained to myself that, as I had read somewhere,
when one does a favor or renders a service to a
person he is all the more likely to have a liking for
that person, and I thought that this unusual antic
of my fancy must be owing to that.

But this revery, or train of thought, was abruptly ended by what sounded like the click of
oars. I listened, and my worst fears were confirmed by hearing voices. I cautiously sprang up
the companionway, and peering over the side of
the schooner saw a boat in which were three men
coming alongside. I at once crept forward and
went down the hatchway of the hold, for I knew
that they were less likely to visit this place than
the cabin. Here I stowed myself away out of
sight, and listened. I was afraid that when they
found my boat they would look for me.

How long I lay there I do not know, as sensations very imperfectly record time, and often make
minutes seem like hours, or the reverse.

After a long time of waiting without hearing
any more from the intruders, for so I considered
them, I ventured on deck, crept aft, looked over
the stern. My boat was gone. I now bitterly
reproached myself for my needless tarry on board,
when I might, as I said to myself, have been in
better business. It was, however, useless to get
blue over my loss. Neither did I long debate the

course I must pursue. I resolved to swim to the shore in order to recover the boat I had lost, or if possible find another.

I first went down into the cabin and lit one of the candles that were in the captain's stores, and then looked the schooner over with the vague hope that there might be a skiff in her hold; but there was none. All that I could find that in the least resembled one was a large wash-tub. I carried this to the deck, attached a cord to it, removed and placed in it my clothing and some of the provisions, and softly getting it over the side of the schooner, swam for the shore, towing the precious tub after me.

I had not, however, taken a dozen strokes, when, on looking back, I saw the schooner slowly swinging from the shore. At first I could scarcely credit my senses, but when I became satisfied that I was not deceived, I returned, climbed up her side to her deck once more, took up the tub, dressed, and then going aft put the helm of the craft hard aport, until she slowly swung around with her bows pointing down stream. An unusually high tide had worked the vessel from the mud.

Once more my hopes rose at the thought that I might be able to get both the craft and myself to the steamer. If, however, I anticipated a clear course with any special favors from fortune, I was out of my reckoning.

Over-confidence, like pride, goes before a fall, and mine was scarcely on its feet before it stumbled.

It was bright starlight; the sky was unusually clear, and I had but little difficulty in keeping my course in the channel. The schooner moved so slowly that I became impatient, and running forward hoisted the jib. This made a creaking sound that seemed the louder because of the still night; but I did not desist on that account. I cleated the sheet, for the wind was fair, and hurrying aft once more took the tiller to bring her on her course (for she had fallen away from it), when from the river banks there was a flash followed by the roar of the gun. A shot came crashing through the schooner, then came a hail from the shore:

"What craft is that?"

"Schooner 'Blanche,'" I replied, "going to try and get out by the Yankee gunboats; and you've hurt the 'Blanche' with your gun."

For a short time there was no reply from the shore; then another voice called out:

"'T won't do; there's no such schooner on the river. Come ashore!"

"Ay, ay, sir," I responded, and then putting the helm a-starboard to give the appearance of obedience, I began to take off my clothing once more, put it in the tub, which I lowered over the side, and then followed it into the water.

The river was not wide, and I was able to reach

the shore opposite to the battery very quickly. Here, after resuming my clothing, and tucking in my pockets all the provisions they would hold, I started up the river bank, chuckling in my sleeves at the Yankee trick I had played on my enemies.

I had not gone far when I heard the guns of the battery banging away at the schooner once more. I laughed at this, but I laughed too soon, for dead ahead of me there came a sharp challenge and the click of cocking a musket. "Halt!" came the order dangerously near me.

I quickly recognized that it was of no use to resist, as the enemy was on both starboard and port sides.

"We uns are watchin' fr ye Yank!" said a voice.

I surrendered with as much grace as was possible, and with a guard before and behind me was marched to a house near by, where, in a large room lighted only by a pitch-pine fire, sat at a table two Confederate officers. One of these was a young and pleasant-looking person, dressed in the uniform of a lieutenant-colonel, and the other was a tall and humorous-looking individual, who was acting as adjutant to the first-named, who was in command of the forces stationed there.

"We uns have got a Yankee spy, kenrel," said the sergeant who accompanied me. The colonel looked at me from head to foot as I said, somewhat angrily:

THE RIVER WAS NOT WIDE, AND I WAS ABLE TO REACH THE SHORE OPPOSITE TO THE BATTERY.

"I am Ensign Johnstone, of the United States navy, sir, and I object to this man's insulting epithet."

"Where is your uniform, sir?" said the colonel sharply, and pointing to my coat, which was still wrong side out.

I unbuckled my belt and passed him my arms and then took off my coat and put it on right side out, as a reply to his question.

The colonel nodded pleasantly, and said, "Take a seat, sir, and explain why you are here in disguise."

I thanked him, took the proffered seat, and replied:

"I am one of the party that made an attack on Secessionville. I got left behind, and not being able to reach the steamer in season she sailed without me, and I have been trying my best to get out of your country ever since."

"Sort o' felt you wa'n't appreciated here 'mong the rebs, I suppose?" said the adjutant.

"On the contrary, sir," I replied, in the same tone, "I felt that they appreciated me too well, after our visit."

The colonel smiled with easy confidence as he said:

"We won't discuss the matter here — this is not a trial, and we will not condemn you; that is for others to do, if it is to be done." Then he said pleasantly, "It was a very gallant and daring adventure, that raid of your gunboat up the river. I would have done as much for the Yanks if I could have the pleasure of getting into their country; but you must n't expect that our folks are going to be pleased at your visit, or feel surprise if they make you suffer some inconveniences on account of it."

Shortly after this some food was brought in that smelled very appetizing.

"Will you join us at supper, sir?" said the colonel politely.

"Thanks," I said: "you have evidently seen service, and appreciate that a man may be a prisoner and yet a gentleman."

"Yes, I was made a prisoner at Malvern Hill, got a shot in the left wing," he said, lifting that arm, which I now for the first time noticed hung rather limp by his side. "I had no cause for complaint while I was with the Yanks. It's about all the vacation I've had since this war began;" and the young colonel smiled.

"Our people," said the adjutant, "have been a good deal stirred up by the visit of your steamer, and between being riled and surprised, they are likely to be powerful unceremonious in the kind of reception they give you."

"Well," I said, "I hardly expect they will shower me with rose-water."

"No, I reckon not," said the colonel; these bomb-proofs are heavy dogs, I reckon, when they have caught a Yank."

After I had been to supper I was sent to the guard-room, which was a shed attached to the building. Here I lay down and slept more soundly than most people do in their beds.

In the morning the courteous colonel invited me to breakfast, allowed me the use of soap and water, and otherwise treated me with as much courtesy as if I had been his friend instead of an enemy.

"I have orders to send you to Secessionville," he said after breakfast. "I suppose you will be on exhibition there for a while."

I thanked the colonel for his courtesy, and then, under guard, was marched away to the town that had so lately been the recipient of so many attentions from the officers and men of the "Spitfire" that I thought it not unlikely they would consider it a matter of honor to return them all on my unworthy self.

I was so closely guarded during this march that there was not the slightest chance for me to get away. The tramp was a long one, and, unaccustomed as I was to such exercise, I was very tired when we halted for the night some ten miles from the town.

The next morning, after an uneventful night, we resumed our march, and reached Secessionville a little after noon, where, like an ordinary criminal, I was consigned to the common jail.

CHAPTER XXV.

TRIED AND CONDEMNED.

I HAD begun to form a very high estimate of the Southern people. The considerate courtesy of the young colonel and the general good treatment by the soldiers who formed my guard led me to believe that I should receive all the consideration allowed by military rules. I had not the slightest idea, notwithstanding the hints that had been thrown out by the young officer, that I should be regarded otherwise than as a prisoner of war. I did not then know that the most vindictive enemy in war is the non-combatant; that those who are fighting with hearty good-will lose all their vindictiveness when their enemies are helpless in their hands; that those who have not had hard fighting are apt to wreak on defenceless prisoners of war, whom Providence has thrown into their hands, all the accumulated hatred of their hearts, which is all the more bitter because they are too cowardly to meet their enemy in battle, where, strange as it may appear, men often gain a hearty respect for one another.

The moment I came in contact with those who had not been fighting I began to receive rough and disrespectful treatment. The Home Guard that had taken charge of me at the town heaped on me insulting epithets, the mildest of which was " Yankee, thief, and abolitionist."

At the jail a young officer of the Home Guard, in a sort of " stand and deliver " style, relieved me of knife, handkerchief, and also of my watch (a gift from my father), and all of my money he could find on my person, though he did not get all, for I had concealed in my shoes two five-dollar greenbacks; and as he did so, with every article taken, he reiterated the remark, apparently for my consolation, " Contraband of war, sar!"

After this ceremony, for the young fellow, with his ritualistic reiteration, evidently intended to make it such, I was put into a closet-like, narrow room, which had not a single window in it, nor apparently any other means of ventilation. The light was completely excluded from it, so that, though it was still day when I was put there, I could not for a time distinguish its size or contents. It had an ill smell as if untidy and filthy persons had been confined there previous to my incarceration.

As I sat in one corner of this pen I heard the sound of footsteps, the door opened, and a flood of light poured from a window in the corridor; and then for the first time in my life I realized how good and beautiful daylight was.

" Whar' ar' y', y' durned Yankee spy?" said the

person; and then there appeared a face over his shoulder, which I at once recognized as that of the young man whom I had heard Mr. Henderson call John Ferold.

"Whew!" he ejaculated; "it smells of the durned Yank. Get a lantern."

"Wouldn't it be well, John Ferold," I said, "to take me out into light and air?"

I heard an exclamation of surprise as the door was slammed, and I thought they both had gone; but they soon came back with a lantern. This was held up while Ferold took a survey of me.

"Yes, it's the same Yankee spy I saw down to Henderson's," he said. "You see he is a spy, else how did he know my name?"

"I should like a decent room," I said. "I should be just as secure, Mr. Ferold, in clean quarters as in this pen, where you have kept negro prisoners, evidently."

"See," he said to the other, "he knows all about this country."

That night I reviewed the circumstances under which I had been captured in the enemy's country, but could see no reason why any such charge as that of being a spy should be brought against me. I at least had been guilty of no conduct except such as I was ready to repeat if I ever got the chance.

It was not until the next morning that any food was given me, and that was a poor quality of cornbread, with water. Yet poor as it was I could have eaten more if I had had it, my long fast had inspired such an appetite; for in addition to a long fast I had both a boy's and a sailor's appetite!

The man who had charge of me was called "Jake," and I do not know that he had any other name; to my surprise he neither abused nor insulted me. He let me severely alone, simply doing what he had to do and saying what he had to say, being scant of ceremony in either act or manner.

On the third day of my incarceration I was taken from the jail and under guard was marched out into daylight. I knew not what it was for, but I was glad once again to breathe clean air and see the light of the sun. I was not, however, prepared for the unusual attention I received, and the excitement that my appearance caused on the streets of the little town.

A large, noisy, and excited crowd had gathered there, reminding me of a gathering on the streets of my native Wichnor to see a circus come to town, only there was none of the good-nature of such a gathering.

Above the rattle of a drum and the shrill shrieking of a fife I could hear muttered curses and exclamations of rage and hatred. Though I marched with stolid demeanor and a firm manner, with my face fairly to the front, I caught glimpses of the angry gestures of men, women, and even children. The crowd had evidently been drawn there by rumors (so I inferred from the remarks I heard) of the capture of one of the Yankee vandals that had stolen the mail and the postmaster's servants, and who had been spying around the town ever since.

"Dangerous-looking customer," said one.

"—— abolition thief," added another.

"Cum' down hyar to steal our niggers and got tooken hisself," said another voice.

"A sneaking Yankee!" ejaculated another; "wonder how he'll like we uns after he's had what he'll git, I reckon."

"He won't stay long 'nough," facetiously said another, "I reckon, to express an opinion after he gits it."

"No," said a citizen with a hoarse voice and a justice's stomach, "there'll be no law's delay; a drumhead court-martial and rope."

This remark gave me for the first time the thought that, in their rage and chagrin at our daring attack on their town, they might execute me if they could find any kind of pretext for it.

The current of my thoughts was speedily turned when, seated in a carriage, I saw Miss Dora Henderson and her guardian. They looked earnestly toward me with the evident attempt to identify me with the Yankee officer they had met under different circumstances, and then Miss Dora bowed to me and smiled, as if to a friendly acquaintance.

I lifted my hat in response, and at the same instant was prodded by one of the guard with his bayonet. The sharp instrument hurt me, but I felt willing to receive its duplicate for another nod and smile of recognition. I was, however, hurried on, and saw no more of her or her guardian. The sunshine seemed to pass, and clouds of sullen hate and rage supplant it; and at the same time there came to my heart and mind a conflict of emotion like an angry storm beating there. Yet there was comfort in the thought that I had friends among my enemies. But the undercurrent of my reflections was:

"Had I lived through so many dangers for this? Was I in my father's home to be treated with this indignity, without sympathy and without any one to defend me?"

Then I found myself passing through a wide doorway, and soon saw that I was at the court-house.

I was conducted to a seat, and a man with a musket stationed on each side of me.

"What have they brought me here for?" I said to one of these men.

"T' be tried, I reckon."

"What for?"

No response was given to this inquiry.

The members of the court began to take their seats; eager, as it seemed, to dispose of me with public applause and popular approval. I thought, as I looked in their faces, that in them was expressed the least of human sympathy I had ever seen.

The judge advocate, who (as I afterwards learned) had been a lawyer of a small pettifogging practice, and also a local politician, conducted the trial as if he were a prosecuting attorney in a criminal case, and then I began to understand my danger.

"What is your name and business?" he inquired.

"Hezekiah Johnstone, sir; I am an ensign in the United States navy, and was one of the crew of the 'Spitfire' that lately paid you a visit."

There was a murmur of inarticulate voices in the court, which I interpreted as that of astonishment that I should dare to make such an admission, and then the red-faced judge advocate glowered at me as he exclaimed fiercely:

"What did yo' cum hyar fo', and what was y'r hyar fo' in disguise?"

"I was here at the command of my superior officer, to assist in destroying public stores; to seize the mails or any other public property or munitions of war. I submit that our acts were those of honorable warfare. There has been an insinuation thrown out that I was acting as a spy. I was accidentally left behind, and have done my best to elude the vigilance of your people and escape; if that is spying, then I am a spy. If I am treated otherwise than as an honorable prisoner of war. I warn you that my shipmates will avenge such acts."

The judge advocate had been growing red in his face, and now ejaculated with great temper:

"We'll show y' what we'll do, sar! Sit down!"

I did so, feeling that no mercy would be shown to me by that court.

After that witnesses were called. One of these testified that he had, as he said, seen me steal the mail at the post-office; that he knew me to be the same person who had stolen the postmaster's servants, and who had insulted the wife of that official.

The young colonel who captured me gave testimony that when I was brought to him my coat was on wrong side out, but also added that he would not call this a disguise. Then the soldiers who had captured me gave their testimony in reference to the facts which the reader already knows.

Thus far the incident of the rescue of Miss Henderson had not been alluded to, and I was glad it had not been, as I felt assured that the so-called court had adjudged me guilty before taking up my case; that it was convened to condemn, and not to acquit.

When I thought from appearances that the evidence was all in, there came from the rear of the court-room a note to the judge advocate.

"Ah!" he ejaculated with satisfaction; "more evidence. Another witness, gentlemen; one of our most respected citizens. Honorable Mr. Henderson will take the stand."

There was a bustle as the old gentleman (who has already been introduced to the reader) came slowly forward, courteously bowing right and left to his neighbors; as he reached me he bowed and extended his hand, and in the most courteous manner said to the judge:

"Excuse me, but I am under peculiar obligations to this young gentleman. He rescued my ward from a most perilous position, and she is very grateful, I assure you, and so am I. There are other reasons."

"We are informed by Lieutenant Ferold that he stole a boat belonging to you," interrupted the judge, with heightened color.

"Ah, yes; the boat! I have not complained of its loss, sar; why should any one else?"

The judge advocate had by this time lost his temper, and the other members of the court frowned and moved nervously in their seats, and one of them, with a long, sharp face, said:

"I protest that this is not a court of compliments, but a court of war to try a Yankee spy for his life."

"I beg your pardon, gentlemen," said Mr. Henderson, looking at the speaker with cool contempt. "In all deference to the person who has just spoken, and to the court, I say all places admit of the exchange of courtesies between gentlemen, and

I have not to learn the correct manners due to polite society and among gentlemen — if that person has."

After testifying to the occurrences that have been elsewhere narrated, he was asked by the judge:

"Do you mean to say that you loaned your boat to a Yankee who was trying to escape?"

Mr. Henderson stared at the speaker, with cool contempt expressed in his manner, and replied in his cool, level, unexcited voice:

"I mean that I have no charge against this man for taking the boat; and I do not know that any one has a right to say he stole it."

"Thanks!" I ejaculated, for his generous words had saved my self-respect.

After giving his testimony the old gentleman sat down, twirled his eye-glasses in his fingers, and looked at the court with the assurance of one who was accustomed to exact respect from all.

Then the court was cleared and its members put their heads together in consultation.

The judge cleared his throat and said:

"This court finds you guilty of all the specifications and charges. It has been proven that you stole our negroes, insulted our women and stole our mail, and committed other depredations unknown to the license of war. You were finally found in disguise within our lines, posted in the names and private affairs of our people. You have been found guilty of trying to incite servile insurrection and of being a spy."

Mr. Henderson had meanwhile left the court without even looking at me.

I was terribly frightened and shaken by this verdict, though I tried not to give those present the satisfaction of seeing it. The members once more consulted together, after which I was marched out of the room and down the street, keeping step in as firm and unflinching a manner as possible.

There was a tumult of voices, and an answering tumult in my own heart and brain.

If there was one feeling deeper than that of indignation, it was the determination that my enemies should not see any fear or weakness in my manner, however much I might feel, and that if I must die I would die as became an officer in the service of his country.

In a moment more I was inside of the jail, with feelings which I shall not attempt to describe.

CHAPTER XXVI.

ENEMIES, YET FRIENDS.

WHEN alone once more in my prison quarters, all the firmness and stoicism with which I had outwardly encrusted myself dissolved before the thought of my impending doom. I had no friends on whom I could call for help in my extreme need, and I had little hope that anything could be done for me if I had had such friends. I had seen enough of war to know that there was little mercy in it. I understood the angry resentment aroused by depredations committed during the raid. I also understood that it was not so much what I had done as it was to prevent similar incursions into their country, and what they were pleased to call Yankee vandalism, — that I was simply the scapegoat; a sort of target on which to score their sense of outrage.

I did not sleep much during the long night that followed, but went over again and again, in a nervous and sinking spirit, the events of the few preceding days, and those of the court which had so unjustly accused and condemned me. I was young and loved life, and did not then appreciate the fact that life is at best but short. Let me not conceal the fact that my mind was so beclouded with gloom that I was indignant, almost to hatred, at my dear father for identifying himself with such a cause, and for being one of such a people.

I had been taught to pray by both my father and mother, but during the months I had been at sea among rough sailors I had neglected to ask God for His protection and care. Up to this time since my capture I had been more proud than fearless; for I was afraid of being thought cowardly.

As the hours of the night dragged on I thought of all this, as I rolled and twisted in nervous agony on my poor bed. But now having given up all hope of human succor, I prayed, as I had never prayed before, for God's help and sustaining power, that I might be able to bear my burdens like a Christian, a sailor, and a man.

After long travail, and when broken in spirit, I had surrendered myself to Him; when I asked no longer for earthly, but for spiritual deliverance, there came to me such an illumination of soul and softening of my pride and resentment, even towards my enemies, that I prayed that they might be forgiven. Then there fell on me such a reaction of peace and joy as I had never before experienced. The burden of agony and gloom that had rested on my mind rolled from me as if it were something material. The terrors of death no longer oppressed me, and I shortly fell into a long and dreamless sleep.

When at last I awoke I was cheerful, and looked without fear at the future.

In a few moments after waking, Jake came in and looked at me curiously as I smilingly greeted him, saying: "Youngster, y' war sleeping powerful this mornin' when I fust come in yere; y' looked so comfortable an' kin o' peaceful that I would n't wake y'! It seemed to me that y' did n't realize."

"Thank you, Jake," I said. "I realize that I have been condemned as a spy, and that I cannot expect any mercy. But I am innocent; and if I die it is for my country. I have forgiven my enemies."

"I reckon they won't forgive *you* much, Yank. But say, Squar Henderson has bin hyar this morning, t' know 'f thar was anythin' he c'd do, an' then I told him yo' war in this nigger hole an' he jist looked mad, an' I 've got orders t' move yo' to a better place. I think he must hev tore 'round some. Come, git out o' hyar!"

The room to which I was conducted was a square, large room with two grated windows facing the west. It had a comfortable bed in one corner, two chairs, and a table. I did not care so much for the latter as for the air and light. Jake astonished me further by bringing me a breakfast of ham, eggs, and coffee.

"The squar wants y' to be well fed, y' see," said Jake; "told me t' git y' what y' needed an' he 'd settle th' bill."

"But," I said, "I can't accept such favors; hereafter bring me the prison fare; that's better than to be in debt. Here's a greenback for the breakfast," for I had concealed this money before being searched, "and if you will get me some pens, ink, paper, and envelopes you can take pay for it out of the V."

When the writing materials came I first wrote a letter of grateful thanks to Mr. Henderson. I said that while I could not accept pecuniary help I should feel under great obligations to him if he would get some letters to my friends, especially those addressed to my father and mother.

I then wrote letters to them and Phil, and to my captain; all of which Jake said he would give to Mr. Henderson. All these I left open, as is the custom in an enemy's country when sending letters under flag of truce; while the one to father was left unsealed that it might not compromise him, and because I had nothing to conceal.

I was informed that I was to be executed the following week, and I thought this delay in execution of the sentence was owing to the interposition of Mr. Henderson, as it could not possibly be out of any regard these people had for me.

During the following days my heart was lighter than it had been, though I yet had seasons of depression and gloom. During these days my time was spent reading from a little Testament which was a gift from father. In it he had marked passages, and in some places had made marginal comments; they were so like my father's utterances that at times it seemed that I could almost feel his presence when I read them, and they were a great comfort to me.

At last Jake informed me that the Richmond authorities had approved of the findings of the court-martial, and that a day had been set for my execution. It was to take place on the following Saturday.

It was a relief to know the worst. Suspense is harder to bear than the worst certainty. Knowing the worst, I began preparing myself for the great change. I prayed for strength to bear all the agony of my ignominious death.

On the morning of that dread day I had got from my knees and was sitting at my table with the little Testament in my hand, thinking of my home, when I heard (or did I but seem to hear?) my father's voice speaking as if to an inner sense, saying: "My dear son, your father loves you — do not doubt it! I am coming."

I started up and looked around my room, expecting to see him. There was no one there but myself, and all was silent. My imagination had played me a trick.

I sat awhile thinking it over, when a dread sound that was no trick of imagination came to my ear: it was the tramp of armed men who came to conduct me to the place of my death.

They halted before my prison door. I heard the command "Halt!" then the jangle of Jake's keys. I rose from the table, and as the door opened said, with a strange calmness, "Come in. I am ready!"

. . . .

As I marched, keeping step with my guard, it was without any outward signs of fear or nervousness, for I was determined that they should see how bravely a Union sailor could die for his country.

It was as beautiful a morning as ever dawned on this lovely Southern land. I looked at the faces I passed, and noted the hate and satisfaction pictured there. In my heart there was a deep quiet or stoicism. It was my last day under God's sunshine (as I then firmly believed), and yet I could not realize it. The measured *tramp, tramp,* of the cadenced step of my guard blended with the roar of voices and the clamor of hateful exclamations as I neared the dreaded structure erected for my execution.

We were halted, and I looked up at it with unquivering nerve. I said to myself, "It is part of my fight in this war to show these enemies of my country that there are men who can die for it bravely."

My hands were tied, and as I stood, with set, resolute face and firm nerves, there came to my ear a sound like the clamor of many voices rolling nearer, and nearer, and nearer. I had commended my soul to His mercy, and said "Now," as a signal of my readiness, when there burst through the crowd around the gallows a man on horseback, covered with flecks of foam and gray with road dust; he reined up, said something I did not understand, and handed a paper to the officer of my guard.

Then my hands were unbound, the order was given to the guard, — "Shoulder arms, forward, march!"—and once more I was conducted to the street, with the word "Reprieved! Reprieved!" ringing out on every side.

Then, and not until then, curious as it may seem, my limbs trembled, and my heart throbbed almost to choking, and I should have fallen to the ground had I not been mercifully held up by my guards.

Once more I was in the jail, and then learned from Jake the circumstances of my reprieve.

"Squar Henderson has been t' Richmond 'bout your business," said Jake, "and has got it put off, I reckon. But I say, it war a right close shave, youngster, but th' all say y' showed a powerful lot of grit if y' are a Yank, an' it 's talked a right lot, 'roun' yere, that y' 've got Southern blood in ye."

I reflected that while there were grounds for hope, as there were evidently some strong influences at work in my behalf, still there was hardly a hope that the verdict of the court-martial would be set aside for a Yankee "nigger-stealer," for it seemed to me that this crime was there considered the greatest a man could commit.

I think the days that followed my reprieve were harder to bear than those that preceded the time set for my execution.

Matters of life and death in the Confederacy moved quickly in those times. I now hoped to hear from my father, if not from my mother and Phil, before the time for my execution arrived.

I was quite nervous for one of my stolid temperament, and I fear that I bored Jake very much about so small a matter as my fate. During this time I wrote out a circumstantial account of our raid into Secessionville, especially contradicting the charges that I was acting as a spy, also that I had in any way insulted the wife of the postmaster. This account I intended for my father.

While intently absorbed in its composition late one afternoon, I had paused in the occupation and laid my head on my arm, when once more I heard my father's voice saying, "Good news, my brave boy! Good news!"

The voice was so distinct and so unmistakably that of my father that, startled, I looked up, expecting to see him standing before me. But there was no one there. It was another delusion. When Jake came in I inquired if any one had been near my room and he answered in the negative, and further said that I was the only prisoner in the building, the others having been given their liberty on condition that they would enlist in the Southern army.

I tell this incident as it occurred, and do not attempt to explain it.

One afternoon not long afterwards I broke the seal of a letter in a handwriting which I knew to be my father's. It was an affectionate letter in which occurred the very words I had heard. My father afterwards told me that he had uttered this sentence aloud as he wrote it. The letter itself was so like him, so unconstrained, that it almost seemed to bring me face to face with him. In it he explained that Mr. Henderson, having ascertained by my letter to him that he was in Richmond, had been there to see him and get a suspension of the sentence.

On the afternoon following the reception of this letter I was reading once more from my Testament. It was the only book I had to read, and I had found therein so much comfort that I had learned to love its promises, and understand them better than ever before. I was absorbed in reflection on what I had read, and I was so oblivious to my surroundings that it was as if I were in some other world; then I heard once more, distinctly uttered by my father's voice, "My dear, dear son!" Fearing to break the spell I did not move, when strong arms encircled me, and I found it was no delusion now, but that my own dear father was with me in reality; brown, thin, and careworn, with stern lines deeply written on his face, but still his own dear self, thrilling me with his presence and his earnest love. God bless him now and forever, in the great hereafter in which he awaits me! After all these years I seem to see his tender look of love, a love that knew no separation of time, space, or country.

The past was all explained. He told me that he had been detained at his home, when he had expected to join us at the North, by the sickness of his father; that he had written letters at that time which he had learned only of late had been intercepted by jealous partisans of the Post-office Department.

That very afternoon I was given my liberty by signing a parole of honor, and this was written by the very official who had acted as judge advocate in the court that had condemned me to death. He was very wordy and obsequious to my father.

As we went out father said: "It is such bomb-proofs as that man, who think to distinguish themselves without danger, that bring reproach to the brave men of our cause."

There were two horses at the door, and Andrew himself gave me a broad smile of greeting as I passed out under the blue dome bright with God's own sunshine.

"We missed Andy at Wichnor," I said, "but we knew he would come to you if he could."

"Yes," said father. "Andy is no fair-weather friend; he goes where I go."

We rode down the street which I had so lately trod as a condemned man, and riding along the river road halted at the very veranda upon which I had carried the dripping form of Miss Henderson.

"Our home is some twenty miles away," said father, "and these friends of mine have invited us to be their guests."

I was about to explain that I had been there under different circumstances, but father smiled and said, "I have been told all about it, Hez, and you will want to pay your respects to these good people, I know."

I was ushered into the house, was introduced formally to Mr. and Miss Henderson, and, singular to relate, I was less self-possessed during this interview than I was on my first visit there.

"I am sorry," said Mr. Henderson, "that you have suffered so much at the hands of our people."

"That's the nature of war," I responded, "and possibly your people may think they have suffered somewhat at my hands; but there is no mistake, I owe you a debt of gratitude that I cannot easily pay, and that I cannot express in words."

I was presented to Miss Dora Henderson by my father; she was very kind in her manner towards me.

"I can understand your gallant conduct, now that I know who your father is," she said, looking up into my face; "you have Southern blood in your veins, and maw gracious! how can a Southern gentleman help being brave, especially when his father is one of the bravest in our country?"

"Yes," said father in bantering tones, "and my gallantry was so misunderstood at one time that the gossips would have it that I was about to marry Miss Dora here;" and then more seriously in a remark to Miss Henderson added: "There is not much difference at heart between Southern and Northern men; they are both brave, but in a different way: the Northern gentleman is less excitable and sentimental, but is more enduring, and my son, I believe, has the good characteristics of both."

"Oh," exclaimed Miss Dora impetuously, "there are none so brave as our dear Southern heroes!" and she gave father such an admiring look that I felt small and chagrined when she continued: "What a kind man our president is! Who but he would have liberated a Yankee incendiary like your son?"

"Miss Dora is grateful for your gallant conduct," interrupted Mr. Henderson, "if she is just a little provoking."

"Maw gracious!" exclaimed the young lady. "Why don't you say we stood by him (isn't that sailor talk?), and would stay by him again if they hanged us, like real Southern hearts?" and there was a mist in her eyes as she added, "And I *was* grateful to you, and would have shown it in the same way, even if you'd been a real Yankee."

"I beg pardon for saying," I replied, "that I am

a staunch Union man, just as father is a staunch believer in the cause of the South; and I believe we respect each other's honest convictions, though we do not understand why others can see questions from a different standpoint than ourselves."

"It is unprofitable to discuss these differences between friends — I couldn't even respect my dear boy if I knew he was fighting against his convictions, any more than I could forgive myself. The Northern and Southern men have honest differences, and are fighting it out like men. I believe too, for one, it is more healthy to let out bad blood than to stir it up."

"What was it about Jeff Davis?" I said, to turn the conversation in a new channel.

"Mr. Davis," said father, with emphasis on the Mister, "God bless him! granted me an interview, and I presented a letter from my general commending me to him. They may say what they have a mind to, but Mr. Davis has a warm heart under that crust of ice; for, when I told him my story, a tear ran down his nose as naturally as if the ice had melted — and when he understood he couldn't do enough for me; said he'd arrange to have you especially paroled or exchanged, and gave me this order to which you are indebted for your present liberty. Northern people misunderstand him: he is a Southern gentleman, and has all their faults and virtues. I shall carry this order to my grave on my breast."

I had some charming talks with Miss Dora, and found her very lovely in her manner, as well as in her person, and that in a way much different from our Northern girls. There was such a frank sweetness, blended with a hectoring, teasing manner, that it made her provokingly charming.

While I could but reprove her secession sentiments, we did not let that spoil our friendliness.

The next day father and I rode to the Johnstone estate, and he showed me many places I had heard him speak of, and among them the place where he and his brother had first met Andy in the swamp.

"I should like to see Uncle Robert," I said; to which father replied, "Perhaps you will if he is alive; there are strange encounters in this world, and it is so narrow that your tracks may cross."

A few days after this I went to Richmond with father, and, after a day's waiting, I took leave of him at Aiken's Landing, below that city, where I embarked on a flag-of-truce boat, and was glad once more to be under the protecting shelter of the flag that I loved all the more because I had suffered for it among enemies and friends.

CHAPTER XXVII.

AT PLYMOUTH.

On arriving within our lines I was sent to the parole camp at Annapolis, where I at once telegraphed to mother of my arrival.

A paroled prisoner is still a prisoner held in trust for the enemy until declared exchanged with the consent of both parties. In the parole camp there was neither occupation nor excitement to keep me from the dreary task of self-analysis and repining. I was therefore but little less rejoiced at my liberation therefrom than I had been to get into the Union lines.

I was declared exchanged on the twentieth of August, but it was December before I reported to the "Spitfire" for duty. Here I was heartily congratulated on my escape from death and my arrival within our lines. "You had a close call," said my young commander, when at his request I had narrated to him my experiences in the enemy's country.

"Yes, sir," I replied, "there was a time when I did not expect to be here again."

"You could n't expect they would be over-pleased at the visit we paid them, and as they could n't get hold of all of us, they made it exciting for you. I learned, however, that you were tried for a spy, and for inciting servile insurrection, and I was preparing to make another raid up the river. If they had hanged you I'd have hanged some of their prominent citizens; I sent a letter to them under flag of truce, to that effect."

"Thanks, lieutenant," I said, "but I can't see that hanging a reb would have mended my neck."

"You are hard to please," said the lieutenant, with a lift to his eyebrows. "It would be a satisfaction to me, living or dead, to get even with an enemy."

Some of my shipmates even expressed a wish that they had been in my place, and I obligingly said that I would willingly have exchanged places with them. When, however, I remembered the face of Miss Dora, I doubted if I had been entirely candid with them.

Phil was overjoyed to see me safe once more, and I believe the dear fellow had really grown thin in his worry over my detention by the enemy. I was almost startled by a resemblance, as I fancied, or an expression in his face, that was like my father. When I said as much to Phil, he replied: "Oh, nonsense, Hez! By and by you'll be wanting to claim relationship with the aristocratic Gurleys."

"No," I said, laughing, "I am not anxious, and perhaps it is a trick of my imagination instead of any real resemblance, and I could n't think more of you, Phil, if you were a dozen times my brother."

"See here," said Phil; "it's getting to be fashionable to have Southern relatives, and I'll have to scrape acquaintance with the rebs and see if they ever hanged any of the Gurleys, or have had any other connections (by rope or otherwise) with our tribe."

"I wouldn't joke about such connections by rope, Phil; it may turn out that you'll get something more than a running acquaintance with the rebs. I found a pleasant side to them, but it wasn't while I was threatened with an intimate acquaintance with their methods of dealing with an enemy — ugh!"

And the remembrance of the time I stood under a gallows sent an unpleasant shiver down my back.

Lieutenant Bell had been given leave of absence to visit New York on business of a confidential character connected with the navy; and I did not see him again until several months later, when I saw him under dramatic conditions, an account of which will be narrated in its proper place.

In January Phil and I were ordered to report to Lieutenant-commander Flusher for duty, and were much excited at the prospect of a change, as sailors usually are at anything that is likely to break the monotony of routine on shipboard.

The steamer to which we were transferred was, to our chagrin, the "Southfield," then lying opposite the town of Plymouth, about ten miles up the Roanoke River. The "Southfield" was commanded by a volunteer lieutenant, and it caused something of a fall to my expectations to discover that she was neither more nor less than an old ferry-boat fitted up with pivot guns and the armament of a gunboat. Another gunboat, the "Miami," side-wheel steamer, was anchored alongside the "Southfield" in the river, with the town on one side and an almost impenetrable swamp on the other. Both vessels were under the command of Commander Flusher, as fine and as brave an officer as there was in the service. He was afterwards killed in an attack of the enemy on the town, in the defence of which we participated.

This little Southern town was at that time in an almost ruined condition. The enemy and our own troops had made attempts to burn it, and there remained only two or three brick buildings used as stores, a church, a few residences and frame buildings used for Union hospitals, commissary depots, and officers' quarters. Besides these there was a medley of low huts made of logs and chinked with mud; or with roofs and sides made of split staves. These buildings were used as quarters for the "raft" of fugitive negroes that came down the river in search of freedom from work; what they got was — short rations and hard times!

The town was garrisoned by Wessell's brigade of about eighteen hundred men, whose tents whitened and enlivened the town from up the river at Warren Neck, or Fort Grey, to its outskirts on the south, where were two redoubts, and to the east beyond Fort Williams at the centre of the town. These forts were connected by earth-works, with the exception of Fort Grey, which was accessible only by a log foot-bridge through a swamp, or by boat on the river.

Among the troops were one Connecticut regiment and two companies of native North Carolinians, also artillery from Massachusetts, and infantry from several other States.

We did not get much liberty on shore, as that privilege was almost exclusively claimed by our superiors.

The Connecticut regiment, we had ascertained, was the one in which our friend Jim Bisbee was a corporal. We had asked for a day on shore, as we were desirous of seeing him and several other Wichmor men belonging to the —th.

It was some time, however, before Phil and I got a day for this purpose. We found Jim in a little stockaded "A" tent all alone in his glory, his tent-mates being on guard or engaged in other duties.

"Wal," said Jim, shaking hands at arms' length in order the better to admire our bright uniforms, "wal, this is somethin' t' brag abaout; 't ain't every day y' see a man that's 'scaped from th' halter, as y' might say. Y' see, I read all abaout

it in th' newspapers, an' I ruther think y' 've got
enough t' tell on t' last y' a lifetime."

Jim was very persistent in having me tell my
experience, and was seemingly hungry for all the
details, especially where, as he termed it, "the
close shave of near onto being hung come in."

"Wal," said Jim, after interspersing my story
with many exclamations, "y'r father I always said
was a good man; if they 'd all ben like him down
thar there would n't ben no war, and I can understand why a Southern man can't find it in his gizzard
t' fight agin his State. But y'r father 's that kind o'
man that if he thinks a thing 's right from his stand-
pint he can see it from another man's. Now, there 's
your granther; he never could understand how
any one could see things diff'ent from what he
did. He bought some tin stuff from me, an' one
of the pans leaked like a riddle. Wal, I had the
all-firedest time y' ever did see tryin' t' make him
see 't wa'n't my fault, but I could n't; he wanted a
new milk-pan; snum if he did n't! I told him tin
pans ware n't infallible more 'n caows. He said I
was a cheat, dummed if he did n't! an' him an' me
b'longed t' the same church, an' in good stan'in',
tu, I swow!"

"But what did cows have to do with it, Jim?"
asked Phil.

"Why," said Jim, with a grin, "y' see one time
th' squire sold a caow t' my ole man, an' that ole
caow up an' died 'fore th' next milkin'; I vaow if

she did n't! Father he goes t' th' squire, an' says he, 'I want my money back, squire; th' caow is dead.'

"'Wal,' said th' squire, 'cows ain't infallible,' an' that's all th' satisfaction father could git; plague if it wa'n't!'"

Phil and I had a good laugh, and Jim continued: "Y'r granther would n't own up any way 'f lookin' at a thing was right but his own. Say, did y' ever hearn tell 'baout his buying eggs o' that there Jot Williams, time I was referee? Did n't? Wal, I 'll tell y'," said Jim, picking his teeth with a long straw as he turned his face reflectively downward. "Jot Williams druv daown to Wichnor with a lot 'f eggs f'r sale — he lived on th' Jinks place aout there. Y'r granther kep' a store in them days daown on Central wharf, and Jot was one of his customers, an' a good one tu, I guess. Wal, Jot he come in one day with a lot o' eggs, an' walked int' y'r granther's store, an' sez he, 'I 'd like t' sell y' seventeen dozen o' fresh eggs, square.'

"'I don't want no eggs,' said y'r granther cross 's a settin' hin, 'an' won't hev 'em at any price, nuther.'

"Jot Williams jes' sot down an' cleared his throat in a kind of a delib'rate way, an' thumpin' th' floor with th' butt eend 'f his whip said, 'Yis, y' du want these eggs, tu, Mr. Perkins, an' ef y' don't buy 'em I won't never come intu y'r store agin, an' y' know I buy a lot o' goods, tu.' Yer granther pulled in his horns an' said, 'Jot, I don't want t' lose a good customer an' fren', an' I won't go back on what I've sed, nuther; what shall we du 'baout it?' an' jis' then I walked intu that store.

"'Here's neighbor James Bisbee, he's a pooty fair man,' said Jot, 'an' we'll leave it aout tu him.'

"''Greed,' said the square.

"So they told me the case, an' I sot in jedgmint on them eggs and hatched aout just as good a d'cision 's could be, I snum!

"'Wal,' I said, 'y' say, Square Perkins, that y' won't hev them eggs at no price?'

"Th' square said 'Yis.'

"'An' you say 'f he don't buy 'em, that you won't never come t' this shop agin 's long 's y' live?'

"Jot said, 'That's what I said, an' I'll stand tu it.'

"Wal, I sot an' delib'rated, an' fin'lly said: 'It's a humly case t' deal with, neighbors, but here's my d'cision: square, you've got t' pay for them eggs, an' at a good market price, an' as y' say y' won't hev 'em at any price, the court 'll take them eggs f'r its fee.'

"Wal, yer granther was kinder grouty over that d'cision o' mine, but Jot Williams made him stan' tu it.

"Jot said I was a second Solomon, but y'r

granther said I was a second-class jackass; snum if he did n't, and that, tu, arter I 'd pulled him aout 't a bad hole!

"Wal, y'r granther held a grudge 'ginst me; an' one day when I went t' Wichnor t' trade I hitched my hoss t' the hitchin'-post front his store an' went in. I had aout in my wagin 'baout as good a lot of eggs as y' cummonly see, an' I put 'em in with a lot o' oats in th' tail o' th' wagin.

"Yer granther 'vited me t' th' stove, polite as a basket o' chips. 'Quite chilly, Mr. Bisbee, f'r the time of th' year,' sez he. 'Take a seat b' the stove where its comfort'ble.' An' then that critter went aout an' hitched his hoss, that al'a's hed his nose in everythin', tu th' tail of my wagin — I vaow tu man he did! And then he come in an' p'lavered jest as sweet as maple sugar. An' when I went aout t' my team, ther was that pesky hoss a-champin' up an' deoun 'nough tu make yer cry — th' dummed critter was jes' a-goin' it in my oats an' eggs, with yaller froth an' specks of egg-shells from th' eend of his pesky nose tu th' tip of his consarned ears!"

"It *was* pretty mean," said Phil, holding on to his sides with laughter.

"Mean?" said Jim, solemn as a funeral. "I jest told him thet a man thet 'd du that 'd steal corn from a blind jackass, dummed if I did n't!

"'Or buy eggs f'r hisself with another man's

money,' said y'r granther." And Jim, relaxing his gravity, crossed his thin legs almost double and laughed at the joke, though it was against himself.

From the time we came to Plymouth, there had been rumors of an iron-clad that it was said was about to come down the river. In March these rumors multiplied, until at last there came one of our spies, with the intelligence that she was about to make an attack on Plymouth in conjunction with land forces from the rebel capital.

General Wessells was so well convinced that there was truth in these rumors that he called for reënforcements. He did not get them, for General Grant needed all the available troops for the overland campaign, that was then just about to open.

CHAPTER XXVIII.

THE ADVENT OF THE "ALBEMARLE."

On Sunday the 18th of April there was an unwonted stir in the little town, for it was reported that the enemy was advancing from the interior on all the roads to Plymouth.

In the afternoon the enemy sent word of his intention of storming the town, and at sundown the little wharf opposite the "Southfield" was crowded with non-combatants who were embarking on a steamer for Roanoke Island. That afternoon the enemy attacked Fort Grey, a mile up the river, and this attack led those of us who were on board to infer that it was to clear the river for the iron-clad. Obstructions had been sunk at a narrow part of the river above for the purpose of preventing the passage of such a craft, but the spring freshets had partially removed them.

On the afternoon of the 19th the enemy shelled the place with a storm of spherical case-shot which riddled the houses and lopped the limbs from the trees in the streets of the little town. On the sides of the houses toward the river were groups of black people who had gathered there for protection, and whose shrieks and wails and prayers could be heard above the uproar of the battle. Our batteries answered the shots of the enemy, and the guns of our boats soon added to the tumult by throwing shell over the town into his ranks. When night came we could see the firefly-like sparkle of his guns in the fields on our right, where under cover of this uproar he was attempting to capture an isolated redoubt. The firing continued with unabated noise until ten o'clock in the evening, when it died away.

Shortly after there came the intelligence that the ram was on her way down the river. In preparation for her coming, Commander Flusher had fastened our two vessels together with long spars, while strong chains hung between them for the purpose of holding the ram, with the intention of sinking or boarding her while so held. We had but little doubt that if we could in this way entangle the iron-clad we should place her at a great disadvantage.

The "Southfield" carried five 9-inch and one 100-pounder Parrots, and one 12-pounder howitzer, while the "Miami" carried more guns than our ship; and although our boats were of wood we believed they would make the passage of the ram difficult, and, it was hoped, impossible.

Both Phil and I, as the reader knows, had taken part in the fight with the "Merrimack," and did not feel so sanguine as did our gallant and fearless commander. We were not certain, however, that the much-talked-of iron-clad was anything more than a "scare."

It was about one o'clock in the morning when a message came from General Wessells that the first craft that came down the river would be the rebel ram.

It was nearly two o'clock when she made her appearance. Then we heard a gun fired from Fort Grey, and shortly after we heard the lookout exclaim, "Here she comes!"

Through my glass I saw a dark-looking craft with a huge volume of smoke pouring from her smoke-stack, which showed that she burned pitch-pine wood for fuel, and could be nothing else than the ram. She came on without firing a single shot, while we steamed up the river to meet her, and to entangle her, if possible, in our toils.

A water battery with a single gun carrying 200-pound shot fired once at the ram; then, without replying to the battery, she was upon us. Either the Confederates had been warned of our plan, or else by accident avoided its consummation, for they steered near the north side of the river, and then by a quick turn plunged the beak of the ram into the "Southfield."

I was standing by the forward gun when this took place, and had just given the signal for firing. Whether the signal was obeyed or not I do not remember (if I ever knew), for the ship began rapidly filling with water, and the chain plates of the "Albemarle," which had become entangled in our framework, carried her bows down with us as we sank.

Amid the crash of timbers, the creaking and straining of the enlocked crafts, the gurgling waters, and the shrieks, and cries, and musket shots, I heard Phil's voice cry out clear and penetrating as we sank:

"Give them one more shot, men!"

Then I was caught in the gun tackle and carried under, in a whirl of water, with the sinking craft.

It seemed an age before I could extricate myself. There was a roaring sound in my head, it seemed as if my brains would burst from my skull, and then I lost consciousness, to regain it as I found myself on the surface of the water. I heard the sharp cries, and the *crack, crack, crack,* of musketry in the conflict.

I found that I had come up between the iron-clad and the "Southfield," and fearing to be crushed or otherwise injured between them I dived, and coming up beyond her on the north side swam for the swamp. As I reached the shore I turned and saw the "Miami" with all steam on headed down stream, followed by the slower "Albemarle."

After floundering around for a while, in an attempt to find dry land, I determined to swim to the opposite side of the river where our forces were. It wasn't much of a swim, but the current was swift and carried me down stream out of my course. I succeeded at last in reaching the shore below the town. The water was very cold, and I was chilled to the bone as I crept through the mud to the swampy river-bank.

My knees were so weak, either from being in the chilly water or from nerve strain, that I could scarcely stand. I found myself on the margin of a narrow stream, a branch of the main river, which swept between me and the town.

With this discovery I sat down to debate with myself what course it was best to pursue. It was fortunate I did so, for the rattle of some timber soon showed me that the enemy was near. I listened and then, not being able to hear what was going on, crept toward the sound I had heard. As I did so there was a tramp of men, and coming near to me was a party bearing a boat or scow on their shoulders; these were followed by others with scows and timber.

I was soon convinced that they were about to build a bridge across the stream for the purpose of reaching our left flank, which was protected by two small redoubts open at the rear.

On making this discovery, I determined to reach the town and give information of the sinister intentions of the enemy. I retraced my steps, and then taking to the water reached the opposite side without accident, picked my way to firm land, and hurriedly walked to the town.

I knew where General Wessells' headquarters

were, and to this I steered without delay. On arriving there I did not find even a sentry before the door. There was a lamp burning in the hallway. I listened, but heard not a sound. The place was apparently deserted, or the general and all his staff had gone to bed.

I was about to leave the house when I saw a glimmering of light through the crack of a door at the farther end of the hall. I opened this door and saw, at a table lighted by a single candle, a young man in the dress of a private, with his head on his arms, fast asleep. It was the mess-room of the general's staff, who had evidently been disturbed while at supper before I arrived. The table was set for a half-dozen people, and was still covered with very appetizing food.

Remembering that one of the maxims of a sailor was, "Eat and sleep when you can," I seated myself at the table, and without awakening the soldier, who I knew must be one of the detailed clerks of the general's office, I helped myself to the food I found there. The coffee was still warm, real cream near at hand, while the chicken was cooked with a skill unknown to my experience on shipboard.

I sat opposite to the slumbering man, enjoying every mouthful, using napkins to wipe away the water that dripped from my sleeves, when a dish crashed on another and the soldier awoke and started to his feet with an exclamation.

"Sit down!" I said, as I helped myself to a toothpick. "Where's the general?"

The young fellow continued to gasp and stare as if he had seen a ghost, until I repeated my question.

"Who in thunder are you?" he exclaimed, "and what are you doing here?"

"I am Ensign Johnstone of the 'Southfield,'" I replied. "I have been eating a good dinner while you were asleep at your post." And drawing my revolver with the water running from the muzzle, I exclaimed, "Speak, you idiot, or I will blow your brains out, if you 've got any in your head!"

Under this inspiration he cried out:

"The general is at Fort Williams; he expects a night attack at any time."

"All right," I said; "come on, we 'll go to Fort Williams; lead the way!"

The fort was not more than a quarter of a mile away, in front of the town, and to this we made our way.

"What were you alarmed about when I awoke you?" I said to the soldier.

"You were as white as a ghost," he replied, "and your eyes shone like a tiger's, and there was mud on your head and weeds in your hair; and you looked wild enough. I ain't afraid of anything but spirits, but darned if I ain't afraid of them, an' I thought you was a ghost."

I was not very much flattered at the description

of my appearance which he gave, though no doubt it was a correct one.

We reached Fort Williams, and when it was learned that I had important information for the general the drawbridge was let down, and I was shown to the presence of that officer. I found him squatting in an "A" tent which was lighted with a candle, and to him I was presented as an officer from the "Southfield." The general glanced me over with a grim smile and said, "Where's your ship?"

"At the bottom of the river, sir, and I've just arrived from her."

The general's stern face took on a sterner expression as he said, "What information do you bring?"

I told him what I had seen on the creek, and what I had heard.

"Very good," said the general; "you did well in reporting this at once."

He then called an energetic-looking officer, and to him gave directions for the concentration of troops at that flank. After this he turned to me and said, "Ensign, you will find some dry clothing in that corner, and if any of it will fit you put it on."

I thanked him, and found a pair of dark-blue trousers, a pair of drawers, a shirt, and some coarse stockings; and after putting them on was more comfortable.

"I am afraid I am taking clothes that some of

the rest of you will miss," I said to one of the staff officers who had come in as I completed the change.

"That's all right," he said; "all we can do in any case is to fight and keep comfortable; we've got to surrender at last, for we can't get away or get reënforcements with that iron-clad in the river."

"You think there is no show for us, then," I said, "and that the enemy will gobble the whole garrison?"

"They have a strong force, not less than ten thousand men, and our line is long and weak. We can't stand a siege without provisions; so it is only a question of a short time when we make our final surrender."

I threw myself on the bare ground and slept soundly until I was aroused by a great din. There were prolonged yells and the sharp crackle of musketry, punctuated with the deep growl of artillery.

"What is that?" I exclaimed.

"Sounds like an attack on our left," said an artillery officer.

The shrill yells of the charging enemy, the roar of heavy guns, with the crackle of infantry firing, continued for a few minutes, and then in the dim light of approaching day, we saw our soldiers falling back through the town, fighting every step as they retreated."

The enemy was in our rear.

Very soon men began to come from the fight into the fort, and we knew that the enemy had carried the town.

Among those who came was Jim Bisbee, accompanied by a lieutenant of artillery in whom I recognized my old schoolmate Burton.

I was requested to take command of a 100-pound gun, which was mounted on a ship-carriage, and I at once set at work changing the gun so that it could be brought to bear on the town, instead of the front, as was the original intention. This was more quickly accomplished than I thought would be possible.

While I was directing this work I was lightly touched on the shoulder by an infantry soldier, whom I recognized as John Nixon. He told me he had joined the First North Carolina regiment (sometimes called the "Buffaloes"), and that his wife, who had been with him at Plymouth, had left on the steamer on Sunday, for Roanoke Island.

I shook hands with him and requested him to assist at the gun.

The shot were now striking in the fort from every direction, right, left, and rear, as well as front, and the prospects looked far from cheerful. I could see the enemy constantly passing on a street parallel to and near the river.

When my gun was shotted I turned her down to point-blank range, and with a savage joy, which only those who are in a tight place know, fired down the street among the enemy, shot after shot in rapid succession. I was glad to make some return for the attentions I had been receiving.

The fighting soon became exceedingly hot. The unexploded spherical case-shot fired by the enemy stuck in the logs which formed the interior walls of our breast-heights, like plums in a pudding. In addition to shot fired from the enemy's light field-guns, those of the iron-clad struck the fort constantly. Nor was that the worst: the enemy's sharpshooters were in the houses and officers' quarters near the fort, endeavoring to pick off our gunners. Nearly every man who stepped up to adjust the primer to my 100-pound gun was either killed or wounded.

In the midst of the fight, I was training the gun to bear on a group of Confederates, the glitter of whose bayonets could be seen on the river street of which I have already spoken, when Dudley Burton came up, and with an important air said:

"Can't you sight that gun farther to the left?"

I pointed to the tramway of the gun-carriage and then pulled the lanyard. The shot went bellowing down the street, and Dudley jumped to the gun-carriage to see where it would strike. In an instant he fell back wounded and bleeding.

A sharpshooter's bullet had struck his cheek bone, and passed down out through his lower jaw. The blood ran from his mouth and I thought he was dead, but I had time only to throw his overcoat cape over his bloody face and go on with my duties, for in a fight there is little time for sentiment or ceremony.

Eleven men were killed and wounded at this gun, and every minute the sharpshooters were making our places there still more uncomfortable.

At about ten o'clock I got orders to cease firing, as the general was about to go out under a flag of truce to confer with General Hoke, who commanded the enemy's forces. They had been associated together in what the Confederates called the 'Old Army,' and it was thought that our general might get better terms than any one else.

As I had lost my hat in the river, I had taken one from a dead artillerist and placed it on my head. During this temporary suspension of fighting, I took it off and found that the top, where it was pinched together, had been almost shot away.

"It's lucky you are an inch too short for the sharpshooters," said Nixon, "or you'd be a right dead man."

In a few moments General Wessells returned greatly enraged.

"What are you dodging for?" he exclaimed to one of the men who ducked his head; "they wont hurt you!"

It was said that the terms of surrender proposed by him had been rejected, and that the old general had come into the fort determined to fight as long as a man could be brought to the guns.

Among all ranks it was felt better that we die fighting than be made prisoners of war; such was the evil reputation rebel prisons had gained among the Federal soldiers.

But the situation on all sides grew more and more desperate, and at last, at 11 o'clock A.M., General Wessells reluctantly surrendered the garrison.

CHAPTER XXIX.

IN THE ENEMY'S COUNTRY.

THE first man who came over the parapet of our works was a slight lieutenant accompanied by a burly and bearded Confederate. Without much notice of the Federal soldiers standing around in the fort, they began at once to ransack for valuables; and in this pursuit they ripped open a feather bed in the general's tent, in search of greenbacks.

I said, "That's the general's tent, and is to be respected."

They both turned fiercely upon me and presented such a comical appearance that I laughed in their faces. They had evidently been eating molasses, for the feathers had adhered to their beards, giving them, to use the mildest expression, a grotesque appearance.

The young officer scowled at me and said in his fiercest tones, "We'll soon show you how we respect you and your general!" and then added with a sneer, "Oh, it's you again, is it? A renegade North Carolinian! You escaped the halter once, but you will be fortunate to get off the second time."

And with this he pointed his revolver at my head, and I verily believe he was about to shoot me down in cold blood, when an officer who had come up knocked away his hand, saying,

"None of that, Jack; these men are prisoners of war and cannot resent your insults. Let them alone!"

"He's a renegade Southerner," snarled the lieutenant, who was the same John Ferold I had seen with Mr. Henderson while I was attempting to escape from Secessionville.

"None of that, I say," repeated the officer, and Ferold, as he met the determined look of his superior, turned sulkily away.

"You are in a scrape again, I see," said the latter, and I then recognized him as the young lieutenant-colonel to whom I had surrendered at Secessionville.

"Sorry to see you in bad luck again," he said pleasantly, "but it is the fortune of war."

Later we were marched out of the fort between two lines of Confederate soldiers, who exchanged hats with us by grabbing ours from our heads and substituting their own. One seized my hat and gave me his cloth home-made article in return. At first I was inclined to throw it away, but on second thought saw that it was a more serviceable hat than my own, and wished I had a gray jacket to go with it, for I was determined not to go to a Confederate prison if I could possibly escape.

From the fort we were marched to an open field, as a preparation for — we knew not what. In the field were gathered not only soldiers that had been captured, but men, women, and children, black, yellow, and white.

As I stood looking at this motley collection of fellow-prisoners, I was slapped familiarly on the shoulder, and turned to resent it, when I was confronted by Phil and Jim Bisbee.

"How be y'? I snum we're all in the same box!" said Bisbee.

Phil extended his hand, and I knew by the looks of his face that he had been uncertain as to my fate.

"I am glad to see you. Where have you been?" he exclaimed, wringing my hand. I told him in brief my experience since the sinking of the "Southfield."

"And I," said Phil, "swam right to the shore instead of down stream after the 'Miami.' But I thought you were at the bottom of the river."

"And I snum, here y' are agin. I might say right 'mong y'r North Car'linians," said Jim. "Say, d' ye think y'r father is 'mong this craoud o' tough fighters, Hez?"

"No," I replied, "and I thank God for that; this is Hoke's division of North Carolina troops on a little excursion after Yanks, and my father belongs to another division of the Army of Northern Virginia."

"John Nixon is around here somewhere," I said; "he put on the coat and hat of a dead artillery-man, and I don't want you to forget that his name now is John Burns, of the —d Massachusetts heavy. You see these rebs might mistake him for one of those 'Buffaloes' they are making inquiries about."

Shortly John came up to our party, shook hands with Phil, and added Jim Bisbee to his list of Yankee acquaintances and friends.

That night we slept in an open field surrounded by a guard.

The following afternoon we were plentifully rationed with Union hardtack and salt pork, preparatory to a march into the interior of the country to — we knew not where.

Having suffered from the want of food while within the enemy's lines during my former experience, I drew all the rations possible; and as there was no great system in its issue I not only got all the hardtack I could stow away in a haversack I had picked up, but I also filled my pockets until they bulged prodigiously. I had told Phil, Bisbee, and Nixon of my intention to escape, and they also, with the intention of joining me in my attempt, drew all the rations they could carry.

To those who laughed at our loads I said, "I guess you don't know how scarce provisions are in the Confederacy." And to this remark even one of our guard nodded in assent.

Jim had what he called a new-fangled frying-pan, with a handle that unshipped, which he was about to discard, but which I prevailed upon him to keep.

Instead of eating of our provisions at our first stopping-place, we bargained with the guard for some "pones," and thus were able to keep our stock good.

It was soon currently reported that the enemy would execute all North Carolinian and negro soldiers. Even before beginning our march we had heard the *crack, crack* of infantry firing, and on inquiring of the guard its purport, were told that they were shooting nigger soldiers that had fled to the swamps.

Twice during the first day's march we were halted and drawn up in single line on each side of the road while Confederate officers with citizens passed down the ranks carefully scanning each face for deserters — as they termed all natives who had enlisted in the Union army. John met their scrutiny unflinchingly, and though one of John's neighbors was among those that made this search, he was not identified. At one time an officer stopped square in front of him, but his uniform, together with his unconcerned manner and perhaps the fact that those around him were Massachusetts men, caused the officer to pass on without suspicion.

At the third halting-place John once more underwent the ordeal of a similar proceeding. They identified several so-called deserters this time, and hanged them to the nearest trees without ceremony.

At Hamilton we were halted in a grove to cook our rations, and here a large number of the people gathered to see the captured Yanks.

They were quite jubilant over our capture, and one of them said, " I reckon that we-uns have got the hul Yankee nation here."

Women and children predominated, though there were also a number of elderly men.

John had a bladder of Scotch snuff which he had picked up somewhere, which he declared was worth more to trade with, among the women folks, than double its weight in gold. He thought it would not be prudent for him to come in contact with the natives, as he might be recognized, and so Phil and I started out to trade the snuff. It was eagerly taken by those who had any food for sale, or bought by those who had Confederate money, so that we reaped quite a harvest, and yet had disposed of no more than a third of it. Nearly every woman in the gathering carried a snuff stick (a chewed pine stick) which she was anxious to dip into our snuff to test it.

General Wessells, in surrendering the garrison, had obtained the concession for his officers and men, that their personal property should be respected; so we had not been stripped, as was often the case under similar circumstances, and we still had our money, knives, and other valuables.

We were watchful now for an opportunity to escape; but John thought we should stand a better chance when not so near a large Confederate post like Plymouth.

At Hamilton we had what Jim called "a committee of the hull tu git aout of the Confederacy," and it was agreed that we would escape at the first opportunity that occurred. Jim, however, at first said, "I heard jest naow that we was goin' t' be sent t' Richmond t' be 'xchanged. I snum I don't want tu lose the chance."

An old soldier who heard this remark said, "Don't you take any stock in such stuff as that. I was a prisoner once before this and got fooled by just such rumors. Every time the rebs would have a slim guard, they'd begin to put up such talk as that. Don't you believe it."

"I reckon," said John, "it's a kind of a Yankee trick they are try'n' to play to make us easy to keep."

"Sho!" said Jim; "y' don't say? Wal, naow, I would n't a thought it of 'em, by gum! I guess I'll take my chance t' make tracks, for if some o' these folks I've sold tinware tu should take it inter th'r heads th't 'cause it's worn aout thet I cheated 'em, likes not 't would go kind o' hard with me."

At last, after a long march, we were halted at Tarboro', on the Tar River, where, it was surmised, we were to be put on the cars and sent down south to Andersonville.

The bank of the river where we were halted was quite steep, and no guards were placed near the water. I took out a small book-map which I had in my pocket, and saw that the Tar River ran by Little Washington, where a force of our soldiers was stationed. In attempting to reach this place we had, however, to take into account the possibility that the same force that had captured Plymouth might also capture it before we could arrive there. John thought this improbable, and gave good reasons for it. So, after discussing all the probabilities, we determined to take this route to freedom.

Along the margin of the narrow stream on which we were halted was a thick fringe of foliage, in which John proposed that we conceal ourselves and remain until the other prisoners were marched off; and then when darkness came, we would stand a fair chance to get away.

One by one we got into this wooded river-fringe, and then worked our way as far down stream as we safely could while the party still remained there. On so doing, however, we found that the guards extended away down to the river on that flank of the camp.

One by one, therefore, we silently distributed ourselves among the undergrowth, with the agreement that when darkness came we were to meet (if not captured meanwhile) at a tall tree which was designated.

I found a little hollow near this tree, where, covering myself with dead leaves, I lay down, listening to the clamor of the many voices that came to me from the camp, and the river that flowed by prattling of Yankee waters beyond.

I must have fallen asleep, for I knew nothing more until I was awakened by a hand on my shoulder. It was Phil, who with John Nixon had come to meet me.

"We can't find Jim," they said in a whisper; "but we will wait for him awhile."

"Do you know where he was hid?" I asked.

"Yes, but he is moved, and the prisoners and their guard have been gone an hour. We ought to be getting along."

We waited nearly an hour, and then not seeing or hearing from Jim reluctantly started without him. Phil said that just as the prisoners were marched away two rebel soldiers had come prowling along the shore; that one of them had come so near him that at one time he thought that he should be discovered; perhaps they saw Jim's long legs sticking out somewhere and took him in."

It was at first debated between us whether or not we had better cross the river and go down on the other side. We concluded that there was not enough advantage to be gained thereby to pay; we should get wet, and our matches would become useless; besides, it would take time.

We therefore began to walk along the river shore

listening and peering into the darkness with great caution until we had got full a mile away from where we started. During this time we had not met a single person. Feeling that now it was safe to proceed with less care, we began to move rapidly in single file down the river.

I was in advance, when, getting out of a path by which we had been moving, I stumbled over what I thought to be a log. I should never have known to the contrary if the supposed log had n't got on to a pair of feet, run, then stumbled, and rolled down the steep bank.

We all rushed forward, pounced on the intruder, and while John and Phil were tying his legs I held him by the throat to keep him from crying out.

"We must buck and gag him," I called out to my comrades, "or he will raise the town."

There came from the captive a gurgling sound, when, thinking that he was suffering from the pressure that I had put upon his windpipe, I loosened my grasp, and putting the cold muzzle of my canteen to his head, said:

"If you move I'll blow your brains out! and I don't want to kill you."

The snorting and twisting continued until I thought he had a fit. The reader can imagine my astonishment when at last he said with a gasp of laughter, "Now stop yer nonsense! I swow it's too all-fired funny, Hez Perkins!"

I was angry, and exclaimed, "I wish I had

choked you harder, you clown you! What in thunder are you laughing at?"

"Wal," said Jim (for it was he), between gasps, and still convulsed, "I swow, it's 'nough t' make a caow laf to have any one tryin' t' blow y'r brains aout with a canteen!" and Jim laughed still harder, in his groaning, chuckling, out-of-breath manner.

"You will bring the whole country around our ears, you blunderbuss!" said Phil, who seemed as much amused as Jim, though he tried to conceal it.

But I was unable to see the fun, and can't to this day when Phil sometimes relates the incident.

"It puts me in mind," said John, "of the sniggering of a nigger we were going t' hang one night down t' our place.

"'What ar' y' laffin' at, y' nigger?' said one of our folks.

"And that dog-goned nigger chuckled an' said:

"'Why, massa, yo' 'mos' hung yo' own nigger; got de wrong one, sah!' and then that or'nary nigger chuckled, and haw-hawed right smart!"

It turned out that Jim had fallen asleep, and when he awoke, thinking that we were gone, he had started off before we did. He had no idea that the persons who had come upon him were other than rebel guards until I called out to Phil.

This foolish affair over, we started on our way once more, and met no other adventures that night.

When daylight came we resolved to go into

hiding during the day in a swamp near the river, in which was a thick growth of weeds and bushes.

We found a safe hiding-place there, and before sunrise kindled a fire, fried some bacon and boiled some coffee, of which we each had a small quantity. Then having eaten breakfast we trampled out our fire, for fear the smoke would attract attention, and lay down on the dry leaves we had gathered, and warmed by the sunshine went to sleep, leaving only one — John Nixon — on guard. We had all learned that to have cool nerves and a clear head, a man must lay up a good store of sleep for emergencies.

CHAPTER XXX.

UNDER TWO FLAGS.

No incident of note occurred during the day, except that Jim deserted his post when on guard to look at the timber in the swamp, and had come back in great alarm, saying he had "seen an alligator big enough to swaller a caow."

When we reproved him for leaving his station as lookout he said with provoking coolness, "I 'll come daown here an' make a great spec cuttin' that timber sometime; there's a all-fired lot o' money in them big trees."

As darkness came on we once more started on our way, searching the shores as we went for some kind of a boat in which to pursue our journey with greater speed and safety. In this we were however unsuccessful; for either there were no boats or they were well hidden.

Thus it was we made so little progress that soon not only were we out of provisions, but also we began to think that we had made a mistake in supposing that we were on the Tar River. It had been over three days since we started, our supplies were nearly all gone, and we were compelled to take some measures to replenish our stock or give up the attempt to get into our lines.

I estimated that we had traveled full thirty-five miles; and, making allowance for the crookedness of the river and the necessary detours we had made, that unless we had made the mistake I have mentioned, we were not far from thirty miles from our lines at Little Washington. It seemed to us that the influence of a Union force at even that distance would be felt, and that we might therefore presume on a certain amount of friendliness towards, or fear of, Union soldiers.

John was the only one of us who did not heartily agree with this view, and he only by saying, "You can't reckon on anything in this dog-goned country since th' folks have gone wild, 'xcept that they'll do somethin' y' don' want 'em to. When people hev no right view of th'r own welfare I reckon they wont respect we-uns."

It was finally agreed that John should interview the people at the first house we thereafter saw (providing it was n't a big planter's estate), and not only trade for food, but also get positive information as to our whereabouts, and of the distance to Little Washington; or if we were off our course, to some other point inside of Yankeedom. We soon saw a house which we knew to be inhabited, by the smoke that came from the chimney. John threw off his coat, borrowed a hat and a canteen which a reb had exchanged with Phil, and said, "If I had a gun I reckon I co'd pass fo' one o' Hoke's men."

Then, equipped with the snuff that was still left, he started out to trade and prospect.

We gathered several other articles from the members of our party, such as jack-knives and combs, but John viewed these disdainfully, and said, "I 'll 'low they may be right good, but I reckon this snuff 'll go better with the women th't don't comb so much as they snuff. An' th' 'll be no men folks 'cept young trash or old uns."

"It looks like a consarned ticklish job t' me," said Jim anxiously, "but w' might 's well be aout o' breath 's tu be out o' fodder, I guess."

We waited patiently for what seemed to be an hour, when we saw John coming hurriedly back with a ham dangling from one hand and a tin pail from the other.

"What's the matter, John?" we inquired in chorus. John made no reply except to pass the ham to me and the pail to Jim and ejaculate, "Scoot t' th' swamp," and with this led the way with such speed that we had to make our legs fly to keep him in sight.

When we were well in the swamp we halted, and Jim, after listening, said, "If they put dogs on our track we must git t' the river right through th' swamp."

But not a sound of a dog was heard, and John then satisfied our curiosity.

"When I got to that house," said John, "I found no one thar but an ol' woman, a young girl, an' a nigger wench; and they war powerful cur'us t' know whar I come f'm. I said I come right f'm Plymouth whar we'd gobbled a right smart lot o' Yanks, and that I'd got a furlough t' see m' folks that lived near Little Washin'ton, an' thet I was all out of grub fixin's an' wanted t' buy some. Said they had n't no eat fixin's, an' then ast me what rigiment I b'longed to.

"To stop th'r 'quiries I begun to talk 'bout th' fight an' said I'd got some powerful good snuff down thar f'r our folks thet I war goin' t' see. An' then I tuck out my snuff and let her take a dip. 'I'll 'low,' I said, 'I'd like to git this snuff t' m' ol' woman an' maw.'

"Soon 's that ol' woman got a dip o' my snuff her eyes shined an' she said peart like, 'Stranger, what d' y' want fo' that thar snuff?'

"'I don't wan' t' sell,' I said, 'but t' 'commodate y' I'll let y' hev' half o'vt f'r pervisions.'

"'What grub fixin's d' y' want?' says she, an' her eyes pulled at that snuff-skin so powerful thet I could n't hardly hold it.

"'Will a ham do yo' any good?'

"'Yes, I reckon,' I said.

"'Stewed chicken?'

"'I reckon,' I said agin.

"'Some pones o' corn bread?'

"'Pass 'm along,' I said impatiently, shaking th' snuff-bladder.

"'It's a bargain,' she said with a snap t'r her

teeth like a steel trap when it shets; an' the ol' woman went out an' brought in the fixin's.

"When I started off I looked back, fo' I suspicioned; an' there w's the ol' woman goin' powerful fas' over th' fields. And then I knew 't was time fo' me to git right smart 'fore that ol' 'oman 'd put th' whole country on my track after that thar stuff."

"Wal, I swum!" ejaculated Jim. "I guess y' showed good jedgment in lightin' aout. Say, le 's have some o' that johnny-cake an' chicken; my maouth seems t' be kind o' waterin' f'r it. What say?"

Though none of us said a word in reply, our stomachs indorsed the suggestion, and we soon were ranged around the tin pail, as Jim said, "drivin' in the pickets on that chicken."

John had learned that we were about two miles above the town or village of Greenville on the Tar River, and, as I had thought, not over thirty-five miles from Little Washington.

We were, however, surrounded by hostile people, whose enthusiasm had been raised to fever heat by the news (that had spread over the region as if by magic) that the Yankee garrison had been captured at Plymouth. We did not know that Little Washington was still in the possession of our troops, but reasoned that there had not been time for the enemy to capture it. It was agreed, whether our reasoning was right or the reverse, that we must risk endeavoring to reach that place. After getting out of the swamp we made a wide detour (though Greenville was on the other side of the river), in order to give the people of that place a wide berth. We traveled most of the day and succeeding night, keeping our course as best we could.

During the next day we came upon some negroes at work in the woods, and from them got several pones of corn bread, and learned that we were a mile from the river and a right smart distance below Greenville. When we offered them pay they would take nothing, though I was well satisfied that they had given us most of the food they had for the day.

We were confident that the black men would not betray us, for there is a freemasonry of misfortune among God's lowly ones. We struck out due north when we left them, and then turned back to the river, which we reached about sundown. We then rested and ate a good supper, and again started down the river-bank.

We had not gone more than two miles when we came upon an old darkey just shoving off from the shore in a flat-bottomed, weather-beaten dory. We opened negotiations at once to purchase the craft. He finally agreed to sell it, with the understanding that if we were captured by the enemy, we were not to tell them where we got it. We also bought one of his fish-lines and a hook, thinking that by the help of these we should be able to replenish our stock of food should we be long detained on our journey.

That night we made good use of our time and muscles, and we judged when daylight came that we had made full twenty miles since we took to the boat.

With the dawn we had more need of secrecy than hurry, so we pulled our little craft into the bushes, in a nook well sheltered from sight, and, being tired and sleepy, first establishing one of our party as guard, we lay down and slept, only awakening when it was our turn to stand watch.

With the night we continued our voyage, and each taking a turn at the oars made such progress that we expected to get into Little Washington before morning. But either the tide set against us, or from some reason we did not understand we failed to make the progress we anticipated, and at daylight had not reached that place.

We were very anxious, and were debating whether or not to lie by for another day, when there came a sharp hail from the shore.

"What boat is that?"

"That's a landman's call," said Phil in a low tone.

I answered the call by replying, "A scow from up the river."

"Come ashore with your scow," was the laconic order.

"I vow we are either lucky or in a tarnation scrape," said Jim.

"That's what I thought; we are inside the Union lines," said Phil, taking the oars and rowing for the shore, where we saw a party of men gathered.

The skiff grounded and I jumped ashore; for I had discovered that the men wore the Union blue. It was the outpost of Little Washington.

The first thing uttered by any one of us came from Jim; it was: "Say, fellers, can't ye give us something nat'ral-like t' eat?"

They complied with Jim's request by conducting us to their rendezvous, where they gave us plentifully of Uncle Sam's rations.

"I smum," said Jim, "this is tu good f'r anythin'."

"Yes," said Phil teasingly, "you can let yourself loose now, corporal, without danger of running on to a hunger snag."

John was as undemonstrative as ever, only saying in his sober manner, "I 'll 'low I 'm right glad t' git hyar."

When we got into Little Washington, and it was learned that we had escaped after being made prisoners at Plymouth, we attracted much attention.

"We have forgotten something, in our joy at our safety," said Phil soberly.

"What is it?"

"We have forgotten to thank God for this deliverance."

As we recognized His hand in our deliverance I felt, as Jim Bisbee said, "that we were in 'God's country,' and under God's flag."

We were treated with great kindness by the officers at the post.

Though it was but a few days since we were captured, it seemed to us as if it had been months, so crowded were the hours with emotions inseparable from such adventures.

We told the story of the sinking of our gunboat and of the capture of Plymouth to a newspaper correspondent, and were interviewed by officers, who thought it possible that the post was likely to be attacked at any day.

CHAPTER XXXI.

WITH OUR FLEET.

The next day Phil and I took leave of Corporal Bisbee and John Nixon, and went down the river to our fleet, then lying at the mouth of the Roanoke, from which the rebel ram "Albemarle" was hourly expected.

The first craft sighted was the "Strikewell," commanded by volunteer Lieutenant Bell, who received us with almost affectionate heartiness, and invited us to dine with him, an honor which will be best understood by those conversant with naval etiquette.

We then learned that we were thought to have been drowned, for though those captured at Plymouth had been allowed to communicate with their friends, and though I had written to my mother of my capture, neither of us had sent a letter to any one in the fleet, and it was therefore thought probable that we had both gone down with the unfortunate "Southfield." We also learned that some forty officers and sailors of our steamer had been rescued by the "Miami" and the other vessels of the fleet.

At the table we told the story of our capture and

escape, and mentioned the hanging of the North Carolinians that had been captured there. I told as a good joke the threat of the young lieutenant to hang me as a renegade Southerner, now that they had got hold of me the second time.

"But you are not a Southerner," said the lieutenant inquiringly.

"No," I replied. "It was a mistake. I have relations who are, though."

"I am a Southern man by birth," said Lieutenant Bell musingly. "I have a number of relatives and friends in the army, and though I believe they are entirely wrong I can understand their way of looking at things. They have greater pride of their States, and also greater family pride, than Northern men — their likes and dislikes are much stronger. They are very brave, and yet it seems to me we are fighting as much to preserve their heritage as our own. If I didn't believe so I would take no part in a war against them."

"I don't understand that," said one of the officers of the ship. "I believe that we are right and they are wrong, and I can't understand how we are preserving anything of theirs."

"Liberty is a common heritage," said the lieutenant, "but what I mean is, that if they succeed in establishing a government of their own, both North and South will come under the control of foreign powers. United we are strong enough to protect ourselves against any nations that can be brought against us; disunited by fighting against each other, we shall finally lose a republican form of government for both. It is a very sad war of brother against brother, and father against son," and the captain looked thoughtful and sombre.

"Yes," I replied, "it is hard to fight against relatives and friends."

Lieutenant Bell passed over my remarks by saying to Phil, "I haven't heard anything of your relatives, Gurley," which I understood was his way of saying that my Southern relatives could be of no possible interest to him.

"I might tell a long story," said Phil. "I have good reasons for believing that my mother's married name was not Gurley; but I know that whatever my parentage I am still myself."

I had flushed, somewhat in anger I confess, at Lieutenant Bell's manner, and perhaps he saw it, for he said in reply to Phil's remark:

"Yes, after you have stripped a man of his artificial surroundings that sometimes give him importance, such as wealth, birth, or honors, you have come down to the marrow of individual worth. The man who has not in some way got this view of himself cannot properly estimate his own value. I am a good deal of a democrat, you see, — but still, blood will tell."

I thought to myself that though he might voice the sentiments of democracy he was sometimes almost offensively aristocratic in his manner, yet I could not lay hold of anything in what he had said or in his manner that was tangibly snobbish, much less personally offensive.

We reported that afternoon to the senior officer of the fleet, and at our request, as we knew its captain, were assigned to temporary duty on the double-ender "Sassacus."

The plan of the Confederates, after the capture of Plymouth, was to take Newberne, and once more open these inland waters to the ships of England. In this plan the iron-clad ram "Albemarle" was reckoned on to coöperate with the troops under General Hoke. Two days after our arrival here the enemy's iron-clad came down to contest the possession of Albemarle and Pamlico Sounds.

I was assured that had we arrived a week earlier, I should have been given command of one of the smaller craft of the fleet, but as all dispositions for battle were now made, it could not be done.

The prospect of sharp work is not an unwelcome one to naval sailors, since it is not only their profession to fight, but is also one of the roads they must travel to distinguish themselves and gain promotion. Men of our race are brave by nature, as has been many times demonstrated in battle by sea and land. It was often said, during the war, that personal courage was the cheapest thing we had. In the navy the officers who were cowardly soon had a chance to get out of the profession and give place to those who, while not seeking danger, did not shirk or flee from it.

On the 5th of May the "Albemarle" came slowly steaming down the Roanoke River to discuss the question who should retain the possession of the sound. The stakes to be played for were large. If our combined fleet could destroy this dangerous craft we should regain possession of Plymouth, and also preserve the inland waters of Pamlico and Albemarle Sounds, and all that this implied.

The vessels waiting to prevent the ram from getting into the sound were the "Mattabesett," which was also a double-ender, the "Miami," "Whitehead," "Ceres," "Commodore Hall," and our own.

As soon as it was reported to us that the "Albemarle" was coming, the whole fleet steamed up the sound to give battle. We had not gone far before we saw black volumes of pitch-pine smoke, which told us that she was coming. At her approach the vessels of our fleet opened fire on her at comparatively short range, to which at first she made no reply. But as she came near her forward port flew open — there was a puff of smoke, a flash and roar, and then a shell struck the quarter of the "Mattabesett," cutting her rail and killing and wounding (as we afterwards learned) six men at her pivot gun. Meanwhile the shot and shell of our vessels were striking the iron-clad roof of the

"Albemarle" and glancing from it like so many marbles from a board. At full head of steam she headed for the "Mattabesett" with the intention of ramming her, but the blow was avoided by a quick turn which the rebel craft, more clumsy, was unable to meet. We then opened on her at close range with our formidable nine-inch guns, but, as Phil afterwards said, "It was like throwing peas at an iron pot." Fortunately for the smaller craft, she paid no more attention to them than a furious bull does to flies when engaged with an opponent.

The din and uproar of the conflict soon became tremendous. It was, however, apparently of little more use to fire shot at the enemy than to snap one's thumb and finger at her.

We were about four hundred yards from her when the captain of our vessel sent orders to the engine-room to cram in oil and cotton waste, and back her. Then the order was given to steer for the iron-clad! With throttles wide open, with the hottest of fires under her boilers, the engine working the pistons at a furious stroke, our good ship shot forward with tremendous speed to ram the rebel craft!

I shall not forget the scene on our decks if I live a thousand years! The men grasping the rail with the nervous pallor of suspense on their faces, the clanking of the engines, the hissing and wash of steam and water, the sharp commands; and then (as we neared the enemy) the order

THE ORDER CAME, "ALL DOWN!" AND WE STRUCK THE "ALBEMARLE" LIKE A THUNDERBOLT!

came, "All down!" and we struck the "Albemarle" like a thunderbolt!

I was sitting on my feet on the deck holding to the rail, but was thrown over and over by the tremendous shock. Our stanch craft quivered, but held fast, and as I got to my feet, I saw through the smoke that the ram, though still afloat, had heeled over, while our bows were torn away and its timbers strained and ripped to the water line. I could hear the click of the engines, which seemed uninjured, and not ten feet away saw the port of the iron-clad open, and a gun's crew, naked to the waist, red, perspiring, and blackened by powder, working like so many demons. Then came a blinding flash almost in my face, and the shot tore and crashed through us.

Both vessels were moving. Our ragged bows were clinging to the iron-clad, with our own prow so twisted that we lay side by side with our stern to her bows.

Another shot ripped through us, piercing the overcharged boilers of our engines. They emptied themselves with a shriek like a wounded creature, filling the forward deck with steam and boiling water. Our ship lurched heavily to port, and then, amid the screams of agony from scalded men and the fierce shouts of the contestants, there came simultaneously a terrible cry and a command: "The ship is sinking! Make ready to repel boarders!"

Our crew with cutlasses and pistols sprang to the bulwarks, and a hand-to-hand conflict took place; but a steady fire from our tops, and a fierce resistance from our men on deck, kept the enemy back.

While assisting in this duty of repelling the enemy I felt a sharp pain in my right side, and my legs doubled up under me as if of paper instead of flesh, muscle, and bone.

I had been struck by a bullet.

I did not, however, lose consciousness. I heard the shrieks, groans, tones of commands on both ships even more distinctly than before.

Thirteen awful minutes passed, while the other ships of our fleet, as if paralyzed at the scene, looked on, with stopped engines. Captain French, of the "Miami," however, who had been fighting his ship at close quarters, came to the assistance of the "Sassacus" and attempted to explode a torpedo under the iron-clad.

While the pivot guns were kept at work almost muzzle to muzzle with those of the enemy, we drifted apart.

The other ships now got into line and fired, and also made attempts to befoul the propeller of the iron-clad with the seine; but like all other attempts proved impracticable.

At sundown the "Albemarle" steamed up the Roanoke River, never again to appear in battle.

She was finally destroyed with a torpedo by the bravest of the brave — Lieutenant Cushing.

It was not until the conflict was over that I learned that Phil had been badly scalded while directing the guns on the forward deck of our ship. I was told that, though so badly injured, he had for some time refused to leave his post, and even then did not until he was forced to do so.

CHAPTER XXXII.

UNDER THE SURGEON'S CARE.

Soon after being wounded I was carried to the cockpit, from where I could still hear the din of the fight.

Upon examination my wound was found to be caused by a bullet striking and breaking the second rib, and then passing obliquely through the right side and out just where the elbow naturally touches the side when pressed down upon it.

Phil's injuries were still more serious, as the upper portion of his body was badly scalded, and it was feared that he was injured internally. The surgeon shook his head as if doubtful of any but unpleasant results, as he cut away his garments to apply white lead, linseed oil, and other dressing. It must have been very painful, but Phil talked, laughed, joked, and cried out only once when the surgeon hurt him with rough handling.

When the surgeon began examining me he did not hurt much, and it is not my nature to cry out with pain. But Phil looked as compassionate as if my hurt was more desperate than his own.

"I am not hurt half as bad as you are," I said, "and here you are pitying me just as if your scald was of no consequence."

"Well, old fellow," said Phil, "you never yell out over anything, but I squeal when things go against my grain."

This was in part true, for I was of a more stolid nature than he, and such people sometimes get credit for bravery when it is a matter of temperament, rather than of courage. I have seen men who were easily startled — who jumped and cried out nervously — and yet were really more courageous than others who were not easily shaken.

While the surgeon was removing Phil's clothing to apply the dressing he came upon the locket of Phil's mother, which he had always worn around his neck.

"Take that off," he said rather crossly; "it will hurt you."

Phil passed an uneasy, restless night, and I heard him call out in his sleep repeatedly, which I thought indicated that he was in great pain. I did not suffer much, though before I got through with that bullet wound the pain was enough for a lifetime.

When the surgeon visited us in the morning I told him how Phil had called out in his sleep. He shook his head at this, and said, "He needs very careful nursing." On renewing portions of the dressing he came upon the locket again, and was very cross about it. "You *must not* wear it," he said; "it is likely to chafe and hurt you."

Phil then handed over the locket to me, saying, "Hez, you keep your weather eye on it."

Then the doctor gave Phil an opiate, and he had fallen into a deep sleep under its influence, when Lieutenant Bell, having heard of our injuries, came to pay a visit to the ship.

And now I must tell of an occurrence which, were it not true, would seem like an invention. Before Lieutenant Bell came I had opened the locket and was looking at the miniature of Phil's mother. The likeness was that of a beautiful woman, dressed in fanciful costume. I still had the likeness in my hand when the lieutenant came in.

"How are you this morning?" he said.

I made a motion towards Phil to indicate that he was sleeping. He looked at him earnestly for a moment, then said:

"We shan't disturb him; if I am not mistaken he's under the influence of morphine."

In reply to his inquiries I told him of Phil's brave conduct, and how he had stuck to his post of duty after being hurt; and as I spoke I laid the locket, still open, on a little table by my side.

"What did the doctor say about his case?" inquired the lieutenant.

"He didn't say anything," I replied; "but I didn't like the way he shook his head."

"There is not so much in that," said he, smiling; "these surgeons usually make the most of a case, so as to get the more credit for the cure of it. I hope that the burn is not serious — the boy is such a brave little fellow: if he lives he may become a credit to the navy."

"Yes," I said, "no braver sailor ever trod a deck; and see, this is the picture of his mother: she looks high-bred enough."

Lieutenant Bell took the locket carelessly in his hand and said, without looking at it, "Yes, I understand: the poor boy has no father or mother, and it is wonderful how"— and here he adjusted his eye-glasses and looked at the miniature in his hand.

I was not prepared for the effect it produced. He gave a cry, turned pale, looked from me to Phil, exclaiming, "Merciful God!"

"What is it, sir?" I exclaimed, almost jumping from my bed with alarm. But the strong man was on his knees at Phil's bed, making inarticulate sounds, and I thought he had gone suddenly insane.

"Who did you say this likeness was?" he asked excitedly. "How did he come by it?"

I said:

"It is Phil's mother; she died when he was a child, and when the old woman he lived with in New York died, he was left alone and drifted to Wichmor. Why, what is it about the picture? Did you ever see her?"

"She was my wife — and this boy must be my son that I have been searching for for years," he replied, and he hung over Phil, his lips moving as if in silent thanksgiving; and by this time I was as much excited as he, and should have been still more so had I known all the facts.

"I will tell you all about it," he said, "when I am calmer, and when my boy is out of danger. Possibly there may be some mistake about it — he may not be my son, though it seems impossible that there should be any mistake about it, for I recognize this locket and likeness as one that my wife gave to me, but which I left with her when I went to sea; but I have a duplicate of it in my state-room. It is without question the one I left with her."

"My father always said," I replied, "that Phil had good blood in his veins."

"The best in the South," said the lieutenant proudly. "No wonder he shows courage; he comes from a race of soldiers."

Mr. Bell stepped out to see the surgeon. When he returned he said, "The surgeon thinks there will be no harm in my seeing the boy this afternoon — that joyful excitement may prove beneficial rather than injurious to him. I want him moved on board of my ship, where he will get the best of care."

"Can't I go too?" I said. "Phil and I have always been together; we have never got hurt except in couples. Mother used to say, when I had stubbed a toe, 'Get two rags, for Phil will be along with a sore toe in a minute.'"

"God bless your mother!" said Lieutenant Bell.

"Of course you will come to keep him company, for your own advantage as well as his; he's still your friend if he is my son."

There was something in his manner of saying this that nettled me, and I growled to myself. "I guess the Johnstones have got as good blood as any Bell that ever rang its own praise."

"What are you growling about, Hez?" said Phil drowsily; then, yawning, said, "I must have been asleep."

"Your father has been here to see you, Phil."

"Your granny!" replied Phil, who seemed much refreshed by his slumber; and then very seriously added:

"But, honor bright, I dreamed of my mother, though; she came, as I thought, and brushed back my hair, as I remember she used to do, and said, 'My dear boy!' and then, plague it! I woke up. But wasn't it a beautiful dream? When a fellow is down he wants some one to coddle him just as marm and your mother used to do. I suspect that I'm a good deal of a baby and not much of a man. But say, old fellow, how is your ventilator?"

"My what, you scamp?"

"Bullet hole, you thick-head!" said Phil, laughing.

"That's all right; but seriously, Phil, — honor bright, and no fooling, — your father has discovered you, and when you heard me growling, it was because he had been patronizing me, just as if I was dirt."

"Just hand me my locket, Hez," said Phil, smiling; and then added, "I guess you have been dreaming too, Hez."

"Yes," I continued, "and it was that locket that did the business; you know father always thought it might. You don't seem to think I am in earnest, but your father has been here while you were asleep."

"Nonsense!" ejaculated Phil.

"Honest, Phil! and here he comes again, I guess." And the door opened and Lieutenant Bell came in.

Phil reached to grasp his hand, saying, "Glad to see you, lieutenant."

"I'm glad to see you," he replied with great emotion; "you are looking better, my dear boy."

Phil opened his eyes with surprise at this demonstrative remark, while the lieutenant continued as he sat down by Phil's side, still holding his hand: "I've got something to tell you. I think — I think — yes, I am positive — that you are my son. At any rate," he said, pointing to the locket that was in Phil's hand, "that dear woman was my wife."

"Well," said Phil excitedly, "but that was my mother. You don't mean to say that what Hez has been telling me is — is — so?"

The lieutenant made no other reply than to fall

on his knees by Phil's side and kiss his face as he reverently exclaimed, "Thank God! thank God! I'm glad to have such a brave boy for my son."

"And I am glad to have a father like you; that is — if it is really so," said Phil hesitatingly; "it seems too good to be quite true, though."

And the father sat holding his boy's hand, saying little, but with an exchange of feeling between them none the less deep, until Phil fell into a deep natural sleep.

Lieutenant Bell laid Phil's hand down gently, saying softly, "God bless you, my son!" The surgeon came in and seeing Phil asleep said, "That's good, that's the effect I hoped for!"

The next day Phil and I were moved to the "Strikewell," where better air and better attendance, it was thought, might be given him. As for myself, I seemed to be of little consequence except as Phil's friend.

Sailors are not reputed to be sentimental, but when the romantic incidents of the meeting between father and son were known by the officers and men of the fleet, we were the recipients of as many indigestible messes as there were cooks. I don't know why it is that when people feel kindly towards you — when their emotions are particularly excited in your behalf — they proceed on the principle that if one is sick they can best express interest for you by stuffing your stomach and putting you in the way of getting worse.

The next evening after the change of quarters Phil showed a disposition to exult.

"What do you think of this? — the lieutenant's state-room, and grub to kill!"

"Beats any story I ever read," I said, "this finding your dad."

"Yes," said the lieutenant, who just then came in and overheard my remarks; "and now that you are a little better, Philip, I want to tell you the story of my life. I am not going to spin a long yarn, but tell it in a few words, so as not to put you to sleep again, my dear boy." And the lieutenant looked at Phil with a soft light in his eyes that seemed to me very sentimental for a man.

"I was born," he said, "in South Carolina, not two hundred miles from this place. My father is — if alive, God bless him! — a slaveholder, but at the same time a humane man who would not do injustice to a servant or any one else. But my brother and myself were sent North to be educated. I was in school in New York city to be trained as a lawyer; my brother in a Connecticut college. My brother married a Yankee girl. My father could n't stand that; sent him a check for money belonging to him from mother, and would have no more to do with him. I fell in love with your mother, Phil, and married her, and when father learned of this he served me as he had my brother. Your mother was of a good English family, but they were impoverished, and she had become an actress. At first I went on the stage, and with my own and my wife's wages we managed to live. When you were born we named you Philip, after her father. Then her health failed, and she of course could not help support me and her child too. I, foreseeing that we should soon come to want, left her the little money we had and shipped as a common sailor on a voyage to China, giving her the advance wages I received. On arriving in China I wrote to her, but never heard from her again. At the time I started on this voyage you were about two years of age. On my return from my voyage I made a thorough search for her and my child, but could learn nothing of them. When I left you boys in New York some three years ago it was to resume the search, but it was without success.

"At the time I shipped on the 'Favorite' it was with the intention of communicating with my father. But at Newberne I learned that my brother was with him, and though I loved them both I was too proud to make any claim on them for recognition while little more than a common sailor. The name I now sail under is not the one I am entitled to by birth. It was because of the prejudice of Southern people against manual labor that I did not take my real name when I went to sea, but took instead the stage name I had used when I was an actor."

During this narrative I had been exchanging

glances with Phil which were almost as good means of communication as words would have been.

"What is your real name, and mine?" said Phil.

"Johnstone," was the reply. "One of the proudest in the State of North Carolina!"

I could restrain myself no longer. "Phil," I said. "Consin Phil. I am coming over to shake hands with you, surgeon or no surgeon," and with this I got out of bed and shook Phil by the hand and then blubbered out between gasps:

"Old fel, you always were as good as gold, and I've loved you ever since you pulled me out of the Wild River; but plague me if I don't someway or other cotton to you just a little more, now that you are my cousin, than ever before."

"I don't understand this," said Lieutenant Bell in amazement; "and you'll get cold, with nothing on but your shirt. But, I say, explain. I don't understand it!"

"Well," I replied somewhat tartly, "my father's name is Rufus Johnstone, Jr., and if I am not mistaken, you are the Uncle Bob I've heard him tell so much about; the same that helped tame the boy Andy."

The scene that followed can be imagined better than told.

I had to tell my uncle the story of Phil's coming to Wichnor, and then to our home, and of my father going South and getting drawn into the Southern side of the rebellion.

"Of course Rufe had to go with our people," said the lieutenant. "but a nobler man or boy never breathed!"

When Uncle Robert said this, I forgave him from that moment some of the Southern Johnstone airs he had been putting on.

CHAPTER XXXIII.

IN THE HOSPITAL.

As the very warm weather was approaching, it was deemed best by the surgeon that Phil and I should be sent to the Brooklyn Naval Hospital, where we could have the benefit of cooler weather, and the most skillful care and attendance. Phil had been growing better ever since he was conveyed to the "Strikeweil," while my wound was healing rapidly, and I should have been moderately contented but for the torture of having the wound reamed out with caustic at every notion of the old doctor.

In June we arrived at Brooklyn and were duly installed in comfortable quarters at the hospital. Here, after a few days, mother and grandfather came to see us. Grandfather — wonderful to relate — had a new suit of clothes, and while in Brooklyn expended several dollars in ice-cream and other luxuries for Phil and me; or at least, whatever grandfather's intentions were, Phil got his share. I had already informed my mother, in a long letter, of our relationship, and the incident by which it was discovered, and hence they were prepared to greet Phil as a relative. Though mother said she could not have liked him any better than she always had, if he had been twice over related, I could observe in her manner, as well as in grandfather's, more deference to the son of Robert Johnstone than to plain Phil Gurley. This is saying nothing to their discredit, for they were simply human.

Grandfather was aging very fast, and with age came a certain softening of many of his harsher traits. It was, as mother said, quite pitiful to see how childishly fond of me he had grown. One trait, recently developed, my mother considered still more alarming. This was liberality in the use of money. At a fair held in Wichnor for the Christian Commission, he had, so my mother told me, given so freely that it was the talk of the town that he was losing his mind. And mother looked so alarmed as she told me this that I was inclined to laugh. Phil slyly said to me he guessed Squire Perkins had had an enlargement of the heart.

Once, when grandfather had insisted on an expenditure for me that seemed to mother needless, for she was very frugal, Grandfather Perkins said:

"Well, Rose, money is well in its way, but since I have seen men and boys like these two sacrificing comfort and everything else for this country, I've made up my mind to be more liberal with money. I see now that I've made a mistake in life in regarding it as the principal thing to be considered, and I am sorry now I have n't given more freely to you and Rufus. Perhaps I have made a mistake in considering money of too great value. Anyway, I've been sorry that I was not more liberal to Rufus and kept him with us. He used to say money should be our servant, and not our master, and I'm not sure but that I've sometimes let it be my master."

This was such an unusual admission for grandfather, whom I'd never before known to admit that he could be wrong in anything, that I became almost as much alarmed as mother. Phil looked over to me and whistled such a prolonged whistle when grandfather went out that mother mildly reproved him by saying, "Philip, you are getting well too fast for your good manners!" And then to me she said, "Your father's way of looking at money came from his never knowing the want of it when he was a boy, while your grandfather had to work and struggle for every cent he got. The true view may be between the two extremes."

During the summer mother came to Brooklyn quite often, and grandfather sometimes accompanied her, and at one time he stayed a week longer than she did.

It was a happy day when, during the latter part of August, we were allowed by the naval authorities to go home to Wichnor on a sixty days' furlough.

When we arrived at Rivermouth, we took passage up the river for Wichnor on one of the excursion steamers that ply between the two places. On its decks were a number of Wichnor people whom we knew; they treated us with great friendliness. It seemed like a family party rather than an accidental gathering.

"This seems a reality and the past a dream," said Phil, looking off on the beautiful banks of the river.

I understood why these familiar scenes had raised a train of memories. I thought, too, of the time when he had first come to Wichnor and to our home; and I asked myself the question, Was it accident, or was it by the direction of a higher power, that he was brought there and finally to his own father?

"God has been in our lives," said Phil reverently, "and has saved us from many perils, to see this dear old town again."

I made no reply, for there was a mist in my eyes and a choking in my throat.

Mother and grandfather were at the wharf to receive us, and we noticed with surprise that the family carriage had a new coat of paint and varnish.

Among those who were on the wharf was Jim Bisbee, who was home on a veteran furlough.

Grandfather invited him to take dinner with us the next day, and Jim was full of reminiscences of our fight at Plymouth and our subsequent escape.

"I snum," said Jim, after being helped to the

second piece of pie, "this is some better 'n a-traipsin' through the swamp — say, naow, ain't it? There was tu or three times when I couldn't tell which was my stomach and which was my back, they was so dummed nigh t'gether; and no one 'zackly knows how good things taste till they've been 'thout 'em. I'll never growl 'baout m' grub ag'in as long as I live. What is throwd away in this taown would stand a soldier in good stead on a long march."

"Yes, if he couldn't get anything better," said Phil with a wink across the table to me.

"This war," said grandfather, "has a tendency to show us that there are some values more precious than silver and gold."

"Good gracious, yis!" said Jim, winking slyly to me: "I'm investing in gover'ment bonds m'self, square. I sold th' Thompson place t' other day an' put every cent on 't in th' stuff; f'r if this gover'ment busts I don't care what happens, an' if it don't bust I think it's a spec wuth somthin' while."

"Yes," assented grandfather, "when a man weighs himself and his interests alongside of his country's existence he's a mean skunk. Hez, I've put ten thousand dollars in government bonds in Wichmor Deposit Society for you; you can begin using it when you like; but" — and here he hesitated — "I'd advise you to hold on to it kind of close; for it's much easier to get clear of money than to keep it."

My mother beamed when he added: "And, Hez. all I've got belongs to you and your mother; my will is made by Lawyer Cute, good and strong."

The days passed rapidly and our furlough soon expired. It was now time for us to report at the hospital again. We met the young people of our age at social gatherings, to which we were invited, and Phil lost his heart to one of Wichnor's fair daughters,—and there are none fairer in the land, —but I could not banish from memory the face of one of the loveliest girls of the South.

Amid pleasures we were brought to a realization that the bitter as well as the sweet must be drank from the cup of life.

We were at the supper-table just on the eve of our departure for Brooklyn, when a telegram was handed to me. It read as follows:

OLD POINT COMFORT, VA., Jan. 18, 1865.
ENSIGN H. JOHNSTONE:
Your father wounded and a prisoner on board of transport bound for Fort Columbus, New York Harbor. He wants to see you and your mother.
ROBERT BELL, U.S.N.

We took the boat for New York that night and arrived there the next morning. Here we obtained leave from the commandant to visit the old fort, and found that the transport with father on board had but just arrived. The officer in charge was very kind to us. He conducted us to a sunny corner where lay my dear father, thin, pale, and desperately wounded. He had received a wound in the defence of Fort Fisher, where he fell into the hands of our forces.

He extended his hands to mother and to me, and there were tears on his dear face as he said, in reply to our questions as to his wound:

"Never mind the hurt; it is worth it all to see you, my dear ones, once more."

I withdrew, that he and mother might be alone together.

When I went to him again I found him calm and, if his face was the index, happy.

He said to me, "Hez, it seems a luxury to be here, wounded and all, after being a soldier so long. They are as good to me as if I were a guest."

Then his face lit up with a stern light as he said, "We lost the fort, but we made a glorious fight!"

While we were speaking Andy came in, greeted me respectfully, and then went straight to the bed of his master and friend.

"Andy always manages to keep up with the procession," said father; "if it had not been for the boy I don't know what I should have done sometimes."

My mother got a boarding-place in the city so

that she could spend a part of each day with father. We soon knew, what he had known from the first, that his wound was mortal.

The second day of our coming the surgeon sent for us hastily. As we went into the room father extended a hand to each of us, and with a brave smile said, " I am on my last march, Rose; " and then, as tears choked our utterance, continued: " Don't feel bad over it, my dears. Think how merciful He has been to bring us together again ! And the other wonderful things He has done for us all ! I would n't have it different if I could."

I could well believe him, for there was on his face a look of peace which I cannot describe.

" Rufus," my mother said, " we have never been enemies, and have always thought of you with love in our hearts."

" I know it, my dear, and I have never doubted it," he said. " I love my native South, and when she entered into this fight, that has proved so terrible for her, I should have been less than a man not to have cast my lot with my own people. I *have* been faithful unto death. I could do no less than I have done, and you, my son, could do no less for the North. I loved the North too. I never had an impulse of hate against it in all my battles. But the war had to be."

" We love you," I said, " if the whole world hates you."

My father pressed my hand, and a smile so tender and beautiful came to his dear face that it did not seem of earth.

After a moment of silence he said, "Be good to Andy; he has been a good servant and friend to me."

And then, shortly after, he became delirious. He seemed to imagine himself at the head of his men in battle, for he cried out, "Stand firm, men! We must drive them back or die here!"

His voice made me tremble, for it revealed my father as a stern soldier.

So, as I sat by his side, he went on during the night. Then as it grew light with the coming sun, there came a change: he was himself once more.

He looked into our faces with the old look of love. The darkness had passed from his mind. The final change was coming.

Again he reached out his thin hands to us, saying, "It's ebb tide, Rose. I see more clearly now. My son, my wife! Dear ones, bless you!"

And then his face was illumined with a light that seemed of that other world, as he said in clear, firm tones: "I see more clearly now, my son. I see that the blood shed by Northern and Southern men has not been in vain. I see a great, united, happy people." Then, as if regarding this prophetic vision with a look of joy that was not of earth, this brave son of the South, my dear, dear father, pressed our hands, and died so gently that he seemed to sleep.

The war was soon over. All our enemies were friends and fellow-countrymen again.

My mother and I, after grandfather's death, settled down in the home that was my father's. Uncle Robert with Phil and his wife are in a beautiful home near us.

As I write these concluding words I hear my wife (once such a little rebel), who is putting my son Rufus to bed, and teaching him this prayer: "God bless papa and mamma, our country and its glorious flag, and all its people North and South, forevermore!" To which my heart responds, Amen!

www.ingramcontent.com/pod-product-compliance
Lightning Source LLC
Chambersburg PA
CBHW051736300426
44115CB00007B/585